JOHN STARKEY, ESA ILLOINEN & KEN WELLS

LOLA

ALL THE SPORTS RACING & SINGLE-SEATER RACING CARS 1978 TO 1997

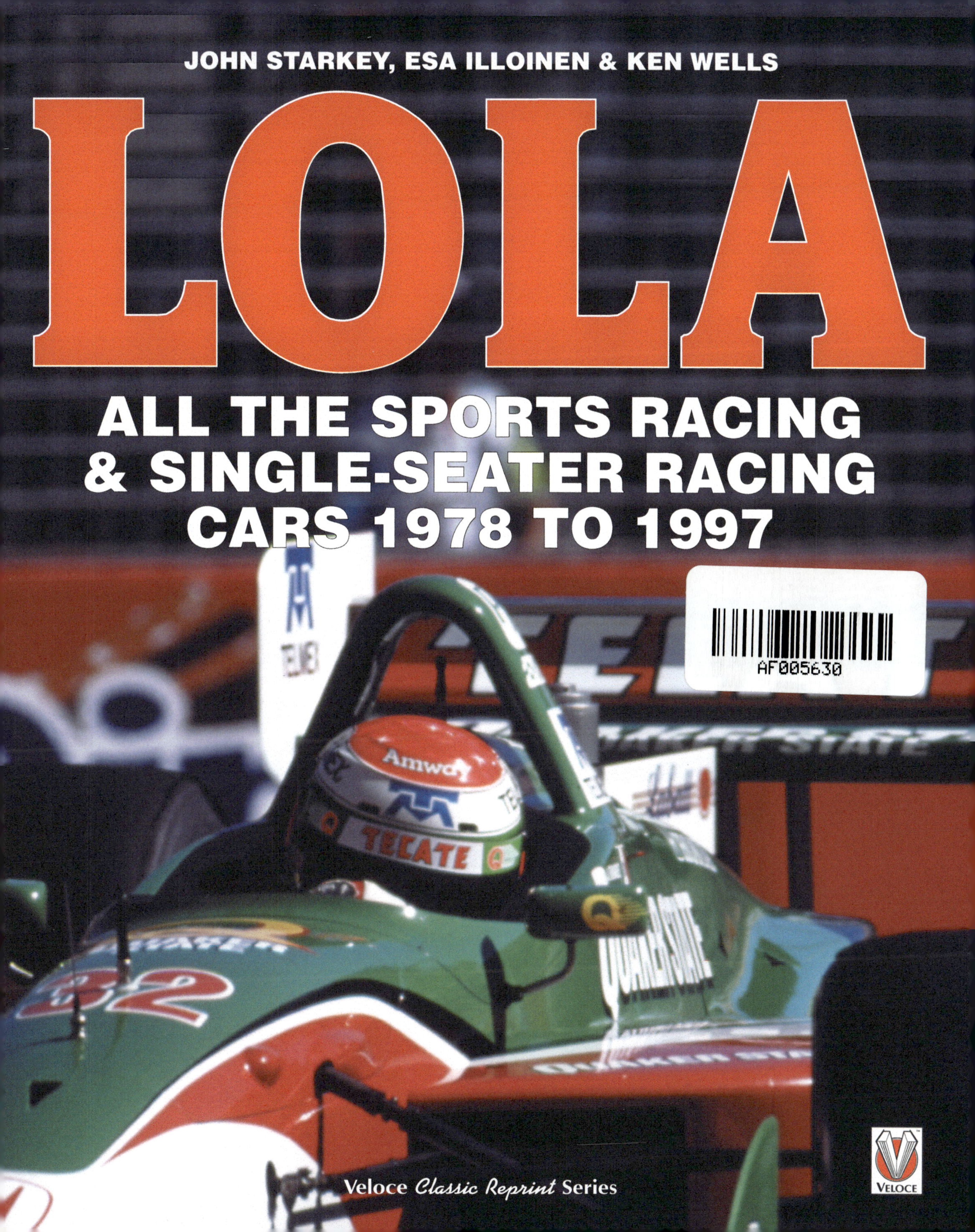

Veloce *Classic Reprint* Series

VELOCE

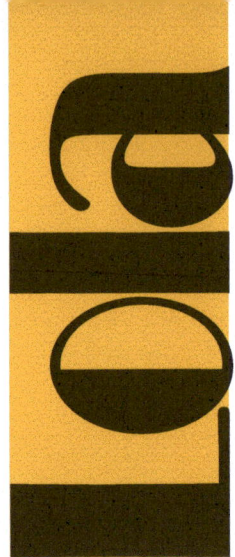

CONTENTS

Introduction & Acknowledgements 5

Chapter 1 1978–1979 7
T332 7
1977 Schkee 8
T333 CS 8
T333 9
T385 11
T390 11
T430 13
T490-492 14
T500 – 1977/79 – Indy 14
T540/540E – 1978/81 – FF 19
T580/582 – 1978/81 – FF 2000 19
T620/622 – 1978/79 – FSV 20
T670/672 – 1978/79 – F3 20
T720 – 1979 – FSV 22
T760 – 1979 – FAt 22
T770 – 1979 – F3 22

Chapter 2 1980-1981 23
T332 23
1980 Intrepid 23
T333 23
T390 De Cadenet 24
T490/T590 24
T500B 25
T530 – 1980 – Can-Am 25
T540 30
T580 31
T580 32
T590/592/592C – 1980/83 – Sports 2000 – 594/594C 32
T600 – 1981 – Group 6/IMSA GTP 33
T770 – F3 39
T850 – 1981 – F2 (Toleman) 39
T860 – 1981 – FAt (Toleman) 41

Chapter 3 1982-1983 42
T332 42
1982 42
1983 42
T333 CS 43
T390 43
T492 43
T530 43
T580 in 1982 43
T592 43
T600 44
T610 – 1982 – GpC 47
T640/640E/642 – 1982/83 – FF 51
T680 – 1983 – FF 2000 53
T700 – 1983 – Indy 53
T760 56
T850 56
T870 – 1982 – F3 57

Chapter 4 1984-1985 58
T332 58
1984 58
T380 58
T490 58
T530 58
T594 58
T600 59
T610 59
1984 – T616 – 1983 – GpC Junior 60
T642 63
T710 – 1984 – IMSA GTP 64
1990 66
T800 – 1984 – IndyCars 66
T810 – 1985 – Nissan GTP 70
T900 – 1985 – Indy 73
T950 – F3000 74
Beatrice – FORCE – Lola-Hart – THL1 75
FORCE – Lola-Hart – THL2 77
T86/50 – 1986 – F3000 79

Chapter 5 1986-1987 81
T86/00 – 1986 – Indy 81
T86/90 – 1986 – Sports 2000 83
Lola-Cosworth – LC87 – Formula 1 83
T87/00 – 1987 – Indy 85
T87/50 – 1987 – F3000 86
T87/90 – 1987 – S2000 89

Chapter 6 1988-1989 90
Lola-Cosworth – LC88 – Formula 1 90
T88/00 – 1988 – Indy 90
T88/50 – 1988 F3000 92
Larrousse-Calmels – LC89 – Formula 1 ... 93
T89/00 -1989 – Indy 94
T89/30 – 1989 – Nissan Group C or Nissan R89C 97
T89/50 – 1989 – F3000 99
T89/90 – 1989 – S2000 100

Chapter 7 1990-1992 102
Larrousse-Lamborghini-Lola 90 – Formula 1 102
T90/00 – 1990 – IndyCar 104
T90/30 – 1990 – Nissan Group C R90CK and R90CP 105
T90/50 – 1990 – F3000 110
T90/90 – 1990 – Sports 2000 112
Larrousse-Lola L91 – Formula 1 112
T91/00 – 1991 – Indy 114
T91/30 – 1991 – Nissan R91CP – Group C 115
T91/50 – 1991 – F3000 117
T91/90 – 1991 – Sports 2000 121
T92/00 – 1992 – Indy 121
T92/10 – 1992 – Group C 125
T92/50 – 1992 -F3000 131

Chapter 8 1993-1997 135
T93/00 – 1993 – Indy 135
T93/20 – 1993-96 – Indy Lights 145
T93/30 – 1993 – Lola BMS Ferrari Formula 1 146
T93/50 – 1993 – F3000 146
T94/00 – 1994 – IndyCar 147
T94/50 – 1994 – F3000 151
T95/00 1995 CART 155
T95/30 – 1995 development – Formula 1 158
T95/50 – 1995 – F3000 158
T96/00 – 1996 – CART 165
T96/50 – 1996-98 – F3000 specification car 166
T96/51 & T96/52 – 1996 – Formula Nippon 168
T97/00 – 1997 – CART 168
T97/20 – 1997-2000 – Indy Lights specification car 169
T97/30 – 1997 – Formula 1 170
T97/51 – 1997 – Formula Nippon 171

Appendix & bibliography 172

Index 173

INTRODUCTION & ACKNOWLEDGEMENTS

This is the second part of Lola's history to date. Just as the first book went to press, in December, 1997, the company passed from the control of Eric Broadley into that of Martin Birrane. Martin is a businessman with many interests, some of which are connected with motor racing: he owns a race circuit in Ireland, besides having raced Lolas and Chevrons for many years, including stints at Le Mans.

When Lola passed into fresh ownership the company's single connecting point to the last forty years was gone. In the first edition of this book I wrote: "He [Eric Broadley] alone is the reason that so many drivers and teams have purchased a Lola. Behind Eric Broadley's quiet exterior is a thoughtful engineer; a man well-versed in the art of designing a fast, sometimes innovative racing car and always a user-friendly car with the added asset of built-in strengh to protect its driver in the event of a 'shunt.'

"Eric Broadley has been overshadowed in his career by other makers of racing cars such as Enzo Ferrari and Colin Chapman, both essentially extrovert people who, of course, are two of the greatest names in motor racing. However, it's arguable that in standing the tests of longevity and time Eric Broadley and his company, Lola, will certainly be seen to be as important, if not more so, than either Lotus or Ferrari." Those words still apply to the Lolas which Eric Broadley designed and, happily, early in the new millennium, we can see that under Martin Birrane's direction Lola has achieved a quite outstanding comeback; something very rare where motorsport is concerned.

In this book we are dealing with the cars that Lola built for its customers between 1978 and 1997. In 1977 (and for a few years thereafter), Lola had been building cars which spanned the spectrum of world racing: Formula Two, Three, CanAm, Indycar, Formula 5000, Formula Ford. In fact, you name it and Lola was building a car (or cars) to suit and to satisfy the demand of customers who wanted a well-built, fast and reliable machine, and with it always a real chance of winning.

This volume tells of the company's move toward specialisation. Since 1979 the sports car world has not thrived as it once did, the modern concentration on single seaters spearheaded by television promotion of Formula One. For Lola, this shift meant almost complete domination of the American Indycar scene; the company profited, together with Bicester-based March, from an almost unbroken series of successes in this area. Indycar domination, together with successes in American-based CanAm (the centre seater variety), and Formula 3000, which effectively supplanted the role of Formula 5000, forced Lola to concentrate ever more on the USA through its energetic agent Carl Haas.

This is very much a book about the various types of Lola racing cars. To prevent it from becoming unmanageable sizewise, the story of the various personalities involved with Lola awaits another volume.

Days gone by ... The two Mark 3 Lola T70 coupés of James Garner's American International Racing team, at Sebring for the 12-Hour race of 1968. (Author photo)

ACKNOWLEDGEMENTS

First of all my thanks to Norman Wells for letting me have the use of the research into Lola racing cars which his late brother, Ken Wells, carried out before his untimely death. Secondly, to Esa Illoinen. Esa, from Finland, took the original manuscript and put in an enormous amount of work, (particularly with regard to the cars of the eighties and nineties), adding pertinent facts and making corrections. Thanks also to Bill Freeman, *Autosport*, Mauro Borella, Eric Broadley, Clive Robinson, Sid Hoole, Mike Ostroumoff, Lawrie Bray, David Hodges, LAT, Sutton Motorsport, John Foden and David Cundy.

**John Starkey
Florida, USA**

Lola

1
1978-1979

Portland, Oregon. No, not 1974 but 1998. Glenn Brown in action in his beautifully restored T332. (Author photo)

T332

The T332 was a Formula 5000 car which enjoyed a long life. Developed from the T300, the T332 continued a line of very successful Formula 5000 cars. Brian Redman, for instance, won the American series three years in a row with T330 derivatives. During the 1978 Tasman series, Warwick Brown won all four of the Rothmans-sponsored races in his ex-VDS team T332. The first race was held at Sandown Park and saw Alfredo Costanzo lead by half a lap up to the halfway mark, only to have a piston fail. Garrie Cooper in an Elfin was second, John Cannon in the March 76B third and Keith Holland in another T332 fourth, despite two spins. In Adelaide for round two, Vern Schuppan in the Elfin was second and Johnnie Walker in his T332 third.

In the Surfers Paradise round, Vern was again in second place but Don Briedenbach took third in his T332. At Oran Park for the final race of the series, McCormack in his McLaren chased hard until a cam follower broke, leaving Allison in a Chevron second and Graham McRae in his GM3 third. Derek Bell could not better eighth in

Where it all began for Lola in the United States. Carl Haas' showroom in Highland Park, Illinois in 1968. Two 160s – the 'Simoniz'-sponsored T163 is on the left – can just be seen in the window. Note that Haas was also the Hewland agent for America at that time. (Courtesy Bob Roemer)

Some of Lola's early 70s designs had an amazingly long life in international racing. The T332 was still enjoying success at the end of the decade.

Alan Hamilton's T430, due to poor handling. Final score was Brown 36pts, Schuppan 15 and Allison 9.

From the T332 was developed a special for the single seater Can-Am series which began in 1977. The Spyder was T332-based, strong and good, and was developed by ex-Shadow designer, Ed Stone, with assistance from Lance Smith. The Spyder, run by the Newman-Freeman team, first appeared in 1978, driven by Elliott Forbes-Robinson. He won twice in 1978 (at Charlotte and Trois Rivières) with no less than Patrick Depailler driving a second entry at the Riverside finale, retiring from second place.

1977 Schkee

After a two year hiatus, when Can-Am returned in 1977, its first race (at St Jovite) was won by Tom Klausler in a Schkee. Another Lola 'special', this car was based on an ex-Gordon Johncock F5000 T332 monocoque chassis. Painted STP Day-Glo orange, it was engineered by Doug Schulz and Bob McKee – hence the name. It had been Schulz's idea to replace F5000 with Can-Am. That the Schkee was fast was never in doubt but, despite this, it was still the only non 'real' Lola in the top ten at the year's end.

Matters were not helped by the fact that the team ran into financial problems very early, and the cars were sold off to Tom Spalding who, with the best will in the world, did not have the knowledge or experience to exploit their potential.

Yet another Can-Am special developed from the T332 was the 1978 Gunn. In 1977, John Gunn had raced a T332CS in the new Can-Am series and his Lola-based, so-called Gunn GG4 scored eight top-eight finishes in 1978, including three fourth places, and was sixth in the final points.

Someone else who excelled at modifying Lolas was Mick Hill of Derby, England, undoubtedly one of the greatest ever exponents of the art of building silhouette Supersaloon big bangers. In 1971, he had built a Boss Capri with a Weslake 4.7 V8 engine and T70 suspension and brakes, which won over 30 times. In 1979, Mick Hill had the Skoda Phoenix, featuring bits from his burnt-out ex-Mike Hazelwood Jaguar XJ8. This had had a 7.0 Chevrolet with suspension from a T332.

Then came Titman Preece's BMW M1. This was the ex-Durex-sponsored T400 which then came third in the Shellsport Championship. Dave Shepherd purchased it late in 1988, flat-bottomed it and won over 30 races.

T333 CS

In 1978, Alan Jones, in a T333 CS, won on the car's debut for the Carl Haas and Jim Hall team at Road Atlanta in the championship first round, with Al Holbert second in the Hogan Lola T333 CS on his first venture into Can-Am racing. Third was Warwick Brown, also driving a T333 CS.

The Prophet, taking part in the 1978 season, was also a Lola special. Based on a T332 chassis, the first car was (apparently) credited to former Penske staffman Lance Smith in 1977 although other – authoritative – reports give the credit to Jack Smith, a former McLaren BMW IMSA man. Fast in a straight line, it was second on its debut at Mid-Ohio in 1978, George Follmer then winning at St Jovite by a clear three laps next time out. Later the car suffered a big accident at Laguna Seca, hospitalising George for a long time. Alan Jones looked like making it two in a row at Charlotte in the next race, but had to pit after tangling with a backmarker. Thereafter, he was unable to make up the ground on Elliott Forbes-Robinson in his Lola-based Spyder NF10 (Newman-Freeman team). Bill Tempero in a Chevron was third and Al Holbert fourth, whilst Jean-Pierre Jarier in a Shadow was forced to retire.

Alan was back to his winning ways at Mid-Ohio for round three. George Follmer, who had won the Can-Am series in 1972, was second in an ex-Brian Redman Lola (already renamed the Prophet), and Elliott Forbes-Robinson took third place with the Spyder. John Gunn was next up in his Gunn GG4 and Howden Ganley finished fifth in a Gulf GR7, which was previously known as a 'Mirage'. The name was not used at the time the car was built, although it was of Mirage heritage. Follmer then won in the Prophet at St Jovite, winning by three clear laps after Jones clipped the 'Redman Hump', bending the suspension and being forced into retirement. Michael Allen was second in a T332 CS, with Warwick Brown third for the VDS team. Alain de Cadenet drove the Mirage into tenth place.

Warwick Brown stayed on form, winning Watkins Glen in a brand new Team VDS T333 CS. He had been second on the grid to Alan Jones, who suffered first a puncture and then a water leak, before finally retiring. Al Holbert was second in the Busch-sponsored Hogan Lola, with Rocky Moran third. John Gunn came fourth in the GG4 and the similar T332 CS of Michael Allen was fifth. Alan Jones then won at Elkhart Lake, initially being chased by George Follmer, who faded to fourth. Brown was second and Al Holbert third. The result was the same at Mosport, except that Elliott Forbes-Robinson edged out Follmer for fourth place.

The race at Trois Rivières was held over for a week due to rain, and Elliott Forbes-Robinson won it in the Budweiser-sponsored Spyder. Brown was again second and Alan Jones could manage only third place. Michael Brayton was fourth in the Wolf and Alain de Cadenet fifth in the British Stamps special once more. While Alan was away at the Canadian GP in Montreal (he was ninth in a Williams FW06, having been second before having to pit with a damaged gearbox, yet still got fastest race lap), Al Holbert took the win at Laguna Seca and Warwick Brown was second yet again to close in on Jones in the points chase. John Morton was third in a Lola borrowed from Carl Haas, and Brian Redman finished fourth in his first Can-Am outing since his big accident a year earlier. He had won another race in the meantime as part of a therapeutic recovery plan! Poor Brian had lost time with electrical problems, but then set a new class lap record.

The big drama concerned George Follmer. Easily fastest in practice, he had a monster crash in the Prophet when the throttle jammed open at 120mph when approaching The Corkscrew, suffering severe leg, back and internal injuries.

Riverside was the final event and the finishing order was Jones, Brown (second for the fifth straight time), Elliott Forbes-Robinson and Holbert. So Alan Jones took the championship with 2712 points, Warwick Brown was second with 2548 and Elliott Forbes-Robinson third with 1674, Al Holbert garnering 1534 points for fourth place. The only British driver, Alain de Cadenet, came 15th in the British Stamps Special.

T333

For the 1979 championship, Al Holbert crashed his T332 CS whilst pre-season testing at Road Atlanta because of a fuel leak and fire. Holbert walked away but the car was destroyed.

Elliott Forbes-Robinson also won once in 1979 in the new Spyder (at Trois Rivières) when he was runner-up in the championship to Jacky Ickx by virtue of some good placings. Keke Rosberg also scored two wins for the marque in 1979, at Road Atlanta and Watkins Glen. The Spyder drivers, especially Rosberg, usually had the speed to beat the Haas-Hall team but not the reliability or luck.

The 1979 Frissbee was yet another modified T332 CS. The original car had an ex-Vel's Parnelli Jones Lola F5000 tub first used by 'Big Al' Unser in 1976. Built during the summer of 1979, the Frissbee was designed by Trevor Harris, who drew the first Can-Am Shadow and the later Nissans. The Frissbee was much lighter than a T530 and had very sleek aerodynamics. The car debuted at Riverside late in 1979, driven by IMSA man Brad Friselle, who had underwritten the project (hence the name Fris-B). After Brad had almost destroyed it in a testing accident early the next year, the rebuilt car showed great promise in pre-season testing driven by John Morton. It was on the pole at Watkins Glen but did not have much luck thereafter. It first appeared in the results in the penultimate round, Al Unser winning from flag to flag from pole at Laguna Seca in 1980.

The Lee Dykstra-penned spaceframe Hogan Busch HR001 was initially for Al Holbert, who drove it to fourth place on its debut at Road Atlanta. However, things got worse thereafter and Al left the thing behind with two races to run in the series. Can-Am rookie Geoff Brabham then took over, not finishing at Laguna Seca due to engine failure and coming fourth at the Riverside finale. It was reported that, although the ground effect car was of Lee's own design and build, the suspension was all Lola …

The initial Prophet was replaced in 1979 by a Jack Smith design, even though he had already departed the team. Smith had been disappointed with the lack of progress and/or direction, although the car scored two second places. Bobby Rahal won at Laguna Seca in 1979 and was generally on the pace on most occasions. The consensus was that the cars were well prepared and clean aerodynamically, but Herb Caplan's team lacked the best engines to really do well.

Incidentally, a new Lola T333 CS at this time cost $50,000, which was why many teams used converted old T332 F5000s instead; it was a far cheaper way to go big-time racing! In 1979, round one of the Can-Am Championship was at Road Atlanta and Al Holbert could not better fourth place in the new Lee Dykstra-designed Hogan Busch HR001 spaceframe car which used Lola suspension. The race was won by Keke Rosberg in a Spyder NF11 from the Carl Haas-entered T333 CS of Jacky Ickx. Elliott Forbes-Robinson was third in another Spyder. Keke had scored by getting ahead of a tense tussle by some demon overtaking when he and Ickx encountered backmarkers.

Charlotte for round two saw Keke on pole but now it was Jackie's turn to win from the second grid slot. Elliot Forbes-Robinson was again third when the chequered flag fell. Afterwards, the positions of the two Spyders were reversed due to a penalty imposed apropos a Rosberg indiscretion with the pace car.

Mosport, in Canada, was the next race on the list and Keke led away from pole position, rooted his tyres, stopped, drove hard to catch up and flew off into the boonies. Jacky Ickx won, Elliott Forbes-Robinson was second and Geoff Lees – in a T332 CS – third.

Alan Jones then returned to the scene to win in Carl Haas' T332 CS at Mid-Ohio, upsetting pole man Keke with his forceful tactics. Who wants to be in F1 if that's what they do? he asked, and was promptly signed up to drive for the Wolf Formula One team by a spectating Peter Warr, the team's manager! Elliot Forbes-Robinson was again third. Watkins Glen finally gave Keke the win he deserved. George Follmer had 'retired' from driving a Prophet, still in pain following his accident, and was replaced by Bobby Rahal, who qualified second on the grid. He then had problems, finishing way down in 17th place. Geoff Lees was second in the VDS team's T332CS, with Vern Schuppan third in the Elfin.

Elkhart Lake was the venue for round six and, by way of compensation for his poor outing in a Ligier at the British Grand Prix, Jacky Ickx won after the front runners fell by the wayside. Keke was again poleman but his engine blew up. So did Rahal's, while Elliott Forbes-Robinson spun his chances away. This let Jackie ahead, never to look back. Geoff Lees was second again, Al Holbert in the Hogan team's car third. Tom Spalding came in seventh in a Schkee.

Brainerd racetrack in round seven went to Jacky Ickx again after poleman Rosberg in a Spyder blew his engine on the warm-up lap. Elliott Forbes-Robinson salvaged second place for the Spyder marque, managed by Masten Gregory. Rahal in the Prophet was third and Geoff Lees in a T332CS came fourth after both had punctures, Geoff also punting off the DES T290 of the two-litre pace-setter Tim Evans. Luckily, both were able to restart.

Forbes-Robinson finally got to win a race, at the Trois Rivières circuit, Elliot inheriting the win when Keke's engine failed just two laps from the finish. Bobby Rahal in the Prophet took the pole and second place in the race itself and Jacky Ickx spun off in heavy rain showers. Elliott Forbes-Robinson and Geoff Lees both spun, only the Spyder restarting, the Van Diemen car being too badly damaged to continue. Whilst Lees' car was stationary, it suffered further misfortune when it was hit by a two-litre car.

Bobby Rahal in the Prophet won for the first time at Laguna Seca in round nine of the series, with Elliott Forbes-Robinson second in his Spyder. Keke Rosberg had taken pole position but then crashed heavily, cracking some ribs and sustaining mild concussion. Undaunted, he took over the car of Randy Townsend to finish sixth. Third man home was Geoff Lees for the Van Diemen team with Howdy Holmes (a rookie) fourth. Geoff Brabham – soon to be the SCCA Formula Super Vee champion – was another Can-Am rookie (with the Buschmobile), but he failed to finish after his engine expired. Brabham had taken over from a disillusioned Al Holbert. Jacky Ickx, who finished eighth, now led Elliot Forbes-Robinson by a single point with but one race to go.

When the chips were down, Ickx came up smiling, winning the race and championship outright. Keke Rosberg had been on pole in his NF11 with Rahal alongside in the Ampex-sponsored Prophet. Keke led until his engine went off song, afterwards colliding with Vern Schuppan in the Elfin. Bobby Rahal was second, Elliot Forbes-Robinson only third, Brabham fourth.

So – Jacky Ickx had 51 points, Elliott Forbes-Robinson 45, Geoff Lees 32, Keke Rosberg 29, Bobby Rahal 25, Alan Jones 9 – from his one and only outing – which he won!

Over three years of championship racing, the Lola T332CS won 19 out of 29 races before handing over its laurels to the T530.

T385

The T385 was the project number of the Aston Martin 'Nimrod' endurance car which was built for the 1981 season (although only debuted in 1982). Claimed to have been basically a T70 monocoque, it has, however, been suggested that the only actual T70 component was the pedal mount. Although widened, the car used the 5.3-litre four camshaft Aston Martin V8 engine. This was a strictly conventional and simple coupé which did quite well at Le Mans (the Viscount Downe car was seventh in 1982), particularly when one considers that this was strictly a 'private venture' car.

One car was run by Viscount Downe's team, the team manager being Richard Williams, and the other by Aston Martin dealer, Robin Hamilton.

For 1983 Hamilton took his operation to the States, where he managed a fifth at Sebring. Ray Mallock comprehensively reworked the Hamilton car, losing some 100kg of weight, among other things. Best Hamilton result was seventh at the Silverstone WEC event.

Hamilton's team was bought by John Cooper, and started 1984 with a seventh in the Daytona 24 Hours. Cooper had to change his plans for taxation reasons, however, and the car became a second entry for Dowe. Both cars were now to Ray Mallock specification. One car was run briefly with a lightly turbocharged version of the Aston Martin V8, but, for Le Mans, both were back to normally-aspirated units. At Le Mans both cars were involved in an horrendous accident on the Mulsanne Straight on Saturday evening. Nimrod driver John Sheldon suffered burns and a marshal was killed. This effectively ended the Nimrod's campaign.

T390

Alain de Cadenet was a stamp dealer who first went to race at Le Mans in 1971, co-driving a Ferrari 512M with Hughes de Fierlant. The pair suffered gearbox problems and retired, but Alain was back again next year, this time with the Duckhams Special designed by Gordon Murray. Alain's co-driver this time was the very fast Chris Craft and they finished a creditable twelfth overall. In 1973 and '74, De Cadenet tried again, now having definitely got the Le Mans 'bug', but he had no luck, the car retiring in both years, first with suspension and clutch problems and then, in 1974, when co-driving with John Nicholson, a broken suspension link pitched the car into the barriers when it was lying sixth.

For 1975, a Lola T380 was used by de Cadenet in lieu of the car bearing his own name. (There was Lola identification, too.) Unfortunately, the T380 proved to be 15mph slower than his previous car! There was nobody from Lola around to help so the team experimented, finally going back to the car's original specification. Chris Craft again co-drove and Keith Greene managed the team. There were all manner of dramas and delays but Chris Chraft was said by the ACO to have set the fastest race lap. Craft and de Cadenet finished 15th, 45 laps down, in a race won by Jacky Ickx and Derek Bell in a Gulf Ford.

The T380 of de Cadenet and Craft came home third at the 1976 event, an outstanding result for a private entrant; just 12 laps adrift of the winning Ickx and van Lennep Porsche 936 turbo, and only one lap off the second-placed Lafosse/Migault Mirage DFV. It was also the best ever Lola result there, before or since, and certainly the best by a true privateer since Cunningham. Sponsored by Tate and Lyle and Hammond's Sauce, the T380 qualified tenth with – because of a slow top speed – the car rebodied with a shorter tail, repositioned rear wing and lighter bodywork. It worked.

For 1977, de Cadenet had a car built, with the monocoque made by John Thompson. There was also input from Eric Broadley, Len Bailey and Gordon Murray. Despite lots of problems,

The Aston Martin Nimrod; in reality a Lola T385 at Silverstone in 1982. A creditable Group C effort, the Nimrod was a brave British attempt to win during a period of Porsche dominance. (Courtesy LAT)

Alain de Cadenet made many attempts at Le Mans and the Sports Car Championship. Here he is in 1979 with a car which was a development of the T380. De Cadenet was usually partnered by François Migault and, at Silverstone, they finished second overall.

including losing 15 minutes early on with a dragging clutch, and then an hour spent repairing the nose after Chris Craft went off at night in the wet, de Cadenet's Tate & Lyle-sponsored car (with Gordon Spice as reserve driver) finished fifth at Le Mans, only 90 seconds behind the third-placed car. However, it was also 230 miles behind the Ickx/Haywood/Barth 936 turbo winner.

In 1978, the new de Cadenet proved much faster in its shakedown testing at Silverstone than the previous year's car. Later, de Cadenet announced that the Cosworth engine had 460bhp, onboard air jacks and Keith Greene still in charge of team management.

The Le Mans entry list for 1978 also showed Simon Phillips there in the 1976 ex-de Cadenet car he now owned, to be driven alongside John Beasley and Nick Faure. They qualified 15th but stopped on the Sunday morning after various gearbox and electrical malfunctions.

Peter Lovett was in the newly-acquired 1977 car, to be shared with John Cooper and Bob Evans. Despite being 19th fastest, they were excluded from the start by the ACO, pruning two cars from the Group 6 class to even up the categories and letting in some slower (French) vehicles at back of grid.

A new car for 1978, shared by Alain and Chris again, qualified tenth and finished 15th, having been eighth late on Saturday evening. By virtue of the company it was running in at that time, if all had gone well it could have been third. Again, alas, it was delayed nearly two hours by lots of clutch and/or gearbox problems. The bodywork logo said 'Made In Britain' ...

In 1979 de Cadenet was at the Silverstone WCM round with co-driver François Migault. However, they qualified fourth and finished second! The race was won by seven laps by J. Fitzpatrick/B. Wollek/H. Heyer in a Porsche 935. Reports said the car was 'new' and in its 'debut' race.

The Le Mans car was said to be based on the 1978 car with a wider track and longer wheelbase, revised suspension geometry and altered weight distribution. Aerodynamics were tidied up, too.

At the Le Mans 24 Hours, Migault had been fourth very early on but pitted after only eight/ten laps, whereupon the team discovered a faulty external oil union apropos the gearbox. A three hour rebuild and/or replacement job ensued and the car was withdrawn. Very sad.

Meanwhile the 'Phillips' de Cadenet, co-driven by Martin Raymond and Ray Mallock under the Fisons Lola banner, qualified 14th, giving the position of best Lola to a French T286. The car misfired from early on and finished 21st. The 'Lovett' de Cadenet, now the SG Lola, had starter motor and gearbox problems, and retired.

Alain de Cadenet and Migault appeared again that summer, at the Brands Hatch WCM round in August. They were sixth after an early stoppage due to starter motor problems.

Lovett and Cooper were seventh in the SGG car, having been third until the last 15 minutes when a steering arm snapped needing hasty replacement after limping in from the outback. SG apparently stands for St George, and there was a big red cross emblazoned across the nose of the white machine...

T430

In the 1979 Tasman series, Alfredo Costanzo, in his T430, modified with a T332 nose, won both the opening two rounds, held at Sandown Park and then Adelaide. The championship was sponsored by Rothmans and was now for Formula One and F5000 cars. Costanzo won both events from pole and posted fastest lap both times. Theodore team mates Geoff Lees and David Kennedy, in an Ensign N175 and a Wolf WR4 respectively, were second and third at Sandown Park, whilst at Adelaide Johnnie Walker in a T332 was second and Perkins, in an Elfin, third.

Round three of the championship was at Surfers Park. Kennedy won by punting off Lees (both in Wolfs) after ignoring team tactics orders. There were some acrimonious scenes afterwards and tempers ran high. Perkins in the Elfin was thus second and Costanzo only third, but needing only to finish in the top eight at the last race to take the title. Warwick Brown (who had suffered a big accident at Sandown) was fourth in a T332 CS converted to T333-2 specification. Unfortunately, at Oran Park for the last round, he had a puncture as a result of the new track surface, and resultant driveshaft failure just before halfway when leading the race, and crashed out. Warwick Brown won the race and Perkins the title with

13

Nick Adams' T492 Sports 2000 heavily engaged in a dice during 1978. (Courtesy Ted Walker)

second place. John Wright was third in another T332. Perkins had 35 points to Costanzo's 28 and Brown's 22.

Later, Johnnie Walker in a T332 won the 1979 Australian Grand Prix at Wanneroo in Perth, and finished second in the third and last round of the series at Sandown Park to clinch the Australian Championship,.

Alan Jones, driving a Williams FW07, won the 1980 Australian Grand Prix at Calder in November. Bruno Giacomelli, in an Alfa, was second and Didier Pironi, with an Elfin, finished in third place. Costanzo, as the best of the locals, was fourth in a T430, ahead of a trio of T332s.

T490-492

In 1978, Sports 2000 had started in the USA, initially as an SCCA amateur series. This meant that Lola T492s sold well over there. The series would go pro, too, in 1980, increasing Lola's share of an extrememly lucrative market. Rod Gretton's T490, chassis number HU7, was tested in *Autosport* on 25th May 1978.

Nick Adams used a McLean Hunter-sponsored Lola Nelson T492 in the 1978 series, finding himself up against the likes of Frank Sytner, Chris Alford and Syd Fox; John Brindley, John Trevelyan and Wayne Wainwright. The T490 and 492 dominated the year, before being swamped by the latest Tigas. Sytner (who wrote-off a tub at Mallory), Trevelyan and John Brindley were all early winners in 1978. Chris Alford scored at Brands Hatch in June, Ian Taylor doing likewise the same month in a small, localised championship at Thruxton, before switching to the opposition! Trevelyan led the championship in July only to lose his STC sponsorship. Then Sytner took over the lead after winning at Oulton. Nick Adams won the Thruxton round in August, and so Frank Sytner won the main Sodastream title for the Howitt Group with 277 points; Trevelyan had 239, Alford 176, Brindley 173 and Nick Adams 132.

In 1979, the Lolas of Desiré Wilson and Jeremy Rossiter came in second and third to Ian Taylor's Tiga in the championship opener at Siverstone's F3 Support race in March. In April Rossiter's T492 then won at Silverstone from Nick Adams' Tiga. Later that month, Richard Morgan in a Tiga won at Oulton Park, with Richard Gretton in second place and John Sheldon third.

This pretty much set the pattern for the season; Taylor doing a lot of the winning with the likes of Nick Adams, Richard Morgan and even newcomer James Weaver, and Jeremy Rossiter in the Spax car and Desiré Wilson in the Kelly Girl Lola T492 often 'best of the rest'. Ian Taylor became the 'Chequered Flag' champion and the series provided close competition with 125bhp from its two-litre engines. Taylor finished with 342pts, Morgan 237, Wilson 211, Adams 158 and Rossiter 134.

T500 – 1977/79 – Indy – 5 built

The T500 marked a winning return to USAC racing for Lola – and how! Rumours of Al Unser having signed with Haas/Hall, and a Lola USAC car, were confirmed at the end of October 1977. Hugh Absalom was chief mechanic, along with Dennis Swan, with the chassis being looked after by Troy Rogers. The engines were built by Franz Weis.

The car itself was narrow and long with the largest wheelbase of the 1978 cars seen at Indianapolis at 110in. The design was otherwise conventional: aluminium alloy monocoque, side radiators, front suspension with lower wishbones and top rockers operating inboard springs, parallel links, radius rods and outboard springs at rear. Outboard Lockheed brakes all around. The gearbox was

The Pennzoil-sponsored Chaparral of 1979. In reality, a Lola T500 IndyCar of Jim Hall's team. (Courtesy LAT)

March 18th at Marchat Phoenix for round one in the Jimmy Bryan 150, but ran out of fuel 13 laps from the finish, when in fifth. Gordon Johncock in a Wildcat won from team mate Steve Krisiloff and A.J. Foyt driving a Coyote. Ontario. Round two and Unser was third behind Danny Ongais driving a Parnelli and Tom Sneva in a Penske. The car itself was then destroyed in practice for the Texas 200 at College Station for round three, a broken halfshaft being suspected. Al had amnesia for four days.

Missing the Trenton round 4, an untested new car was built for the Indianapolis 500, but the driver and car were unable to approach Unser's pre-crash testing speeds. They still started fifth and, after battling awhile, took the winning lead on lap 145 when Danny Ongais blew his engine. This was the first Indy win for Chaparral legend Jim Hall, who reputedly reworked the T500. There was excitement in the late stages, when Al Unser hit a wheel in his pit, damaging the right nosefin. The damage slowed him down somewhat and his lead was eaten into by Sneva. Sneva was second (as per the previous year), eight seconds in arrears, with Gordon Johncock third. It was the first Indy 500 win for the Ford Cosworth DFX. (Unser had also won there in 1970/71, both times in an Offy-powered Colt Johnny Lightning Special, an undisguised Lola copy built by George Bignotti.)

Danny Ongais won the Mosport Round 6 on (the then) only USAC road course in North America, but Al crashed out of third place after hitting the guard rail and the car was destroyed.

Hewland 4-speed. The dimensions were as follows:

Overall length 179in
Overall width 44in
Wheelbase 110in
Front track 57in
Rear track 61in

In 1978 first tests of the car showed imprecise and unpredictable turning into corners. The T500 debuted on

Another new car was then built for Milwaukee and round 7, but after leading, Al ran dry of fuel after 144 out of 150 laps, dropping him to sixth place. Milwaukee saw the maiden USAC win for Rick Mears in a Penske, which also ran out of fuel as he crossed the line.

The Pocono 500, round 8 saw Al start tenth and finish 24 seconds clear of Johnny Rutherford in a McLaren and Sneva in a Penske. Unser had nine stops to their 12 and 14 respectively; He paced himself, not using up tyres, and did not need to make any rubber stops at all, only fuel. Rick Mears missed the race as Mario Andretti was back from F1 for a while. He did not finish.

On to Michigan and Al had an engine let go, whilst at Atlanta for round 10 it was like Milwaukee all over again as Unser ran out of fuel (only this time he did not lead!) and Mears won. Returning to College Station, the battle was between the two Texans with Foyt in a Coyote getting it over Rutherford. Steve Krisiloff was third but, in the post-race press conference, was promptly flattened by Foyt for suggesting that A.J. had passed him under a yellow.

Milwaukee for round 12 saw Ongais win, Unser managing only fifth. Ontario saw Foyt out in a Parnelli, the only man to go over 200mph, but he stayed in midfield as he qualified on the second day. Sneva thus got pole but crashed out early on. Foyt retired on the first lap with gear selection problems, so Johnny Rutherford led until his engine blew. Gordon Johncock then fought the lead with Al Unser, gaining the upper hand just before the last pit stops, and led until his fuel tank ran dry five laps from home. Big Al Unser won again! (Writing IndyCar history with the Triple Crown sweep of three 500 milers in one season. Unser was in the same chassis he'd used to win Indy. It had since been crashed at Mosport and rebuilt, with modifications to the rear suspension and relocated shock absorbers. The changes improved turn-in, but Unser was still not happy.) Second was Pancho Carter, after a big spin, five laps down, and only five cars made the finish. Al, who had started on third row, now led the championship from Sneva and Johncock.

Danny Ongais won the return encounter at Michigan in September, coming from the back row in his Interscope Parnelli. Unser, alas, wrote off his third chassis of the year when trying to squeeze between Spike Gehlhausen and the wall, after the Eagle's Offy blew an engine and spun on its own oil, leaving Al nowhere to go.

Mario Andretti had just won the World Championship and celebrated with victory at Trenton, his first USAC win in five years. Foyt was on pole with the Parnelli. Near the end, as championship contenders Unser and Sneva battled, they both tried overtaking second-placed Johnny Parsons in a Lightning Offy, touching wheels in the process. Chastened, Parsons stayed ahead but Tom beat the Lola to the line. Phew!

The team was now working hard to overcome instability problems, changing suspension geometry and moving pick-up points, etc. They made the car better but not good, with Al declaring 'there is a design fault'.

A.J. Foyt won at Silverstone in what he admitted was an outdated and overweight old Coyote, the race culminating with only 38 of its scheduled 52 laps having been run, due to rain. Danny Ongais had been on pole again, with Unser second. Obviously Al's F5000 road racing experience was put to good advantage. Unfortunately, he broke a crown wheel and pinion after only 26 laps, and was classified tenth, with championship rival Sneva third behind Mears, both in Penskes.

Rick promptly went one better at Brands Hatch one week later – but only when Ongais' clutch broke after the Hawaiian led all 83 out of 100 laps, and with a full one lap advantage on the field. Al did not even get that far; his clutch exploded as the team took the flag on the rolling start. Sneva avoided an errant spinner early on to take second in a Penske 1-2.

For the final at Phoenix, Ongais again dominated the field, but fell foul of a new pitlane safety ruling which caused him to lose time, eventually finishing fourth. Johnny Rutherford won from Foyt and Johncock. Al was fifth, but this was not enough to take the title, despite Sneva being only 16th, having lost 17 laps with a broken turbo.

Tom Sneva was thus the first ever USAC champion without a win. Sneva had amassed 4153pts, Unser 4031, Johncock 3548, Rutherford 3067 and Foyt 3024.

In 1979, the Sherman Armstrong team ordered three new Lola T500/79s for the new USAC season, CART having split away to do its own thing, except at Indy. In 1978, Sherman Armstrong had run a Wildcat for Tom Bigelow but now the team was paying out £93,000 for three new cars before the season had started. A fourth chassis was sold to Carl Haas, for CART, as he had now split from Jim Hall and the Chaparral effort.

At Phoenix for the CART Champioship first round, Al Unser was in the Lola T500 for its intended last outing in the team before the new Chaparral appeared. This was BS Fabrications-built and John Barnard-designed. Al qualified tenth. Brother Bobby was on pole in a new Penske PC7, but Gordon Johncock won in an older PC6 from Rick Mears in a PC7, with Johnny Rutherford in a McLaren taking third. Al Unser – with the Lola still not having overcome its handling problems – was fourth, and Bobby Unser fifth. All the cars used Cosworth DFX engines.

The Ontario speedway saw the first round of the USAC Championship, which was easily won by A.J. Foyt in a Parnelli, whilst Tom Bigelow was sixth with his so-called Lola T500B. USAC Championship round two was at the Texas 200 where Foyt won again, and it was George Snider's turn to grab sixth for SA and Lola.

Atlanta was the next CART venue for rounds two and three of the championship, and both races were won by Johnny Rutherford. Al Unser, still in his Lola, qualified seventh. Lee Kunzman led in a Parnelli (he'd been sidelined earlier in his career by big accidents involving bad burns, etc.), but failed to stop near the end of the race for fresh tyres and was caught by Johnny Rutherford a lap from the finish. Kunzman still managed second place. Out early in the second race with gearbox problems, Salt Walther tried the same trick but to no avail, he finished well beaten, and Al had a new set-up on his car which allowed him within 0.5 seconds of Johnny Rutherford with but two laps to go. Then a turbo hose blew and Rick Mears was thus second, Al Unser third.

The Indianapolis 500 was round four of the CART Championship and round three of the USAC title chase. Al Unser qualified on the front row in the sensational new Chaparral 2K. Janet Guthrie, sponsored by Texaco Star, qualified 14th (the first woman, in 1977, this was her third time on the Indy 500 grid), and Tom Bigelow thirtieth (he was just at the back, because he was a second weekend qualifier), in their Sherman Armstrong T500B DFXs. Alan McCall worked for the team which was also represented by the Wildcat Offy of rookie Howdy Holmes, who was 13th. Both the Lola drivers complained of handling problems or, as it was known, 'Unser's twitch.'!

Al led from the start until lap 104 when an oil seal failed and let all the lubricant out of the gearbox. (He was black-flagged.) Rick Mears won for Penske in a PC6, with A.J. Foyt in a Parnelli second and Mike Mosley, driving an Eagle, third. Howdy Holmes was seventh, the first non-DFX-engined entry, and Tom Bigelow 14th. Janet Guthrie blew a piston after only three laps.

The next races (rounds five and six) of the CART Championship were held at Trenton, and both were won by Bobby Unse. USAC had its next race at Milwaukee. Victory here went to Foyt with Tom Bigelow in third place behind Bill Vukovich. Foyt had led the first ten laps before Sheldon Kinser, in a Watson Offy, passed him. His car later blew up.

The Pocono 500 was won again by A.J. Foyt. Howdy Holmes' Wildcat would have been second if not for an oil leak. Ongais retired, Jim McElreath in an Eagle-Offenhauser was second, and Larry Dickson, in a Penske-Cosworth PC6, who was sitting in the pits, out of fuel, when the chequered flag was shown, was third! Janet Guthrie had qualified fourth, alongside Bigelow on the second row with Larry Dickson in a Penske. Sadly, her clutch burnt out at the start. Tom Bigelow was eighth despite an 'off' caused by avoiding Gary Bettenhausen. Jim McElreath, driving an Eagle, was second and Dickson third.

Rounds seven and eight of the CART title fight were held at Michigan. The first race was won by Gordon Johncock and the second by Bobby Unser. No Lolas featured.

The Texas Speedway saw the next round of the USAC Championship and it was Foyt again. He led but hit some debris, letting Bigelow ahead but it didn't last. Tom came second, Sheldon Kinser third and Roger McCluskey fourth in a Lola T500.

Watkins Glen was next for the CART circus and the race went to Bobby Unser. Al had been on pole in the Chaparral 2K, but could only manage fifth. Rick Mears

'Perdigao'-sponsored Formula Ford 2000 of Placido Iglesias at Brands Hatch. (Courtesy LAT)

was second and Gordon Johncock third, also in Penskes.

There were no Lolas at Watkins Glen, but there sure enough was one at Trenton next time out for the CART's round ten after Al destroyed the Chaparral in practice at turn three. The team wheeled out the Lola, brought along as a spare, and still on its settings from Road Atlanta, and started preparing it to race again. Bobby had the pole but, in a thriller of a race, had to give best to Rick Mears, with Tom Sneva third in a McLaren. Again, Al could only manage sixth.

Milwaukee was USAC's round seven and Roger McCluskey won. Pole position had been taken by Tom Bigelow in the second Sherman Armstrong T500, and the race was between him and Roger McCluskey after Foyt blew up when leading just after half way. McCluskey, who was USAC Champ of '73, promptly retired, having become the first person other than Al Unser to win an IndyCar race in a Lola (as opposed to a Colt) since Graham Hill in 1966. 'Vuky' Vukovitch was third in a Watson Offy, then came the Lightning Offy of Johnny Parsons and Janet Guthrie. Lola 1-2-5: what a great finish to the season! Foyt 3320 points, Vukovich 1770, Bigelow 1305.

CART had several more rounds to go, Ontario being round 11. CART was proving to be much more dramatic and unpredictable than had been forecast, the last USAC round notwithstanding. Rick Mears was on pole from Al Unser in a replacement Chaparral 2K, with Bobby and Mario Andretti next. Bobby then won from Rick and Mario (all in Penskes) with Rutherford fourth for McLaren. Al was fifth and John Barnard was present to oversee the Chaparral

Michigan was CART's round 12 and Bobby Unser won from pole to chequered flag, whilst Al crashed the Chaparral due to a puncture. Road Atlanta saw Rick win again from

'Gordy', Bobby and Wally Dallenbach, all in Penskes, with Al Unser finishing fifth. The next race was at Phoenix for CART and went to Unser in the Pennzoil Chaparral 2K, with brother Bobby six seconds adrift and Rick Mears third, clinching the inaugural CART title. Bobby had started from pole with Al alongside.

The works Penskes of Bobby, Rick and (occasionally) Mario did 5607 of a possible 5700 racing miles! Rick Mears had 4060pts, Bobby Unser 3780, 'Gordy' Johncock 2211, Johnny Rutherford 2163, Al Unser 2085 and Danny Ongais 1443.

Two weeks later Al announced he was to drive for B. Hillin's Longhorn team in 1980. His replacement at Chaparral was Johnny Rutherford.

T540/540E – 1978/81 – FF – 106 built

Designed by Eric Broadley and Tony Gilliard, the T540 had a simple tubular space frame chassis, suspension by double wishbones at the front, top links with lower wishbones at the rear.

Overall length	140in
Overall width	64in
Wheelbase	94in
Front track	56in
Rear track	56in

In 1977, Mike Blanchet (later to become Lola's Managing Director), raced the 'works' development car with some success, including a fourth in the 1977 Formula Ford Festival.

For 1978, the Esso FF1600 series was easily won by Peter Morgan in a T540E who was also fourth in the RAC FF1600 series – beating the likes of Roberto Guerrero and Mike Thackwell, despite not having much money. Peter Morgan was also APG Driver Of The Year. *Autosport's* seasonal review suggested Lola could have done well with more cars out there fighting with Royale, etc. ... Come 1979 and Andy Ackerley and Julian Bailey were the main exponents, but, with most of the cars headed for the USA, not many competitors were interested in developing a Lola for Dunlops when they could buy something else. Sadly, while Julian Bailey went on from tenth in the BRSCC Dunlop Star Of Tomorrow points to become a F3000 winner and F1 driver for Tyrrell, none of the nine above him did much of note ...

T580/582 – 1978/81 – FF 2000 – 19 built

The T580 series was based on the existing T540, using its chassis. Designed by Eric Broadley, it featured a tubular space frame, suspension by way of top rockers and links and lower wishbones all round.

Overall length	163in
Overall width	61in
Wheelbase	94in
Front track	50in
Rear track	51in

In 1978, Mike Blanchet debuted the T580 at Silverstone in June, achieving fastest lap and finishing seventh. Proving himself a very consistent driver thereafter, Blanchet won the Allied Polymers Group round at Brands Hatch on August Bank Holiday Monday, leading from flag to flag. Second was Syd Fox and third Desiré Wilson. They were backed up by young Brazilian Placido Iglesias.

The T580 contingent went to the Benelux race at Zandvoort, where Mike qualified fifth and was dicing for the lead with Ron Kluit when he spun, taking both of them off. Blanchet later won at Mallory, taking first heat (second in latter edition to Rick Gorne in the Reynard in the battle of the sales directors!), and first overall. David Leslie (Van Diemen), was second with Chris Skellern (Crossle) third. Mike Blanchet finally finished third in the Lord Taverners' FF2000 points and eighth in the BAF FF2000 series despite missing some races. In 1979, Maarten Henneman won the Benelux FF2000 race at Zandvoort and eventually became the Benelux FF2000 champion.

Peter Morgan (ex-FF1600) came second to David Leslie in a Reynard in the BARC FF2000 opening race at Brands Hatch in March, and won both the following rounds which were held at Brands Hatch and Mallory Park, but could only manage fourth at Donington in June. After this, Peter Morgan had a big accident at Snetterton which put back his progress as he was already on a shoestring, despite some works assistance.

Ray Edge was fifth at Snetterton in October, while championship challenger Morgan was again out of luck. The final points were: David Leslie 101, Peter Morgan 72, Simon Kirkby 70 and Tim Wallwork 35.

T620/622 – 1978/79 – FSV – 26 built

The T620 and 622 had the same basic tub as T670 FSV.

In the USA in 1978, Tim Richmond won the Phoenix 'Mini Indy' Formula Super Vee in March. This was the first year that Lola mounted a big threat to SCCA FSV honours, and the team certainly went out in style with Herm Johnson winning all the last three rounds. Alas, it was not enough to wrest the title from Bill Alsup in an Argo, who won by 114 points to 99. Thereafter, American FSV virtually becomes a Ralt benefit; indeed, practically a one-make series.

Back in Europe for 1978, Arie Luyendyk won at the Nürburgring Formula Super Vee in a Rotel car. He left Formula Super Vee for the bigger and brighter lights of Formula Three. After that, it was Indy-bound for Luyendyk.

T670/672 – 1978/79 – F3 – 9 built

The T670 shared the same basic tub as the new T620 FSV, and much of the testing of the new Formula Three car was done by Mike Blanchet and Nigel Mansell. Aeros were very much like a revised T570 F3 car. A team of two 'works' cars for the upcoming British Vandervell and BP Formula Three Championships was announced in December 1977.

In 1978 Arie Luyendyk was loaned the works car for European Formula three at Zandvoort in March and finished sixth, but Luyendyk was unable to start at the Nürburgring for the second round due to a cracked tub sustained in practice. Luyendyk then sold his Formula Super Vee in order to concentrate on F3 with Roger Heavens. He was advised to switch to a Ralt but preferred to stick with Lola, for now. Luyendyk placed sixth at the Österreichring and fifth at Zolder. He used a Ralt at Monaco and did not even qualify!

Jean-Louis Bousquet did qualify a T670 at Monaco but broke a wheel on the first lap of the first heat. Elio de Angelis won after punting off Patrick Gaillard, both in Chevrons.

The ex-Luyendyk car, incidentally, was used by Lola as a development vehicle for the forthcoming new Formula Super Vee. Later on in the year it was returned to Formula 3 specification for Slim Borgudd to use, overseen by Eric Broadley himself.

After experiencing problems with his new T770 at the start of the 1979 season, Mike Blanchet switched to a modified and re-coded T642 model at Silverstone in the European Formula 3 round, as did Alain Hubert. Mike qualified 14th, immediately behind Nigel Mansell, and was 11th in his heat but failed to finish with a misfire in the final. Brett Riley, in a March Triumph, won from Chico Serra.

In May, Mike Blanchet finished tenth in the Silverstone Formula 3 round and was ninth at Cadwell Park a month later. He was then tenth in qualifying for the British Grand Prix support race ahead of Guerrero, Mansell and Prost in his Vega-powered car. Alas, the engine died on the first lap. Pole man Mike Thackwell beat his front row partner, Serra.

Mike Blanchet in a T672 Toyota was fourth to the Marches of Stefan Johansson, Chico Serra and Kenny Acheson at the Silverstone Vandervell British Formula three round, despite

Silverstone and the Lola T670 Formula Three car of 1979. (Courtesy LAT)

finishing in the Woodcote boonies with them all when a cloudburst flooded the track on lap 13. Inglesias, driving another Lola, was fifth; the only F3 championship points Lola gained in 1979 were when Chico Serra won the title.

T720 – 1979 – FSV
The T720 was another similar design to the T770 Formula three car.

T760 – 1979 – FAt – 1 built
Yet another design from the T770 F3 stable, the T760 was bold but unsuccessful.

Alo Lawler won on the debut of T760 at Mallory Park from pole position. He had been given the winner's trophy when the race was stopped after 31 laps, but then told it was going to restart! Luckily, he won the other 19 laps.

T770 – 1979 – F3 – 2 built
The T770 was a needle-nosed new car launched in February, 1979. It featured inboard suspension and aerodynamic sidepods in keeping with the newly-discovered ground effect principle. Eight cars were ordered, all for abroad, by the end of the month. The prototype was subsequently slightly damaged by Mike Blanchet in an 'off' in the damp at Snetterton. It had been tested without front wings and with a low mounted rear wing. The prototype (and the subsequent rehashed T670) had a Toyota engine in testing but raced a Chevrolet Vega unit until the money ran out.

In 1979, Philippe Alliot debuted his new T770 Lola Renault at Magny-Cours in the European Formula three series. After being seventh early on, he spun out and then had the engine fail. Alain Prost won in a Martini Renault. Next, at Silverstone, his heat was won by former Lola man Placido Iglesias, but in the final Alliot went no further than the first lap after an accident with N. Mansell. At Monaco soon afterward, Phillipe failed to qualify, being even slower than Alain Hubert's T670. Mike Blanchet, however, carried on in the British F3 in a T672

A re-designed T770/2 appeared in 1980. This now had a wide, sportscar-type nose which housed a radiator. Skirts had been banned, which necessitated major modifications. Blanchet was competitive in early races: third in the British F3 opener at Silverstone, second at Thruxton one week on.

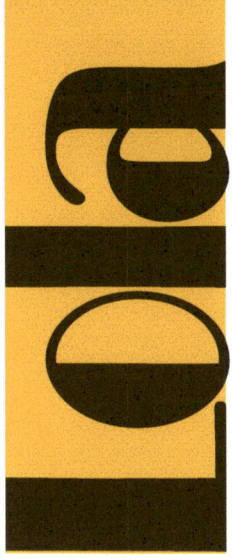

Lola

2
1980-1981

T332

In the USA, Lola T332-based Frissbees were seen in the Can-Am series, winning twice thanks to Al Unser in 1980 and Danny Sullivan in 1981, then Horst Kroll in 1985 and Paul Tracy winning the final Can-Am race ever, at Mosport, in 1986.

Frissbees also formed the basis for the Galles GR3S with which Al Unser Jr won the 1982 Can-Am title with four victories.

1980 Intrepid

Built from funds supplied by 'Jack Daniels' heir Garvin Brown, the 1979/1980 Intrepid GB1 of Danny Sullivan was also a Lance Smith design (see Prophet and Spyder), and T332 based. Smith, however, decided to ignore modern ground effect thinking and settle for a 'simple' wedge to acquire the required downforce: it didn't. [See Leon Mandel's book *Fast Lane Summer* for details, including how others called it the Insipid ...]

It was second at Watkins Glen '80 – flattering to deceive – before being replaced by a Lola T530. End of the line for the Insipid ... The marque was not to be found in records beyond 1980, having already shown its age viz-a-viz T530s, let alone others. 1980 Spyder reports were that Newman-Freeman were foregoing their Spyders for 1980 and buying four Chevron B51s to run with works blessing. Alas, it fell through when the manufacturers liquidated in the aftermath of Derek Bennett's death in 1978. They bought Lolas instead, but an old Spyder was resurrected for Stephen South at Brainerd and Trois Rivières (the T530 was not repaired from the Brainerd crash) when the throttle jammed. Part of Stephen's left leg was subsequently amputated and Rosberg replaced him.

In 1981, Rocky Moran got three thirds with the old car, whereas David Kennedy and John Morton both notched a fourth, and returnee Tom Klausler (replacing David Kennedy) a fifth in new Frissbees. At the final round in Las Vegas, Danny Sullivan scored a maiden Can-Am win, aboard his T332C-based Frissbee.

T333

Randy Lewis was fifth in his T332 CS at Sears Point in 1980 at the end of the first round of the Can-Am Championship, whilst eighth was Skeeter McKitterick in the ex-Jacky Ickx version. R.J. Nelkin was third at Mid-Ohio for the second round in a race of attrition. Nelkin took part in a few more Can-Am races without repeating his luck, before crashing and retiring.

Brian Redman and David Hobbs won the non-championship, IMSA-run Lumberman's 500 at Mid-Ohio in mid-season, beating the John Morton/Hurley Haywood Frissbee (delayed with battle damage when overtaking a Corvette), and the Gianpiero Moretti/Jim Busby Elfin. Driving a T430 in 1980, Costanzo was fourth ahead of a trio of T332s as the best of the locals in the Australian Grand Prix at Calder Raceway on November 16th. Alan Jones, in a Williams FW07, won, Bruno Giacomelli, in an Alfa, was second and Didier Pironi, driving an Elfin, third.

T390 De Cadenet

Missing from the 1980 Daytona 24 Hours, Alain de Cadenet and Desiré Wilson appeared at Brands Hatch for the World Championship Six Hours on the 16th of May, qualifing fifth and finishing third, splitting a Lancia Beta Monte Carlo 1-2-4. The race was won by Ricardo Patrese and Walter Röhrl. Poor Martin Raymond (of Fisons Lola fame) was killed when he was struck by two cars whilst working on his vehicle – the gearbox had seized – out in the country. The race was stopped and restarted. The *Autosport* race report said that, during practice, the team needed to change from 15in to 13in rear wheels "from De Cadenet's previous car", i.e. the 1977 one.

The De Cadenet Lola, with the same driver pairing, then won at Monza (with 183 laps) from Henri. Pescarolo and Jürgen Barth, also on 183 laps in a Porsche 935, with Patrese and Rohrl one lap behind on 182. Alain de Cadenet was only 13th on the grid after both drivers had 'offs' in practice. When Capoferri retired, Vittorio Brambilla in the Osella led, only to crash with 16 laps completed. The battle was then between the Porsche and the Lancias. De Cadenet was third at the halfway point and then Desiré took over, taking the lead as others pitted. Pescarolo eventually overhauled her and pulled 18 seconds clear, only to have to pit for fuel with two laps left, the team mistakenly thinking it was a six hour event. Trouble was, it was 1000kms! Pescarolo shot back onto the track but was still ten seconds behind at flagfall.

Next time out, at Silverstone, Alain and Desiré won again! It was May 11th. Reverting to 15in rims, Alain was not happy that his Cosworth DFV engine had endurance race characteristics, so the gear ratios were altered to suit. Second was the Siggi Brunn/Jürgen Barth-driven Porsche 908/3, which was overhauled in the final hour. Wilson got a one lap penalty for missing the chicane when she missed a gear, so she and Alain won not by a lap but by 0.82 seconds – close!

Also seen at Silverstone was the ACR of Lola stalwart Andre Chevalley Racing. Based on a T380 but with widened chassis, the brakes were not powerful enough for such a heavy car. Nevertheless, it qualified second thanks to Patrick Gaillard, who was sharing it with Andre Chevalley and François Trisconi. They started the race late due to ignition problems, but later had the fastest race lap to their credit for quite some time. Sadly, they retired the Longines-sponsored car with a broken clutch.

Alain and Desiré were joined by François Migault at the Le Mans 24-Hour race. They qualified sixth but Desiré flipped the car at the Virage Ford bends. The ACO stopped Desiré racing, having conveniently lost her time, and, as qualification depended on the average time of all the drivers, she made the team vulnerable. Sadly, the team then had no choice but to drop Desiré. A *fait accompli*. During the race itself, the car stopped early on the Mulsanne with electrical gremlins – a legacy of the shunt – but climbed to fourth place after ten hours. A broken crossmember at breakfast lost the team an hour, finally dropping the car to seventh overall.

Jean-Michel and Philippe Martin teamed up with Alain de Cadenet in a De Cadenet at the 1981 Silverstone 1000 kilometres in preperation for Le Mans. The team qualified 12th but the electrics died on the rolling start lap. For the Le Mans 24 Hours, the team managed to qualify 19th on grid (immediately behind the Kremer-built Porsche 917K/81) after an unspectacular two practice days, but the engine blew on the Mulsanne Straight. The 1977 de Cadenet was back again, under the DRA banner for Nick Faure and Vivian Candy and Martin Birrane but, having qualified a respectable 26th, early overheating and then fuel pump problems restricted the revs. They were finally put out in the night when the gearbox casing split, spewing out its contents. Very terminal.

At the Brands Hatch 1000kms in September, Richard Jones and Leon Walger qualified 12th but, after suffering water loss, Walger had two spins and finally hit the barriers at Surtees too hard to continue.

In 1980 the Capoferri DFV debuted at Monza, using a Bellasi-designed – and Lola-inspired – chassis. It took pole with Renzo Zorzi and Claudio Francisci driving, and led from the flag, but was out after only three laps with a water leak and seized engine.

T490/T590

Early in 1980, a Sports 2000 T490, with a bluff nose and enclosed rear wheels, was driven in Brands Hatch testing by former Crossle man John Cotton. It looked akin to a T590 and Trevelyan's 1978 'Lola Brick'. A garage proprietor from Bostons, Lincs, England, Tony Dickinson raced a Skoda 130RS silhouette car in the Wendy Wools, the ASCAR, and similar championships in 1980, driving a Lola T490 Sports 2000 formerly used by Teddy Toleman with an ex-Henton, two-litre Hart 420R engine. This replaced an earlier and heavier T296-based device and it won on its debut at Snetterton on May 11th, beating the T492-based 1300cc Skoda BDA of David Auger. Dickinson continued to win over the next three or so years, taking class and high overall placings in the Wendy Wools Championship. Syd Fox ran Desiré Wilson's old T492 in 1979. He placed third in the season starter, and a good run in the Brands Hatch World Championship for Makes Six Hours followed.

In the season opener at Silverstone, Frank Sytner won in a new T590, but T492s were next up thanks to John Brindley, Syd Fox and John Sheldon. Rossiter, in a T590, was fifth after a spin, whilst Taylor had his engine blow and did not take the start. (In 1980, Fox had a T492 rebodied by the TDC team with an extremely low rear deck. For the latter part of the season, Don Halliday took over driving.)

At the aforementioned Brands Hatch World Championship for Makes Six Hours, the Sports 2000 category was won by John Brindley and John Sheldon with ninth overall from the Divina Galica/Mark Thatcher Tiga.

Ian Taylor, driving a Tiga, then took charge of the Championship, winning the Derwent TV title. In 1981, there were some outings for the older car with class places but without much success. John Sheldon was, however, one who showed well in a T492.

T500B

For 1980, CART and USAC joined forces to run a championship together, and Johnny Rutherford won the first race at the Ontario Motor Speedway from pole, in his first race for Chaparral. Al Unser qualified third on the grid but had to retire due to CV joint failure. Sherman Armstrong tried to switch to March Orbiters from T500s, and Longhorns were officially sanctioned (and paid for) Williams FW07 copies.

Come the second round, the Indianapolis 500, Jerry Sneva qualified fifth, rookie Greg Leffler 23rd and Tom Bigelow 31st, all in Sherman T500Bs. Thirty second was Gary Bettenhausen in a Sherman Wildcat Offy, and a fifth Sherman entry for Howdy Holmes did not make the race. Johnny Rutherford won again with Tom Sneva second, having driven from the back row of the grid with Gary Bettenhausen doing likewise to follow Sneva into third. Tom Bigelow placed eighth and Leffler tenth; Jerry Sneva crashed on lap 130 after clipping the wall whilst running fourth.

Milwaukee was the venue for round three of the championship, and Al Unser was third on the grid with a Longhorn as usual. Longhorns used sliding skirts, but it was the beginning of the end for these: in a season peculiar for its political wranglings, skirts were allowed in qualifying rounds, originally scheduled as CART races, and banned in the ones billed as USAC rounds! Bobby Unser won from Johnny Rutherford, repeating the victory at Pocono for round four. Jerry Sneva qualified sixth in a T500B and was amongst the leaders when his electrics failed, forcing him to retire. Howdy Holmes was eighth in another T500B.

No Lolas featured in the overall results in the next five races, and Howdy Holmes crashed the Orbiter at Ontario, breaking some ribs. Michigan saw an Andretti win with Bobby Unser and Rick Mears backing up a Penske 1-2-3, whilst Mexico, round 11, saw Rick win and Johnny Rutherford fail to finish for the first time all year. Phoenix was the final race of the series and victory went to Tom Sneva from Mario Andretti and Gary Bettenhausen's Orbitor. Bill Alsup spun his Penske, collecting Greg Leffler in his T500 along the way. Johnny Rutherford wound up champion, winning the title from Bobby Unser and Tom Sneva. By 1981, the T500 was outdated and had given way to much newer machinery.

T530 – 1980 – Can-Am – 10 built

Two weeks after the Chevron B51 first saw the light of day (just before Christmas 1979), the new Lola T530 Can-Am was announced. This was Lola's first real ground effect Can-Am car (or any ground effect car, for that matter), and was meant to replace the triple title-winning T332 CS.

Shaken down by Patrick Tambay and Brian Redman, the new 'big-banger'

Geoff Brabham driving the VDS team's Lola T530 in 1981. (Courtesy Bob Roemer)

The T530 was a big bruiser of a closed-in, single-seater for Can-Am racing in 1980. This is the ex-Danny Sullivan-driven car, now racing in HSR events.

sports-racer featured a monocoque chassis with wide, ground effect sidepods. The Chevrolet Z28 5-litre engine was semi-stressed with its own steel frame, and the bodywork – in polyester and Nomex – had been fashioned in the SERA wind tunnel. Featuring front-mounted water radiators, the T530 had a central nose duct above the splitter, which allowed air into the brake cooling ducts. The sliding carbon fibre skirts were mounted about 12in in from the car's sides. Front suspension was by lower wishbones and upper rockers with inboard springs/damper units, and at the rear by lower parallel links with fabricated upper links and outboard springs/dampers. Brakes were by Lockheed/Girling and were huge (10.9in diameter by 11in width), ventilated discs with twin four pot calipers at the front, single four pot calipers at the rear, mounted outboard at the front and inboard at the rear.

A Hewland DG300 five-speed gearbox was used and the 31 US gallons of fuel were contained in the sidepods, along with the twin oil coolers. Front wheels measured 13in diameter by 11in width and rears were 15in diameter and 18in width. Two batches of five chassis were planned to be built. Two of the first five had already been ordered by the Haas/Hall team, and two more for Geoff Lees by the VDS team of Count Van Der Straten.

Overall length 182in
Overall width 83in
Wheelbase 106in
Front track 70in
Rear track.................................. 64in
Weight 1650lb

The T530 became renowned for its heavy steering, but also for its strength and stability. Writing in *Classic & Sports Car*, Willie Green tested one in 1987 and reported: "It looks big and heavy, and by heavens, so it is. And it's very, very quick ... And the odd thing, of course, is that you're sitting in the middle of a sports car. This isn't a problem, but, like that feeling of being in the middle of a glass-fibre movable field, it is unusual. In fact by the time you get down to the serious business of driving the beast you forget all about it. You start up and pull away with a little helpful push from the mechanics – this isn't a racing start, so no histrionics. Drop the clutch, a whiff of throttle and you burble out of the pits, all relatively undramatic.

The first thing you notice is that the throttle pedal is incredibly heavy: You've been told that regular drivers Andrew Ratcliffe and Mike Wilds like it that way. Wait and see ...

"Out onto the circuit and you give it a test blast on the throttle. The result is, literally, explosive. The engine peaks at 600bhp or so at 7000rpm, and it's got torque coming out of it like jam out of an over-filled doughnut, great gobs of it. This is sheer brute force, a dragster in dress.

"Chonk up through the gears, and notice another personal irritant: in true Lola fashion the gear lever knob is free to rotate, which I hate. I'm always slightly worried that my hand could slip on it, miss a change in the heat of the moment, during a race, and the result could be at best a blown engine, at worst an off. In a big way, because if this device gets away

The VDS team developed the Lola CanAm theme with the introduction of its own VDS-001. (Author photo)

from you, then you've got problems. To put it mildly.

"And it doesn't take long to find another irritant, too. The spring/damper units are inboard, sharing your foot room, and the pedal box is a mite crowded. So crowded, in fact, that after only a few laps both ankles are bruised after being banged up aainst those springs.

"By now you're half-way round your first lap, and you've begun to appreciate some of the qualities, the characteristics, of this mega-device. That power, that torque: The track is damp and slippery, and that throttle pedal, the weight of it, doesn't help when you are trying to control it with the right foot.

"Because the lovely thing is that you can. This is not just a point and squirt car, although you could probably put up very respectable lap times by driving it that way. The adhesion, considering the track conditions, is surprisingly good, you *can* put all that power and torque down. What's more, you can really hang the back out, chuck it around, play with it. It really is quite controllable even if the steering is heavy – but, again, you get used to it very quickly, and you appreciate how much better it is after a short acquaintance.

"But ... controllable it may be, but you've got to stay in charge of it. As has been said, if it did get away ... More to the point, though, is that it is pointless throwing it around like a Formula Ford or some such. You're going to be considerably faster by keeping it neat and tidy, getting all that power down progressively, not dissipating it in wild wheelspin, nor scrubbing it away by going sideways. So, in a corner, it's off brakes, set it up, then feed in the throttle, keeping it nicely balanced, no wild sawing of the wheel, stay neutral, and you've gained a couple of yards on the opposition without thinking. Of course, the higher your exit speed the faster you are down the straights: and fast in this is *bloody* fast, let me tell you. I saw the full 7000rpm on the Silverstone Club Circuit back straight, and you'd better believe that it not only feels fast, it is fast. Someone calculated it as 160mph which is highly exhilarating, superbly exciting, but could turn into sheer terror if the brakes weren't up to it. They are, almost unbelievably so. There's a touch of vibration, common with ventilated discs, no problem, but when you stand on the stop pedal – it does. You can go deep, deep into the corners, then hit the brakes and it's like running into a brick wall – that speed just vanishes. Pedal pressures are fine, too, easy to modulate.

"After a few laps you've become acclimatised to that blinding acceleration, that incredible stopping power, that amazing adhesion, and you begin to look at other factors. You've been using third for Copse, second for Becketts: With all that thumping torque you could happily take both in one gear higher. But there's that throttle response, or rather the heavy pedal. Thus it's better to keep higher up in the rev range, because the torque is more progressive there. You're not going to get a great big chunk of it when least expected. That heavy linkage is bothersome: I reckon I could knock off at least a second, maybe two, were it lighter, more delicate.

"Six or so laps, and I'm down to a 54secs time. Not bad for a track test in somebody else's car. Last October Mike Wilds drove it at the Peterborough M. C. meeting, coming up against John Foulston's T530, both going for the outright lap record. Mike had problems but recorded a 49.5secs fastest lap in practice, so honours went to Foulston who equalled the record at 50.1secs. With a lighter throttle, perhaps one or two personal tweaks, I wouldn't mind having a go myself ...

"As you roll into the pits your mind runs back over some of the things you've noticed. Maggotts is flat: Just, but flat. There is a slight fluff as you change up into fourth but it is not worrisome. You really *do* need some padding around the ankles to prevent the ravages of the springs. You can brake with the best and outbrake the rest. The deep baying of 5.7 litres of Chevrolet power.

"It's a man-sized, mega-macho, car, big, heavy but agile with it. It's the total opposite of the Lotus 72, which was all delicate, finger-tip: This thing you pick up by the scruff of its neck, use muscle power for steering throttle, brakes. Brute force, but don't treat it wth ignorance because it'll kick."

The T530 prototype was lost on the USA railroad system en route to its new team, and quite a few days were wasted as they hunted it down!

For the 1980 season, pre-season information revolved around the fact that Tambay had tested a T530 at Rattlesnake Raceway in February and was soon under the lap record and signed onto the Haas/Hall payroll, who had ordered the first two cars. The VDS team ordered two more cars for Geoff Brabham, and Bobby Rahal was also supposed to have a T530 to go with his rebuilt Prophet (itself a rebuilt T332/333 by Jack Smith), with the possibility of a new ground effect Prophet to follow. There was also the return of the (updated) Schkee for Tom Klausler. Paul Newman's team (in which Bill Freeman had left and the cars were now engineered by Barry Green), was to forsake Spyders for Chevron B51s but, unfortunately, with Chevron in receivership, Paul Newman had to buy two more Lola T530s for Stephen South and Elliott Forbes-Robinson. Even by their first race they were heavily revised, most visibly with cutaway sidepods. Another T530 was sold to Ricardo Londono of Colombia, and yet another by R.J. Nelkin, whilst Garvin Brown bought yet another to replace his Intrepid for Danny Sullivan to drive.

At the beginning of the season, opinion on how the T530 would fare were divided, some 'experts' believing that the older T332 CS was probably able to penetrate the air better than the blunt-nosed T530. Also, the new car had front end lift/understeer compensated for by downforce; hence the heavy steering.

Sears Point was the first race of the new season and was easily won by Patrick Tambay from Elliott Forbes-Robinson in his T530 and Rahal's Prophet. Geoff Brabham was fourth, also in a T530. Patrick Tambay had taken pole position and led throughout in the Magicolor-sponsored car. Tambay's car was almost standard, unlike many of the others. John Morton in a Frissbee (itself a much modified Lola, re-designed by Trevor Harris) shared the front row but failed to finish. Skeeter McKitterick was eighth in the ex-Jacky Ickx T332 CS, now painted yellow.

In this race, Tambay drove chassis number two, with the original number one car there as a back-up, Forbes-Robinson had number five and Steven South number seven for the VDS team. The only non-Lola based car in the entire 'big division' field of 21 was Al Holbert in the CAC-1, a Lee Dykstra-designed car.

Round two was at Mid-Ohio and Tambay won again as the others crashed or retired along the way. Bobby Rahal had been on the pole but soon fell out with ignition problems, and Stephen South did not even get beyond the pace lap. Elliott Forbes-Robinson retired on lap two with an engine malfunction. Al Holbert was second in the CAC-1 with newcomer R.J. Nelkin third in an old T332 CS: Nelkin went on to do a few more races without any more glory, crashed himself and soon disappeared from the scene, saying it was too expensive. Gary Gove was fourth in a Ralt.

Mosport saw Tambay win again from South, with Geoff Brabham third for the VDS team. Bobby Rahal had been on the pole but he crashed.

Watkins Glen, and it was Patrick again with Danny Sullivan second in the Intrepid and Al Holbert third in the CAC. This race was remembered mainly for the pitlane crash between John Morton in the Frissbee and Geoff Brabham driving the VDS T530, as both accelerated away from leading pitstops, eliminating both cars.

Round five was at Elkhart Lake and, for the first time, not won by Tambay. This was because Tambay was at home, recovering from illness. The race was won by Al Holbert and was the first non-Lola victory of the reconstituted formula. Geoff Brabham was second, Elliott Forbes-Robinson third. Stephen South had been on pole. Geoff Brabham had been alongside, despite wrecking his race car and needing to use the spare for the event. Mario Andretti was substitute for the indisposed Patrick Tambay. He was fifth on the grid but out after 18 laps with a broken throttle return spring whilst lying third.

Brainerd Racetrack, round six saw a comeback win for the unbeaten Tambay. Al Holbert in the CAC was second with Elliott Forbes-Robinson third in the VDS T530. Rahal in the Prophet was fourth and Danny Sullivan took fifth on his first outing in a T530. Stephen South had a front wheel break in practice, so used an old NF11 but crashed again.

Poor Stephen South had an even worse accident at the next race, in practice for Trois Rivières, which resulted in partial amputation of his left leg. The throttle had jammed open on his Spyder, the Lola not having been repaired. Patrick Tambay won from Al Holbert and Bobby Rahal, despite a deflating tyre.

Road Atlanta for round eight and Geoff Brabham won for the VDS team, with Danny Sullivan's T530 and Bobby Rahal in the Prophet next up. Patrick Tambay was only fourth but had secured the title, despite having his first race defeat. The engine had gone off a bit ...

Keke Rosberg replaced Stephen South in Newman's team, while Tiga revealed its new CA80 using a Formula 2 chassis and the ubiquitous Chevy V8. There was also a new Intrepid GB1-05 for Danny Sullivan, based on a BRM 210 monocoque chassis by Hepworth.

At Laguna Seca Vern Schuppan debuted the Tiga but the engine blew in practice and the car failed in the race due to brake problems. Al Unser won in a Frissbee – which used one of his old F5000 T332 tubs from 1976! Keke Rosberg took pole and second place, Elliott Forbes-Robinson was third and top regular in a T530.

Al Holbert won the Riverside finale from Elliott Forbes-Robinson, Keke and Tambay, all in T530s. Holbert won by 0.65sec despite bad brakes and bad tyres as Forbes-Robinson closed in. Earlier, Geoff Brabham and Keke Rosberg had led until colliding. Geoff retired but Keke went on, the nose of his car eventually ripping off in the slipstream.

So, at the finish, Patrick Tambay took the championship with 61pts, Al Holbert 40, Geoff Brabham 26, Elliott Forbes-Robinson 24 and Bobby Rahal 19.

Previewing the 1981 season to come, former Formula Atlantic star Jeff Wood became the new, full-time Haas team driver, with Patrick Tambay unable or unwilling to do more than two or three races due to his F1 commitments with Theodore. Tambay had decided against Can-Am as Carl Haas had no sponsorship, and was beginning to seriously consider Indy. Tony Dowe (who had been lured away from Newman the year before) remained the team's chief mechanic. The VDS team had decided to continue with the highly modified T530 until the new, T530-based VDS-001 was ready; Tony Cicale was working hard on the project, mainly a totally re-shaped body, as the team engineer. Al Unser and Teo Fabi were destined to have March 817s for the Newman team, Al Holbert a new CAC-2 (eventually), and even a Frissbee for Dave Kennedy. Graham McRae had a new car, for Reynolds and Needham, and Pete Lovely a FW07B to come at Mid-Ohio for Gary Gove.

The T532 superceded the T530, and was stiffer, with new suspension, and better aerodynamics.

Teo Fabi won Mosport – the first round of the 1981 championship – easily in the March 817. He led from pole position with only Geoff Brabham's VDS T530 on the same lap. Danny Sullivan was third and Jeff Wood fourth, also in Lolas. Geoff had his old T530, not his new car. At Mid-Ohio, Fabi won again with Brabham again having to be content with second. Moran, in a Frissbee, was third and Al Holbert fourth. Danny Sullivan was the top T530 in fifth place (Sullivan's car was the ex-Rosberg/Nelkin T530); Jeff Wood was sixth.

Part of the reason for the March's success was that Robin Herd took a personal interest in the cars, which were lighter than the Lolas. Randy Lewis used the CAC-1 and Al Holbert the CAC-2.

Watkins Glen for round three of the championship saw Teo Fabi on pole again, but during the race he suffered piston failure and the win went to Al Holbert in the CAC-2. It was a weekend of crashes: Gary Gove destroyed the Lovely-entered FW07 car (breaking his leg in the process), and Jeff Wood the brand new T532. Al Unser had gearbox seizure in the race, causing one crash and then another as he cruised back to the pits. Geoff Brabham led but his gearbox died out on the track. Danny Sullivan took over the lead but broke a wheel passing a backmarker. Al Holbert inherited the lead and won. Danny Sullivan was second, Moran, in the Frissbee, third and Kennedy, in his new Frissbee, fourth.

For the Elkhart Lake race, it was Teo Fabi's turn to have an accident, going into the trees at the fifth gear kink when the rear wheels locked up. Amazingly, Teo was unhurt and next day went fastest of all to take pole position! However, he missed the race due to black eyes acquired from the practice accident. Geoff Brabham won in the

Later life. Bob Roemer's T540, now used for vintage racing. Bob had just overtaken the Swift when the photo was taken. (Courtesy Bob Roemer)

VDS T530. (It was to be his only Lola success of the 1981 campaign), with Jeff Wood second in a T532. Al Unser was third for March with Al Holbert fourth in his CAC-2.

The VDS-001 was revealed to the press in August. Built at Santa Ana, it had been designed by Trevor Harris around the centre of a Lola T530 monocoque, with aerodynamics by Tony Cicale. The fuel cell, roll bar and engine mountings were Lola based, but the rest was new. It had outboard brakes and suspension all round, the front also being derived from the T530, though the rear was Harris-designed and the car had been fabricated by Jack Smith. Team manager was Steve Horne and the engines were to be built by Weis motors. The new car complied with the 1982 no skirts rule. Geoff Brabham said that it was easier to drive than the Lola, carrying more downforce.

Brabham proved his claims by taking the new car to Edmonton for round five and winning first time out. He beat Teo Fabi for pole position, breaking his run of all four so far, but the March led early on, only for a punctured tyre to explode as Geoff Brabham challenged for the lead on lap 46. The two cars collided and Fabi was out. Brabham spun and continued. Danny Sullivan, in the T530, was 37 seconds in arrears at the finish; John Morton in his Frissbee was third and Jeff Wood in the T530 fourth.

Al Holbert won Trois Rivières, Geoff Brabham was second in a T530, saving the VDS for next time, with Jeff Wood in his T530 third. But it was Fabi who came out tops at Mosport, despite a recent appendix operation. Bobby Rahal was second in the other March, replacing Al Unser because of date clashes. Geoff Brabham took third in VDS-001 and Klausler was fourth in the Frissbee. The best placed Lola was Paul Macey in fifth with an old T294 BDG. Jeff Wood had been fourth at one point in the race but retired.

Riverside for round eight was next. Al Holbert won, with Jeff Wood second in the T530 and Klausler third. Randy Lewis, driving the CAC-1, was fourth and John Morton fifth for T332-based Frissbee. Geoff Brabham had led in the VDS-001, and Fabi dropped out from pole position when a wheel fell off. Danny Sullivan tried a T530 but raced a new Frissbee, the suspension failing on the second lap. Jeff Wood also swapped the lead with Al only to be pressured into a last lap mistake, letting Al Holbert through to win. So near, yet ...

Laguna Seca saw Teo Fabi win again; Holbert took second, Geoff Brabham was third in VDS-001 and Morton and Klausler fourth and fifth for Frissbee, with Wood sixth.

At the final round in Las Vegas, it was finally Danny Sullivan who scored his maiden victory aboard his T332C-based Frissbee. Teo Fabi was second after a tremendous year and Geoff Brabham was third in VDS-001, taking the championship. Bobby Rahal in a March was fourth with the Frissbees fifth and sixth for Morton and Klausler. Al Holbert was seventh and Jeff Wood eighth, ending a disappointing season. Holbert had finished eight of the nine races he had started but his places were just not high enough.

Geoff Brabham had 487 points to take the championship, Teo Fabi had 456, Al Holbert 420, Danny Sullivan 303 and Jeff Wood 256.

T540

In 1980, Ian Khan won the Aintree ELS FF1600 qualifying race on the second of August and was fifth in the overall combined event later that same day. Kevin Gillen replaced his Martlet DM3 with a T540E to take fifth place in the Dunlop 'Star of Tomorrow' series behind Tim Lee-Davey in his Tiga.

The 1981 specification was for a tubular steel space frame chassis with front suspension by unequal length wishbones, while the rear had top links with reversed lower wishbones and twin radius rods and Armstrong dampers, mounted outboard. Brakes were Lockheed calipers with solid cast discs and Lola rack and pinion steering was used. Bodywork was in GRP.

The first round of the 1981 Dunlop-Autosport 'SoT' championship saw T540Es for Mark Peters, Mike Hawkins, Mike McCrea, Trevor Ruddenham and Chris Bullimore, all via Team Touraco. The best result was Peters in seventh place, although Hawkins won at Brands Hatch in April.

Mark Peters led the Dunlop-Autosport 'SoT' championship by mid-August despite not winning a race (Royales won the majority), but then slipped back in the Slush Puppy car, maybe by virtue of a little over-exuberance. At around the same time, however, he led the BARC Junior points chase. *Autosport* said his: "smooth

and flowing style is the hallmark of a natural".

Mark won at Lydden in September to extend his BARC lead – he and Steve Kempton in a T540E both winning heats – and then finished first and second in the final. Peters then won his first Dunlop-Autosport victory, at Oulton Park later in the month to move back to second place behind Dave Button in an Image in the 'SoT' points race. He then won the BARC race at Snetterton to take the championship. At the Thruxton 'SoT' finale on November 7th, Peters' car jumped out of gear on lap four, was rammed by a follower who rolled(!), but Peters carried on to claim third and won the 'SoT' title. In November 1981, Maximo Oliveiri won the International Formula Ford Grand Prix at La Chinita in Venezuela aboard a T540, beating the likes of Mike Roe and John Paul Jr.

T580

1980 and Henneman won the European FF2000 opener at the Nürburgring, with Huub Vermeulen third in another T580. Henneman then set the fastest lap but failed to finish at Zolder at the end of May. By mid-season, Vermeulen led the European FF2000 Championship.

At the end of August, Mike Blanchet was fifth at Zandvoort, with Huub third, in a race won by Fred Krab in a Delta. Delta opposition filled the top six with Jim Vermeulen seventh, also in a T580.

In the same year, Norman Paine and Nick Cole campaigned T580s with gusto in Formula Libre and/or monoposto races, whilst Rob Cooper won the Silverstone Motorcraft FF2000 race in June, and then was second in the Cussons Imperial Leather race at Brands Hatch soon afterwards, as well as taking a third at Mallory Park. At this point, Cooper was lying fifth in the championship to Richard Trott as the best non-Royale. He then won at Mallory Park in late July, holding off the Reynards of Martin Brundle and Frank Bradley, besides winning at Snetterton, too. He finished third in the final points in both the Imperial Leather and Motorcraft FF2000 Championships, both titles going to Richard Trott in a Royale.

The T582, new for 1981, was designed by Eric Broadley and Bob Marston, who later moved to Royale. This car's most striking feature was the unusual, boxy look – the result of uncompromising pursuit of a clean venturi, as well as it having a tall, square opening for the front mounted radiator. The T582 had a tubular steel space frame with front suspension by top rockers and lower wishbones, and the rear had top links, top radius rods, bottom wishbones and track control links. Armstrong dampers, inboard at the front and outboard at the rear, were used, whilst braking was taken care of with Lockheed calipers and solid steel discs. Lola rack and pinion steering was fitted and the bodywork was in GRP. The price for a rolling chassis with gearbox was quoted at £6750 plus VAT.

The Lola T492 Sports 2000 car of 1982. (Courtesy LAT)

The first production car was for Ian Briggs and Penistone. The first early shakedown tests by Mike Blanchet at Silverstone showed that Lola had a very good car in the T582.

Briggs won the Formula Ford qualifier at Brands Hatch on March 1st in an older T580; Dave Coyne, in a Delta, took the Pace-sponsored race on the same menu from Rob Cooper in a T580. A week later Briggs won the Pace round at Thruxton in his T580. Then, on March 28th, Briggs won in the T582 at Oulton Park, causing Lola to put an advert in *Autosport* to celebrate and drum up more business. He also won at Oulton Park in April. Rob Cooper won at Brands Hatch on May 3rd but, by now, Tommy Byrne in his Van Diemen was regularly showing a clean set of heels to Ian Briggs, Mike Taylor, Rob Cooper and co.

T580

In 1981 Huub Vermeulen won the Zandvoort FF2000 race. He subsequently finished eighth in the final EFDA FF2000 with 26 points, with fellow T580 campaigner Peter Elgaard tenth.

Tommy Byrne won from Kris Nissen in a Delta.

T580', though now outclassed, still had the occasional victory: Nick Cole won the Formula Libre race at Lydden in September 1981 and the Cinque ports Flying Club round there in October, whilst Huub Vermeulen was third in the Golden Lion and Netherlands FF2000 Championships, which were won by Basil Mann from Ron Kluit. Both men were in Deltas.

T590/592/592C – 1980/83 – Sports 2000 – 84+ built – 594/594C

The T590 was a Sports 2000 car and was announced to the press in November 1979. An all-enveloping body enclosed the rear wheels. Early tests were encouraging; the new car was needed to combat the almost total domination by the Tigas of Ian Taylor, Richard Morgan and James Weaver. Narrower and lower, the new T590 was lighter than its predecessor, with a lower centre of gravity and different suspension. It also had a longer wheelbase and reduced frontal area. The T590 was due to start going to customers in December.

Testing showed the T590 to be very quick straight away. Improved straight line speed probably helped, and was achieved by a considerable reduction in frontal area compared to the T490/492 series. Lola pointed out that the T590 set a precedent for the 'lay down' driver position in a small sports car.

At the start of 1980, three T590s appeared in February's pre-season Brands Hatch testing: one for Jeremy Rossiter, one for Nick Cole, and one for Alan Humberstone. Frank Sytner won the series opener at Silverstone in the new T590, with T492s second, third and fourth. Rossiter, in a T590, was fifth after a spin. Ian Taylor's engine blew up and he failed to start, but got his own back at Thruxton the next time out, beating Frank Sytner into second place. Sytner had collided with Rossiter en route, dropping him to fifth place at the finish.

For the third race at Mallory Park, Frank Sytner took the lead from Taylor on the last lap, with James Rossiter in third place. At Oulton Park for round four, it was a Taylor-Weaver 1-2, Rossiter again coming third. Frank Sytner had three collisions over the weekend! (A measure of how closely fought this championship was.) Ian Taylor and James Weaver repeated their Oulton Park result at Brands Hatch on Easter Monday, whilst at Silverstone all the Tigas and Lola T590s were adjudged illegal due to the battery cover not making cockpits 'symmetrical' as per the regulations. Luckily, the problem was resolved. Frank Sytner and James Rossiter were second and third behind James Weaver, who won despite a very optimistic overtaking try early on by Ian Taylor which put the series leader off the track.

Soon it was Chris Alford's turn to win in a T590 whilst, as Taylor got back on top at Donington in mid-season, David Leslie debuted another threat – the Crossle – into a promising fourth place. Mike Blanchet joined the ranks, finishing third to a Taylor/Weaver Tiga 1-2 at Silverstone in mid-September (beating Rossiter in a T590), and was soon to win himself, at Snetterton in October.

Abroad, Peter Sadler, an ex-Ford GT40 driver, won at Jyllandsringen in his T590 in August, beating a whole host of Tigas. Despite this, Lolas were well beaten over the season and Ian Taylor became the 1980 Derwent TV champion.

New for 1981, the T592 was designed by Eric Broadley and Bob Marston and had an aluminium and steel monocoque. The front suspension featured unequal double wishbones, and the rear had top links allied to reversed lower wishbones with twin radius rods. The uprights were cast aluminium at the front, cast magnesium at the rear. Lola rack and pinion steering was fitted, and the brakes were Lockheed calipers with solid iron discs. The T592C was for SCCA American racing and hillclimbs, and was a worthy contender. Wheelbase was 95ins; front track was 56ins; rear track was 56ins. The price (rolling chassis with gearbox): £8250 plus VAT.

Kurt Thiim won the Derwent TV supported opener at Silverstone on 29th March in the debuting March 81S. No Lolas were in the top six. An ominous start ...

A track test of Geoff Farmer's much modified T590 versus Tiga SC81 was carried out by Desiré Wilson in the Autosport Formula Ford Yearbook supplement. She was much impressed and said how much she looked forward to the new T592.

Hans Edvinsson, driving a T590, won the EFDA Euro-Sports 2000 at Mantorp Park from Stanley Dickens in a T590. There was only one non-Lola in the top six. Fifth was the T590 of Charles Zwolsman, now run by the EuroRacing works team.

Jeremy Rossiter, Peter Sadler and Geoff Farmer won the Oulton Park Enduro 200 by seven seconds from a whole pack of Tigas (who had won round one). Rossiter and Farmer also won the Brands Hatch Enduro.

Edvinsson won the EFDA Sports 2000 race at Zandvoort from Ros de Giaxa de Salvi, Stanley Dickens and Jim Vermeulen, all in T590s. Stanley Dickens won at Donington in round three on June 7th, beating the Tigas, with Edvinsson, in a T590, fifth. Then it was de Salvi's turn at Zandvoort, with Jim and Huub Vermeulen next up. De Salvi also won the final there in September. Stanley Dickens became the EFDA Euro-Sports 2000 champion with Edvinsson second.

The Rossiter and Farmer-driven T590 qualified 13th at the Brands Hatch WEC 1000kms on 27th September, only one place behind the Jones and Walger De Cadenet, but two places adrift of the class-leading Ian Taylor and John Sheldon Tiga. The T590 of John Webb and John Brindley qualified 23rd, and an old Swedish T492 was 25th. All the Lolas had problems, leaving the honours to go to Tiga again.

The best T590 in the final Derwent Sports 2000 points was John Brindley, tenth (he had bought a Tiga mid-year). John Sheldon became champion. The T590 did do better on the continent, though, winning not only the European title (see above), but also the Scandinavian, Benelux and Dutch crowns, (Ros de Giaxa di Salvi with Huub Vermeulen second and Jim Vermeulen third).

The prototype of the T592 won the SCCA Run-offs with Larry Campbell driving.

T600 – 1981 – Group 6/IMSA GTP – 12 built

The T600 was designed by Eric Broadley, assisted by engineer, Andrew Thorby, and employed a full-length aluminium, honeycomb-bonded and riveted chassis (monocoque panels fabricated from flat panels of aluminium skin bonded on to aluminium honeycomb, using epoxy film adhesive and hot cured in a press), which was very rigid. For ground effect, the T600 sported full-length venturi tunnels made (as was the body) of glass reinforced plastic and Nomex by Harley plastics of Sawtry, Huntingdon. (Authoritative sources say composites were only used by the factory for venturi underbodies – other body panels of composite construction were later fitted by customers.) The doors hinged forward. In WEC and Le Mans outings just a smallish hole was opened in the roof to qualify for Group 6 instead of IMSA GTP. The rear wheels were enclosed by 'spats' to keep the all-important airflow from being interrupted. Early aerodynamic studies for the bodywork were by Max Sardou (ex-T530) and SERA, and then later at Imperial College. Another similar feature to that of the T530 was fuel carried in side sponsons.

The Interscope team's Chevrolet V8-powered T600. At one point Interscope owned three of the 12 T600s produced by Lola. (Author photos)

Suspension was by double wishbones over Bilstein coil spring/damper units all round, with adjustable anti-roll bars front and rear. Rear spring/damper units were set partially within wheel wells to clear venturi tunnels. Wheels were cast magnesium with alloy steel hubs, and steering was by new offset Lola-designed rack and pinion. Braking was looked after by ventilated AP discs with Lockheed four-pot calipers, all mounted outboard, and BBS 16in diameter wheels were fitted. A Hewland VG five-speed transaxle was used for the first car, which was prepared for IMSA racing with a 5.7-litre, Chaparral-built Chevrolet engine and 600bhp plus. The Cosworth DFV would use a DG type gearbox. Rolling chassis were supplied with a fitting kit, including exhaust to suit.

IMSA-prepared T600s weighed 900kg, Group 6 cars 800kg. Cost was £30,000 minus the engine.

Overall length	186in
Overall width	78in
Overall height	41in
Wheelbase	106in
Front track	62in
Rear track	61in

First shown as an artist's impression in *Autosport* in mid-December 1980, the T600 was intended for the 1981 Le Mans 24 Hours and the IMSA GTP series, and then Group C, which was to be introduced in 1982. Actually, it was not Group C legal as the long venturi tunnels left the central flat bottom area too small. Apart from the Aston Martin Nimrod, this was to be the first coupé since the glorious T70s. *Autosport* also mentioned that Guy Edwards would run an open car (just that little hole in the roof) in all the European rounds of the 1981 World Championship for Makes. Early tests of the T600 were to be conducted by Brian Redman, and the new car would have built-in jacks and be capable of using a variety of different engines, e.g: Chevrolet V6 or V8, Cosworth DFV, turbos, etc.

With the first car already putting in impressive test lappery in the USA with Brian Redman (he lapped Riverside quicker than Geoff Brabham in the VDS T530), the Ultramar-backed car for Guy Edwards and Emilio de Villota was announced at the London Hilton in April, 1981, complete with a 'Racing For Charities' idea. This was the second car built and was to be Cosworth-powered. It had been prepared by Ian Dawson with 'works' blessing, and was due to debut at Mugello on April 12th. Ford's new Group 'C' contender, the C100, was announced at the same time.

When the World Endurance

Championship got going in Europe it was Osella who dominated, Giorgio Francia and Lella Lombardi winning the Mugello race from pole position. The Lola got into the act next time round, when the teams went to Monza, but the T600 suffered from being unable to generate sufficient heat to its Dunlop tyres, which were ostensibly designed for the heavier Porsche 935s (having switched from planned Pirellis). Suffering a split fuel tank, the Lola qualified only fifth using the first of the Cosworth DFLs, a 3.3-litre developing 518bhp at 9750rpm. Unfortunately, at around half distance, a damaged driveshaft assembly caused de Villota to pull off the track when placed third. The race was won by a Porsche 935, with Osellas in second and third places. Eddie Jordan was fifth, sharing Siggi Brunn's Porsche 908/3.

The next round in Europe was the Silverstone 1000kms, and the T600 was now on Goodyear tyres as fitted in the USA for IMSA racing. These worked much better, and a demon effort by Guy Edwards put the Lola on the front row of the grid next to the Porsche 908/80 of Jochen Mass, Reinhold Joest and Volker Merl, after de Villota ran out of fuel in the second practice session. In this race, Mass spun off at Woodcote on the first wet lap, leaving Guy Edwards to lead for nearly three hours, chased by the Lancia Monte Carlos, Porsche 935s, 908s, etc. Hans-Joachim Stuck did an epic job from midfield with the BMW M1 to get into second place before problems arose, the Lola leading by a full lap when the engine suddenly stopped, leaving de Villota to walk home again. A fuel stop had been due but the T600 had not picked up what was later discovered to be five gallons! Edwards and de Villota would have a newly-designed fuel system for Le Mans ...

The race was won by Harald Grohs, Walter Röhrl and Dieter Schornstein in a Joest-built Porsche 935 from the Derek Bell, Steve O'Rourke and David Hobbs IMSA BMW M1, and the Siggi Brunn/Eddie Jordan Porsche 908/3. Eddie Jordan, incidentally, achieved the fastest lap of the race.

Next on the agenda was the Nürburgring 1000kms, but the race was stopped after only 17 laps due to the fatal crash of Herbert Müller in Siggi Brun's 908/3 (Eddie Jordan's usual car). Poor Herbert spun and hit the parked Porsche 935 of Bob Akin after Bobby Rahal had gone off in it. The Lola was classified eighth. The race was won by Nelson Piquet's and Hans-Joachim Stuck's BMW M1 after the Mass/Joest 908/80 pitted just as the red flag was shown.

For the T600, Le Mans was not a good race. Juan Fernandez Garcia was nominated as the third driver in Guy Edwards' team, but the car could only qualify twelfth fastest. The reason for this lowly showing was that the car was slow down the Mulsanne Straight with a best of only 191mph. This was primarily due to drag caused by the venturis, which gave away masses of speed to the Porsches. The T600 was, however, quick through the corners, but there weren't enough of them at Le Mans then to make up the loss. It also appeared as though the high speed aerodynamics were lacking. Come the race, de Villota was in trouble as early as lap three with clutch and gear linkage dramas and, although these were not fully cured, he decided to press on somewhat circumspectly. Guy found the bodywork starting to break off about halfway through the race, and the car eventually finished 16th without second or fourth gears.

(Engine vibration was the cause of serious problems. Also, in those early days of ground effect, designers had yet to appreciate the fact that the drag generated is a serious handicap on the Mulsanne Straight. The T600 was a prime example of this.)

Sadder still was the Cooke-Woods Racing/Garretson car. This had a Porsche 3.2-litre turbocharged engine installation which sat too high in the chassis due to the height of the venturi tunnels. This Lola was completed in the paddock just prior to the race and a CV joint broke on the Wednesday on the first practice lap. The mechanics fixed the problem on Thursday and the car was tested on an airport runway but, as time went by, Bobby Rahal needed to try to qualify in the dark, without venturis and with the turbo boost non-operational, giving only half the power the engine was capable of. With these problems, it was no surprise that the car failed to qualify within the allotted time span. Brian Redman was, however, philosophical about the fact that yet another chance to win the only endurance event which had eluded him had gone. The Porsche unit was never tried again and Cooke-Woods Racing acrimoniousy split from Garretson as a result of the disaster.

Laguna Seca, 2nd May 1982. John Paul Jr started from pole position in his T600, and won the IMSA-sponsored Monterey Triple Crown. Danny Ongais, behind in the Interscope-entered T600, started alongside John Paul and finished second. (Courtesy Phillip A Salazar/IMSA Collection)

The race itself was won by Jacky Ickx and Derek Bell in the works Porsche 936/81 from a pair of Rondeaus, thus avenging their defeat of the previous year.

Life suddenly improved for Guy Edward's T600 at the next event on the calendar, as the car – fitted with a Cosworth DFV engine – won outright at Enna. Pole position had gone to the Facetti/Finotto Ferrari 308GTB twin-turbo, with the Lola second and Osellas in third and fourth places on the grid.

At the start, Facetti took the lead but almost crashed at the chicane, letting de Villota through. The Lola needed more fuel stops than the others and, as the track melted in the heat, the Osellas kept the pressure on. The T600 finally won by two laps. Francia and Lombardi were second, Gimax and Moreschi third.

A complete reversal of this form happened at the Watkins Glen race, where the car missed out on all of the first day's practice due to a fuel tank leak. A replacement tank had to be flown in from Carl Haas in Chicago. A rebuilt Le Mans Cosworth DFL engine was installed for this event and the car qualified seventh for the race. In the early stages, Guy and Emilio kept to an appropriate pace as the turbo cars (mainly Porsche 935s), pitted to replenish their fuel tanks or needed to turn down the boost, seeking the necessary economy, so the T600 then found itself ahead. Just short of the two hour mark, Guy Edwards was squeezed by a backmarker, hit the kerb, took off and flipped. He remembers the ticking electrics, the smell of fuel, the marshalls shouting but not coming any closer. Finally, he kicked his own way out through the screen, shaken but okay. The race was a Lancia 1-2.

IMSA cars featured at the Mosport and Elkhart World Endurance Championship races. Both were won by Harald Grohs and Rolf Stommelen in their Andial-run, Howard Meister-owned Porsche 935; Brian Redman was second both times. In the first race Brian was only 22 seconds behind the eventual winner and, in the Wisconsin encounter, just two minutes. Eppie Wietzes partnered Brian Redman for the first event, where they started from the rear of the pack after having missed qualifying due to their engine being delayed by an air traffic control strike. Ted Field and Bill Whittington were third in another 935, and Chris Cord and Jim Adams would have been fourth in another T600 but a head gasket failed on their engine. They made up for this at Elkhart Lake, though, placing third behind the Cooke-Woods Racing T600, this time with Sam Posey sharing the driving with Brian. No less than four Porsche 935s followed the Lolas home, and both events counted for the IMSA Championship.

The final round of the World Endurance Championship was held at Brands Hatch on September 27th. This was called the Flying Tigers 1000, and the T600 of Edwards and de Villota was second on the grid to the new Ford C100, designed by GT40 collaborator, Len Bailey, and driven by Manfred Winkelhock and Klaus Ludwig. A throwback from the past was the Kremer Porsche 917K/81, which had qualified in third place; it was driven by Bob Wollek and Henri Pescarolo. Guy Edwards' Lola was almost entirely new after the Watkins Glen accident, with a new tub and bodywork.

The new Ford led early on in the race but went out after 64 minutes with gearbox problems, handing the lead to Bob Wollek in the 917. For 12 laps, the appreciative crowd was treated to the sight of, essentially, a 1970 car leading a race in 1981! The Porsche lasted but 12 laps more, however, leaving the Lola to win again. Bob Garretson and Bobby Rahal were second in a Porsche 935, Bob Garretson thus winning the inaugural Drivers' crown, and Derek Bell and Chris Craft were third in a BMW M1.

In America in 1981, Brian Redman's T600 was run by Ralph Kent-Cooke and Roy Woods, themselves Porsche 935 privateers from Mountain View, California. The car was looked after and prepared in the workshops of Bob Garretson, who had prepared the previous year's championship-winning Porsche 935 for John Fitzpatrick. Bob Garretson, Brian Redman and Bobby Rahal shared a Porsche 935K3 to win the 1981 Daytona 24 Hours. It was the start of a good year for all concerned with the exception of the Le Mans debacle.

The first race of the IMSA Championship was held at Laguna Seca, just one week after the T600's Monza World Endurance Championship debut. Brian Redman had qualified on the third row of the grid but, in the race, he remorselessly closed in and passed the Porsches as they had to refuel or turn their boost down. The T600 took the lead with only seven laps to go, stretching the margin on John Paul Jr's 935 to 11 seconds at flagfall for a popular win. John Fitzpatrick, in another 935, finished in third place.

Brian Redman was now feeling very comfortable in the Lola and won the next two races as well, by which time Carl Haas had orders for ten more cars! John Paul Jr was to have a pair, Interscope three and Chris Cord another. Come the Portland race in early August, the Le Mans disaster was behind them (see above), and Cooke-Woods Racing parted from Bob Garretson. Unaffected, Brian Redman notched up his fifth victory of the season overall and fourth in the T600. John Paul had put his Lola on the pole and led, only to trip over a backmarker, spin and be unable to restart. Gianpiero Moretti of Momo fame was second in a Porsche 935, and Bobby Rahal in another Porsche 935, was third, with David Hobbs fourth in a BMW.

IMSA specification T600s represented Lola at the Mosport and Elkhart WEC races, which have been covered in the first part of this chapter; both events also counted for WEC and IMSA Championship points.

Road Atlanta was next and Brian Redman was firmly back on the IMSA trail with yet another win. Ted Field was second, a lap behind the Lola with his Porsche 935. The season ended at Daytona in late November when a backmarker blew up in a huge cloud of dense smoke, immediately in front

Brian Redman in the Cooke-Woods-entered Lola T600 at the Daytona Finale in 1981, where he placed second to John Paul Jr. Brian led by one second going into the last banking, but George Alderman's Datsun engine blew in front of them spraying oil and smoke. Brian lifted, John Paul Jr didn't. Afterwards, Brian remarked: "That's the difference between a 21-year-old and a 44-year-old!"

The T600 of 1981. First of the ground effect GT Prototypes, the T600 was a very good car which wrested superiority from the Porsche 935 and, in Brian Redman's hands, won the IMSA Championship. (Courtesy Steve Poole/IMSA Collection)

of Brian Redman as he tried holding off John Paul Jr in the run to the chequered flag. Brian lifted off the throttle, John didn't. "That's the difference between a 21-year-old and a 44-year-old," said Brian afterwards, and announced his retirement at the year's end. Throughout the year, Brian had never been on pole position or posted the fastest lap, relying on racecraft to get himself to the front when it mattered. Brian Redman had 213 points to take the championship, John Paul Jr was second with 131, and John Fitzpatrick third with 110.

T770 – F3

Over the winter of 1979/80, a modified car called the T770/2 was built, with much input from chief mechanic John Church. Mike Blanchet was to drive it again, this time with backing from SDC of Bedford.

Mike Blanchet qualified fourth at the Silverstone opener, finishing third behind Stefan Johansson and Kenny Acheson in Marches. Nigel Mansell was fourth. Then, for round two at Thruxton, Mike was fifth on the grid behind Stefan and Kenny, but ahead of Robert Guerrero and Nigel Mansell. In a typical Formula Three slipstreamer, Guerrero won both his and Argo's first big race from Blanchet by less than 0.9secs, with Johansson another 0.3secs in arrears.

Thereafter, for Lola, things deteriorated and the Marches and Argos pulled away. The Lola was off the pace and midfield qualifying became the norm. At Silverstone for round five, Mike Blanchet was seventh on the grid and at the finish. This was the first of seven, seventh place finishes that Mike Blanchet posted, always just out of the points as the year progressed. His frustration was exacerbated by the fact that, for the British Grand Prix support race, he was only 0.7secs from pole, but 11th on the grid. Stefan Johansson won the Formula Three title, with Kenny Acheson second and Roberto Guerrero third.

T850 – 1981 – F2 (Toleman) – 6 built

Announced in mid-October of 1980, Lola was commissioned to build a 1981 version of the Toleman TG280 Formula Two winner, plus variants for Formula Atlantic and the Can-Am two-litre class.

The plan was initially to build ten F2s with Hart or BMW power.

Brian Henton had won the previous year's title, from team mate Derek Warwick, both in works cars. Third had been Siegfried Stohr and seventh Huub Rothengatter, both privateers. The Toleman team management realized that the team would be too busy with the new Formula One project to be able to get involved with Formula Two, hence the move.

Designed by Rory Byrne, the customer version was that of the previous year's F2 championship-winning Toleman TG280. It featured an aluminium tub, and front suspension was by top rockers and lower wishbones, the rear employing upper cantilever arms and lower wishbones. As was normal Lola practice, a batch of ten was laid down.

Overall length	165in
Overall width	72in
Wheelbase	99in
Front track	58in
Rear track	56in

The Lola-built TG281 (T850) made its world debut at Suzuka, Japan, on March 8th, 1981, with a second place by Kazuyoshi Hoshino in a BMW-powered car from Matsumoto's March win. Hoshino then won round three, also at Suzuka and again with a T850. Hoshino was also third with the Lola at Suzuka in F2 in September, behind two Marches.

In Europe the first cars were delivered to the Alan Docking-Matt Spitzley team only five days before the first race, so, not surprisingly, the new Tolemans disappointed at the Silverstone season opener, which was won by Mike Thackwell in a Ralt Honda on March 29th, the eve of his twentieth birthday. Jim Crawford was fourth in a Toleman TG280 from 1980. The works team of Docking-Spitzley for Stefan Johansson and Kenny Acheson was struggling.

It was all change the next time out, at Hockenheim, where Stefan made his way up from 13th on the grid, past local hero Manfred Winkelhock on the last lap, to score a great win. Mike Thackwell was third.

Roberto Guerrero won the Thruxton round which was marred by a big accident involving Mike Thackwell. Stefan Johansson was sixth for Toleman in T850-03, while Kenny Acheson failed to finish in the sister car. Fredy Schnarwiler was eighth in chassis number 06. Guido Pardini was also T850-mounted, but dropped out when in midfield. Johansson was then fourth at the Nürburgring, with Kenny Acheson sixth to claim his first points. Thierry Boutsen had won for March.

On to Vallelunga and it was Eje Elgh's turn to win in the Maurer with Stefan second for a Swedish 1-2. At Mugello it was Teo Fabi in the March who won, with the Tolemans nowhere in the frame as Thackwell returned on crutches to finish fifth.

Geoff Lees became the seventh different winner of seven races when he clinched Pau. This time it was Kenny Acheson who suffered the most, breaking a leg in a controversial accident with Michele Alboreto, whilst Stefan Johansson could not better eighth. Carlos Rossi upheld Toleman honour with fourth in an old TG280. Problems continued to mount for the works-backed Lolas, with Stefan being tipped upside down at the start of the Enna round, travelling two hundred yards on the rollover bar. Having started from midfield, Thierry Boutsen won with Jo Gartner in a TG280 sixth and Scharnweiler, T850-mounted, seventh for Lola.

Geoff Lees then won at Spa with Boutsen second on his home turf; Eje Elgh, in a Maurer, was third and Jim Crawford in a TG280 sixth. Jo Gartner, in a TG280, would have been third but was punted off with five laps to go. Stefan Johansson could manage only 14th, having run with the leaders until a sidepod broke, ripping a tyre. He was very fast thereafter with the sidepod tied up with string! Geoff Lees then made it three wins from four starts at Donington, with Teo Fabi, in the March BMW, second, Manfred Winkelhock, in the Maurer BMW, third. Stefan was fourth in an ex-Henton TG280. Michele Alboreto won at Misano for Minardi BMW, but Geoff Lees took second place and the Formula Two title. Mike Thackwell, driving a Honda-engined Ralt, was third. There were six different makes in the top seven, Jim Crawford was the last of the bunch in his original Toleman again. Stefan Johansson was ninth in a TG280B. Pardini had the only T850 but failed to finish.

The final race of the championship was at Mantorp Park and Stefan Johansson came home first in his TG280 in this year of home winners!

Geoff Lees was second, six seconds in arrears, with Kenny Acheson a gritty third in this first race of his comeback. Thierry Boutsen was fourth, second in the championship standing.

Lees 51pts
Boutsen 37pts
Stefan 31pts
Fabi/Elgh 29pts
Thackwell 22pts

T860 – 1981 – FAt (Toleman) – 2+ built

This was the Formula Atlantic version of the T850. Designed by Rory Byrne. Suspension as per T850.

Overall length 165in
Overall width 72in
Wheelbase 96in
Front tack 55in
Rear track 56in

Lola 3
1982-1983

T332

By now, the T332 was well past its prime, the only notable success occuring in 1983, when American driver Dave Williams won the CC Libre Championship in his ex-Tom Belso car, with Mike Connor fourth in another T332.

1982

In the ailing Can-Am series, Al Unser Jr won Road Atlanta (round 1) for Galles Racing in a Frissbee Chevy on his Can-Am debut. Rick Galles had purchased the rights to the marque from Brad Friselle at the end of the previous year. He also hired Trevor Harris, the designer, too. Unser then won again at Mosport for round 2 where Poleman Patrick Tambay, in the VDS-001, tripped over a backmarker and was put out of the race, before going off to Ferrari. Holbert won Mid-Ohio, round 3, in VDS-001, with John Morton fourth and the John Kalagian example seventh. Holbert won again at Elkhart Lake where Unser debuted the new Galles GR3 on pole position, but retired in the race itself. Al Holbert then won at Trois Rivières. Al Jr returned to his winning ways at Mosport for round 6 with more Frissbees fourth (Morton) and sixth (Kalagian). Next time out, at Riverside for round 9, Holbert won in the VDS-001 and Unser was second in the Galles GR3. Another GR3 was fourth, courtesy of Geoff Brabham.

A new winner for Las Vegas was Danny Sullivan in a March. At Laguna Seca for the last round, Al Unser Jr won in his GR3. Little Al was taking up where his old man left off. Al Holbert finished second.

Unser	540pts
Holbert	500pts
Sullivan	390pts
Roos	173pts

1983

Jacques Villeneuve won in a Frissbee at Mosport in round 1 of the championship, from Jim Crawford in an Ensign, with another Frissbee fifth for Horst Kroll. The race was marred by the death of Michael Allen. Round 2 was at Lime Rock: Michael Roe was second in a T333, with Jacques Villeneuve a delayed 12th; Monk was fourth and Kroll fifth. Jacques Villeneuve and Dr Charles Monk (the latter having switched from a T290) were then second and third at Elkhart Lake for round 3, before Jacques Villeneuve won next time out at Trois Rivières with Kroll fourth. Michael Roe, in the VDS, was on pole for Mosport but spun out after a puncture. Second to Jim Crawford at Mosport, Villeneuve won at Sears Point to clinch the title. Michael Roe was third at Sears Point. He had both Galles Frissbees used by Unser Jr, as no new cars were built.

Horst Kroll then took up the Frissbee mantle. Having come fifth in '83, he was third in '84, second in '85 (with one win, the title going to the Frissbee of thrice winner Rick Miaskiewicz), and title winner – at last – in the final year of 1987, with a single victory in the four race series. Paul Tracy won the last ever Can-Am race to date, in a Frissbee, at Mosport. Total roll call thus far was nine victories for the marque.

T333 CS

In 1983, Michael Roe was third in the Can-Am opener at Mosport Park before switching allegiance to VDS. Bob Meyer was fifth at Lime Rock in the second round and Meyer scored two more top ten finishes.

In 1984 Charles Monk was third in the first round of the Can-Am challenge at Mosport, and then fourth at Dallas in round two, with another fourth being scored at Mosport in the seventh round of the Can-Am. Finally, he was second in the finale at Texas, just losing out to Crawford in his March 847. This late charge was not enough to stop Michael Roe in the VDS, nee Lola, winning the title.

T390

A so-called de Cadenet Lola, designed and built by ADA, debuted at the Pace 6 hours at Silverstone in May 1982. This appeared to have the pontoons of a Lola of unknown derivation. In actual fact, the car was commissioned by François Duret. The design was by Chris Crawford and was based on a mid-70s T390 show car. The coupé bodywork was fabricated by Marchant & Cox of Hastings, England. This car's stubby looks earnt it the pet name 'Morris Minor'. The engine was a 3-litre DFV. It was called a 'De Cadenet' because this enabled the team to take over a similarly named Le Mans entry. The front suspension was Lola based, the rear coming from de Cadenet. Driven by Mike Wilds and Bernard de Dryver (what a great name!), it qualified 20th and was unclassified in the race. This car was entered as a 'de Cadenet 82' for the Le Mans 24 Hours race and the drivers were Mike Wilds, Ian Harrower and Francois Duret. At Le Mans, it had a new nose and better brakes. It qualified 45th out of 55 starters, but ran out of fuel around midnight. *C'est la vie* ...

In 1983 Duret/Sheldon/Harrower led Group CJ at Le Mans on the Saturday afternoon, but were subsequently unclassified after lots and lots of problems. They had been quicker than the class-winning Mazdas, but not as durable.

T492

In 1982, Peter Hall, a 22-year-old newcomer from Lincolnshire, impressed all who saw him with his handling of a T492 in Sports 2000, taking lots of fifth and sixth places as the top Lola in a field dominated by Tigas, etc. This was Martin Colville's car, previously raced by John Brindley, which was prepared by Hall & Fowler. Tiga and Royale ruled the bigger leagues in 1983, but Lola fared well in the pre-80 series driven by the likes of John L.Webb (T490) and Peter Hall in a T492 – both early class winners.

T530

In 1982, Rex Ramsey proved to be the main T530 stalwart as Lola fortunes took a dive.

In Britain, John Foulston and Les Cocks raced an ex-Tambay T530 in the Thundersports race at Brands Hatch on April 4th, but suffered differential problems. These were soon sorted out and they won at Snetterton on May 2nd. John Brindley and Les Cocks won at Brands Hatch on the 30th of that month from Kennedy and Martin Birrane in the Ford C100. (Martin Birrane is now Chairman of Lola Cars.)

T580 in 1982

The T580 was being outclassed, despite posting the odd result, such as Julien van Dievoet being eighth in the EFDA FF2000 at Zolder as the Deltas and VDS dominated. Huub Vermeulen, in a T580, took second to Cor Euser in a Delta at Zandvoort for round two of the Golden Lion Trophy (also Round three of the German series) FF2000. Jaap van Silfhout and Peter Elgaard were also in the points, Elgaard finishing sixth at the EFDA Jyllandsringen race in late August, a young man named Ayrton Senna da Silva leading home a Van Diemen 1-2-3-4.

Back in Britain, Martin Woods won at Lydden in the Flint Motors FF2000 from Peter Boutwood, both in T580s, on June 3rd, and Woods did it again there the following weekend. David Jacklin won the Sabre Fabrications FF2000 at Thruxton in July, the first three were T580-mounted, and Martin Wood won the Flint round at Lydden in August.

T592

For 1982, the T592 was to have a strenthened monocoque – mainly around the cockpit area to prevent flexing – revised suspension and lightweight alloy front uprights. Made in riveted and bonded aluminium with steel reinforcement, the T592 had a tubular engine frame with the front suspension comprising twin unequal wishbones, and the rear suspension of single top link and lower wishbone.

Bilstein damper/coil spring units were fitted at each corner, and a two-litre Ford Pinto engine was the standard offering. The new price was to be £9500 plus VAT for a rolling chassis. The new car was officially announced in January 1982.

Geoff Farmer posted the fastest lap at Brands Hatch on March 7th, but Tigas took the honours; the best Lola placing was a T492 in fifth, which proved to be the way of the season. However, Hans Edvinsson did win the EFDA Sports 2000 race at Hameenlinna in June in a T590. The Jyllandsring race was a Tiga 1-2 for Thyrring and Kurt Thiim, with a Lola 3-4-5 for Hans Ernst, Edvinsson and Charles Zwolsman, all in T590s. Huub Vermeulen was second and Hans Edvinsson third in the EFDA Sports 2000 at the Zandvoort race. Mike Taylor won in a Royale, but Edvinsson led the championship.

Mike Blanchet and Geoff Farmer teamed up in a T590X to take second place to Eddie Jordan and Richard Morgan in a March in the Oulton Park Sports 2000 Endurance on July 10th. Edvinsson won the EFDA race at Mantorp Park in mid-July and the Lucas Nordic Cup for the second time in three years (he had been runner-up in 1981) by winning all but one round. The T594 was introduced in 1982 and listed at £9975 plus VAT for a rolling chassis. It was with this updated version of the model that Larry Campbell took the American title with, the car having greater downforce, cleaner aerodynamics, better cooling and better brakes.

This car was eligible for Thundersports and American C-sports, plus some Italian national series, and could accommodate the Mazda rotary, Volkswagen or Cosworth BDA engines. The T594 employed a stiffened monocoque with F3 wheels and tyres. A Hewland 5-speed, Mk9 gearbox with limited slip differential and ventilated four pot calipers was fitted. A full width rear wing and extended nose splitter were the main differences from the previous model, and the T594 could easily be restored to Sports 2000 trim.

The car's UK debut was at Thruxton on July 24th. Sporting a Mazda rotary engine, and driven by Peter Lovett and Jeff Allam, it was in third place until it suffered a puncture. Lovett and Allam were then second in the Thundersports Trophy at Donington in August, to Kennedy and Crawford in their C100, with Mike Blanchet and Tony Dowsett taking third place in a T594C with 1.6-litre Volkswagen engine. Mike Wilds had been leading in a T280 but that caught fire.

That Lola stalwart, Hans Edvinsson, was third in a T594 in a race at Falkenberg on July 10th, which was won by a Tiga. Edvinsson then won at Zandvoort from Hans Vermeulen in a T590, and was third in the EFDA Championship to the Tigas of Cor Euser and Thorkild Thyrring. His was the only new model T594 in Europe. Edvinsson had also placed third behind the Tigas of Thorkild Thyrring and Leif Lindstrom in the Scandinavian finale at Karlskoga, fourth place in this race being taken by the T590 of a certain Ronnie Peterson ... not to be confused with his F1 namesake. Elsewhere, Huub Vermeulen drove his T590 to become Dutch Sports 2000 champion, whilst Lobenberg, in a T594, won the SCCA Run-offs, beating a host of Tigas.

T600

Two World Endurance Championships and five Stateside victories meant that 1981 had been a good first year for the Lola T600. However, as Lola and its customers turned their attention towards 1982, it became apparent that, not only had the new Ford C100 shown initial promise, but the March 81G and the Porsche 956 had also been announced, as had the Lola-designed and built Nimrod with which they might beat the T600 if those at Aston Martin had anything to do with it. Times were going be a lot harder for Lola, starting then.

For the opening race of the American season, Jim Adams, Eppie Wietzes and Ralph Kent-Cooke qualified seventh at the Daytona 24-Hour race with a 5.7 Chevrolet engine installed. Bobby Rahal's new March Chevy 82G was on pole position, but Porsches were first, second and third at the finish. The Lola T600 suffered multiple problems and retired.

At the Sebring 12 Hours, the car took third place when David Hobbs helped with the driving after his own car expired after only 7 laps, only to have total electrical failure with two hours to go. Porsche won again, with the March second. John Paul Jr made it three victories from three race starts by taking the 60 lap race at Road Atlanta, too.

At last came a victory for Lola, at Riverside for round four of the IMSA Championship. Ted Field and

The Cooke-Woods-run Lola T600 in 1982 at the Daytona 24 Hours. The T600 had won the IMSA Championship the year before in Brian Redman's capable hands. In 1982, however, the Porsche 935 (JLP-3) of John Paul Jr did most of the winning (he occasionally used a T600 also). (Courtesy Steve Poole/IMSA Collection)

Bill Whittington won with the sinister black Interscope car, beating Al Holbert and Harald Grohs' Porsche 935 by two full laps. The T600 of John Bright and Ralph Kent-Cooke was delayed when a burst tyre smashed the bodywork, and then the engine overheated. Chris Cord and Jim Adams, in a T600, had been on pole but collided with John Paul Jr, now in another T600, at the first corner and hit the barriers.

Back in England, Lola Cars had a T600 installed with a 4-cylinder BMW engine for sale due to a customer change of plan in May. The car needed only bodywork changes in order to take part in Group C racing. Karl-Heinz Becker bought the car and campaigned it for many years. Lola also offered its 1981 works car built around a one race old monocoque which had won at Brands Hatch.

John Paul Jr won the Laguna Seca race by 21 seconds in his new Lola

T600 from the Danny Ongais-driven T600. John Fitzpatrick, in a 935, was third and Ted Field, in another T600, fourth. Then at Charlotte a fortnight later, John Paul Jr won again, this time using his Porsche 935 (which he shared with his father). Jim Adams drove his new T600, rebuilt around a new tub after the Riverside crash, and Danny Ongais crashed out. It was Porsche again at Mid-Ohio but this time it was John Fitzpatrick who won, with Lolas second, third and fourth, courtesy of Ongais, Field and John Paul Jr. Danny Ongais had taken the fastest lap and led until two laps from the end when the battery died, forcing him into the pits. John Paul Jr had been on pole but lost time with a broken throttle.

Lime Rock for round eight was almost a case of deja vu: John Fitzpatrick won again (flag to flag) in his 935, with John Paul Jr, Ted Field and Danny Ongais the new order behind him.

Daytona belonged to Ted Field and Danny Ongais in their T600. They won by two laps after John Paul Jr's Porsche went up in flames, but the race held at Brainerd saw him return in triumph with Danny Ongais forced into second place and Ted Field taking third. Klaus Ludwig took the honours at Sears Point in the Ford Mustang, but it was back to reality when John Paul Jr did it again (for Porsche) at the one hour Portland race. Ted Field was second and Don Devendorf third in the Electramotive Datsun 280ZX.

John Paul father and son teamed up in their Porsche 935 to take the Mosport six hours, with Chris Cord and Jim Adams second. Ted Field and Danny Ongais had led before their engine blew, ending their run. Porsches were back again with a first and second at Elkhart Lake, but the big news there was the new Jaguar XJR5 finishing in third place for Bob Tullius and Bill Adam. Chris Cord and Jim Adams were fourth with fuel feed problems.

John Fitzpatrick and David Hobbs, in a Porsche, won the Mid-Ohio race by two laps from Chris Cord and Jim Adams in their T600. John Paul Jr, again driving a Porsche, was the first retirement, but still won the title. Ted Field and Danny Ongais, in another T600, had been on pole position but their engine broke.

Not down for long, John Paul Jr won the penultimate round of the IMSA Championship at Road Atlanta, with Chris Cord not getting beyond the warm-up lap and Danny Ongais again retiring whilst leading. However, Ongais got his revenge at the Pocono 500 Mile race, sharing his T600 with Ted Field to take a one lap win over the John Paul father and son 935, with everyone else at least 12 laps back.

The season ended in fine style with Ted Field and Danny Ongais winning again at the Daytona Three-Hour race on November 28th. Danny Ongais had put the new Chevrolet V6, turbocharged T600 on the front row next to the John Fitzpatrick and Bob Wollek Porsche 935, and led until the suspension was damaged by yet another blown tyre. Field and Ongais then carried on in the V8-powered car, and went on to win by 40 seconds from the pole-sitting car.

John Paul Jr............................235pts
Ted Field................................167pts
John Paul Sr
& John Fitzpatrick..................125pts

In the 1983 IMSA Championship it became obvious that the T600 was becoming dated. Ralph Kent-Cooke, Jim Adams and John Bright could only manage sixth place at the Daytona 24-Hour race after having hit the wall early on after a collision with the similar Interscope T600. The Lolas had qualified sixth and 11th respectively, and the black car was eventually put out by a repeat of its qualifying days engine problems.

John Paul Jr was on pole at Miami (with Brian Redman), but the race was black-flagged after only 26 laps due to rain when the car was lying second. Danny Ongais had crashed the turbo Interscope entry while leading in the wet. The V6-engined Lola had also been seen again, but to no avail, as it did not feature in the race itself.

Ralph Kent-Cooke and Harald Grohs were fourth at the Riverside Six Hours in a 5.8-litre T600 on April 24th, and Bruce Leven and Hurley Haywood were ninth in the Porsche-powered T600. Hurley Haywood followed up with fourth place at Laguna Seca the next weekend and a fifth place at Portland.

Johns Kalagian and Mills had been third in the former's T600 5.8 Chevy at Brainerd for round 11 of the IMSA challenge; Kalagian repeating the result in a solo run at Sears Point the next time out, where the similar Bob Lobenberg/John Morton car was second to the

Holbert/Trueman March Porsche. John Kalagian and John Lloyd placed third again at the Daytona Three Hours.

In Europe, Karl-Heinz Becker was fifth at Zolder in a 1.4-litre turbochrged BMW T600, then finished in sixth place at Mainz in mid-May, and took yet another sixth at Diepolz. Becker had several points scoring finishes with the BMW-engined T600 in 1982/83 in rounds of the International German Racing Championship, and carried on racing the car for ages.

T610 – 1982 – GpC – 2+ built

Just as it had become obvious that Lola would not be competitive in Group C with the high downforce/high drag T600, April 1982 saw the announcement of the T610, with a debut scheduled for Monza later in the month. Guy Edwards and Rupert Keegan were to be the drivers in a full works team.

Although incorporating many lessons learnt from the T600, the T610 was notably different; amongst the visual features, a central nose wing to provide more downforce being obvious. There was also a low-slung rear wing. The Group C minimum screen height rule accounted for a peculiar teardrop-shaped window above the actual screen – this allowed the car to be run very low. The T610 featured a monocoque made of aluminium honeycomb with aluminium skins, but the floor panel had carbonfibre pre-preg skins. Carbon composite bodywork consisted of woven glass pre-preg over Nomex honeycomb (as this core material would adjust better to complex shapes); metallic honeycomb, however, was used in flat areas. The fully-stressed venturi underbody was glass pre-preg over aluminium honeycomb. Only highly stressed parts like the wings were made of carbon-fibre composites.

This was very likely the first fully enclosed car to have a composite chassis and entire body made of a sandwich structure, and it was slab-sided in the ground effect fashion of the day. The venturi tunnels started behind the cockpit, as demanded by Group C rules. There was also a central fuel cell.

The Ford Cosworth 3.9DFL engine was mounted on a subframe attached to the monocoque's bulkhead, and a Hewland VG gearbox/transaxle was bolted to the engine. Unlike other cars which had the Cosworth DFL engine, the T610 did not suffer from vibration, denoting correct installation. The T610 had less ground effects than the T600 IMSA car, but was reckoned to be a lot faster down the Mulsanne Straight. The outboard suspension was similar to the T600, only tidier.

By the time of the T610's announcement, it had already been tested at Snetterton and Donington, and Eric Broadley said that the car was "a big move for us" but necessary

One of the two Lola 610s built in later life. At this point, the original Cosworth engine had been replaced by a Chevrolet V8. (Author photo)

if Group C racing turned out to be as big as was expected.

Ambitous plans included Ralph Kent-Cooke having a second car for an unretired Brian Redman, and A.N. Other to drive at Le Mans

The first round of the European Group C championship for Lola took place at Monza on April 18th. The scrutineers claimed the screen height was incorrect but allowed the T610 to go out for practice, where it qualified ninth, exactly one second shy of the Ford C100, three and a half seconds behind Hans-Joachim Stuck in the Sauber C6DFL which was leading Group C, and no less than six and a half seconds in arrears of the pole sitting Group 6 Lancia. Group C was, of course, essentially a formula which favoured a fuel efficient car in the race proper, but practice was a no-holds-barred affair where one could see the real potential of the cars.

The T610 appeared for the Sunday morning warm-up with moveable 'kickpads' which prevented bodywork damage when kerb-hopping. (The scrutineers suggested these constituted 'movable aerodynamic aids'.) Eric Broadley offered to fix them but was told not to touch anything until informed by the scrutineers, who returned within

Silverstone, 1984. John Bartlett bought one of the ex-Cooke-Woods T610s and used it in the Thundersports series in Britain. Fitted with a Cosworth 3.3DFL engine, it suffered numerous problems. Here it is at the Silverstone World Championship round. John Bartlett, Steve Kempton and John Brindley qualified 27th, but were forced out with throttle problems.

15 minutes of the start to announce that the car would not be allowed to start. Jeff Hazell, the team manager, told the scrutineers that the disqualification had to be in writing, which duly arrived just three minutes before the flagfall. Guy Edwards did one lap and was then black-flagged. A Rondeau won from fourth on the grid.

The Silverstone Pace Six Hours was the next race for the Group C cars on May 16th, even though the racing world was still stunned by Gilles Villeneuve's death the previous weekend. It was at this race that the Nimrod Aston and the Porsche 956 debuted, making it possible for two Lola products (the Nimrod was a Lola design) to go head-to-head.

Once again, the Lancia Group C car won in what turned out to be a fuel economy run. The T610 featured lower and longer front bodywork and a shorter rear end to compensate for complying with the rules, and this gave a better top speed but was bad for engine cooling. Guy Edwards qualified eighth but, after being sixth early on, the Lola fell back to 16th place due to clutch, brakes and wheel problems.

The Nürburgring was the setting for round three and was the final shakedown test before Le Mans. There was a poor field, most teams preferring to concentrate on preparation for Le Mans, but this was no excuse for the T610 to be out-qualified by an old T296. The Lola featured bigger brakes and better cooling, but was still too heavy. It was, however, fast on the straight bits and qualified eigthth, but after running with the leaders, the T610 (besides Rupert Keegan almost being disqualified for ignoring a red flag) had repeated alternator problems which dropped it down the field.

So, then, to the Le Mans 24-Hour race, which also counted towards the Group C Championship, and to which Nick Faure had been drafted in as the third/reserve driver. The car now sported new front aerodynamics, including a new nose in which the central wing had been discarded, and rear wing following time in a wind tunnel. The T610 qualified tenth, being fast on the straight, despite breaking the undertray in practice because of too much downforce, but was slow through the corners – exactly the opposite of 1981! Indeed, it was the fastest non-turbo car at 228mph. The Lola was third at the start and led for a lap as the other competitors made their first pitstops. Sadly, a head gasket blew inside six hours and the car was retired in a race dominated by Porsche.

Ralph Kent-Cooke, Brian Redman and Jim Adams used a second T610, a brand new car which had been built up by John Bright at Lola. This had the old style front end, as there was insufficient time to fabricate new parts, and so this T610 was ten mph slower on the Mulsanne Straight. The team qualified 18th after Ralph Kent-Cooke had an off in practice. Come the race itself, the engine would not start, and so this T610 joined in late from the pit road. Thereafter, the car was very quick but ran out of fuel on the track after just 90 minutes and was disqualified.

This car was later entered in the Elkhart Lake Can-Am race, the first Group C car to appear in the series. It gave a disappointing performance, Jim Adams qualifying 12 seconds off the pace. He retired after just four laps in the race. There were suspicions of sandbagging, as some suggested this was a deliberate ploy to have the rules changed in favour of Group C equipment.

The Spa-Francorchamps 1000kms, not held until early September, was the next event after Le Mans, and Guy Edwards and Rupert Keegan qualified 12th in 'race trim' as the Porsche 956s ruled again. Rupert Keegan was disqualified after 30 laps. He had come in to replace his car's nose cone which had been damaged by a spinning Jaussaud in the opening battle, and left the pits through a red light. Guy Edwards drove a stint whilst the team argued, but it was to no avail and the T610 was black-flagged again.

The works team missed the races held at Mugello and Fuji, but which only counted for the drivers' title, and so the final outing was at the Brands Hatch 1000kms in October. With more revisions – including a hideous flat plate nose wing and severely truncated tail – as well as rear suspension mods, the team qualified tenth and finished seventh, its best result of the year. Guy had been the first spinner in a very wet first part before the race was stopped after the two Ford C100s collided, that 'race' being won by the epic Hans-Joachim Stuck in a Sauber C6 BMW. Lola was initially disqualified as a non-runner when the race was stopped, but the results were allowed to stand after it was decided that the car was in too dangerous a position to try restarting it at that time. The team made up some time at the restart but was unable to overcome the deficit of the first part.

The team was assessed as seventh in the championship points due to three being gleaned at Silverstone. Porsche topped the list thanks to the Nürburgring result, Rondeau was second and Nimrod, the other Lola product, third.

For 1983 in Europe, there was talk early in the year of running a car with Guy Edwards if the money could be found. Ralph Kent-Cooke, Jim Adams and François Servanin did take their T610 back to Le Mans and qualified 28. They got up to 11th place in the night, but overheated the engine in a BP-sponsored car which had been rebuilt at the factory by John Bright.

In 1984, John Bartlett bought the ex-Cooke-Woods car for the Thundersports series in Britain and fitted it with a Cosworth 3.3DFL engine. John Bartlett, Steve Kempton and John Brindley qualified 27th at the Silverstone WEC round, but missed the cut by ten laps after suffering throttle problems. That seemed to set the tone of the season. Prepared by Colin Bennett, the trio of Kempton/Migault/Servanin qualified 41st at Le Mans, immediately behind two T616s, after a practice crash. The engine failed after six hours. Kempton/R. Andreason/M. Cohen-Olivar started and finished round 5 of the WEC at Brands Hatch in 14th, with 176 out of 238 laps completed, running the final quarter *sans* rear bodywork after it fell off and Kempton completed the job with an off!

The WEC finale at Sandown saw John Bartlett paired with R. Jones and David Borroughs. They were the penultimate qualifier of 30 cars entered and were unclassified (again) on 120 laps out of 206.

Both pages: The Lola T610 at Spa-Francorchamps, early September, 1982. Driven by Guy Edwards and Rupert Keegan, the car qualified in twelfth place, but was disqualified for leaving the pits through a red light.

T640/640E/642 – 1982/83 – FF – 39+ built

Mike Blanchet had been seen testing a new 'high-tech' Formula Ford 1600 in December of 1981, the car showing promise at Silverstone. Similar to the T582 FF2000, without a wing or venturi structures, the T640 series featured a slim spaceframe with inboard suspension and wide track. It was intended mainly for the USA (the first ten cars were bound for there), but there would be European and UK versions as well. The price for the T640 was quoted as £5800 plus VAT for a rolling chassis.

The T640 made its debut at Sebring in Florida – and won. Michael Andretti was the driver in a car run by the Carl Haas racing team. It was the same chassis that Mike Blanchet had tested in England. Andretti also won at West Palm Beach and *Autosport* said "We can guarantee that you will be hearing a lot more of Michael Andretti in years to come."

Easter saw the European debut of the T640E. Julian Bailey had led most of the Snetterton race in a Lola using a Minister engine. He had led from pole position but dropped back to second after a clash and spin, the race being won by Maurício Gugelmin in a Van Diemen. Another Brazilian in another Van Diemen RF82 won the day's FF2000 round. His name was Ayrton Senna da Silva (he didn't shorten his name until 1983). Bailey made amends by winning the 'Champion of Brands Hatch' race on April 12th, taking pole and the fastest lap. After five Townsend Thoresen races, Andrew Gilbert-Scott was leading the championship in a Reynard, but was second to J. Oxborrow in a Ray in the 'Champion of Brands Hatch' title. Bailey was fifth.

Mark Peters was to run a new Lola for Auriga, having severed his Touraco/Royale links. This was the third such car, Andretti having raced the prototype, with the first two production machines going to Julian Bailey and Julian Pratt and run by former Formula Two winner and Formula One driver, Dave Morgan.

The Formula Ford 1600 T640 series was very successful, helping to launch the careers of, amongst others, Julian Bailey, Maurício Gugelmin and Michael Andretti.

Bailey won the Oulton Park race and Pratt was sixth on June 5th, and was soon leading the Townsend Thoresen Championship. Peters was on pole for the Donington round on July 4th, but was punted off by John Booth, as was Pratt. Bailey won, adding to his wins at Brands Hatch, Snetterton and Oulton Park. Bailey then won the RAC British Formula Ford 1600 race at Mallory Park to close in on the leader Maurício Gugelmin. Bailey won from Pratt at Brands Hatch on August Bank Holiday Monday, both in T640Es.

Peters won the 'Birmingham Mail & Post' FF1600 series at Donington with three out of six victories. He also won the Townsend Thoreson race at Brands Hatch on September 26th, clinching the Townsend Thoresen Championshipship. Peters had 219 points; Gugelmin in the Van Diemen had 207, and Rick Morris in a Royale had 173. Meanwhile, in the RAC British FF1600 series, Maurício Gugelmin won, finishing up with 90pts. Bailey had 84, Rick 65 and Peters, in a T640E was sixth on 29.

Julian Bailey won the Formula Ford Festival at Brands Hatch. Rick Morris in a Royale was second as always and John Pratt in a T640E was third. Maurício Gugelmin was vying for the win with the top two but rolled, and so it was 21-year-old Julian's 21st race of the year and 13th win. All in all, with only three Lolas out there against numerous VDS and a host of Royales, the results were excellent.

For 1983 the revised T642E car was developed from the slimline T640E, but it was made more durable with cast aluminium uprights, stronger suspension and bigger brakes. The price quoted in November 1982 was £6150 plus VAT for a rolling chassis.

Andrew Gilbert-Scott won the 'Champion of Brands Hatch' round from pole on March 6th and set the scene for the season. Colin Stancombe was fifth in a T640E. Gilbert-Scott then won twice in the same day at Thruxton using Minister's famous 'Patch' engine, while John Pratt, in a T642E, was third.

Graham de Zille then won one race at Donington with Gilbert-Scott the other later that afternoon. Pratt improved to second place behind Gilbert-Scott at Oulton Park on April 1st, and finally beat him at Brands Hatch on April 10th; Gilbert-Scott won at Castle Combe in-between these races with John Penfold in a T642E sixth. Gilbert-Scott and Pratt then shared a win apiece at Snetterton and, by the end of April 1983, Ayrton Senna had nine wins to his name.

Colin Stancombe and Peter Rose took old T640Es to a second and fifth respectively at the 'Champions of Brands Hatch', and BP Superfind Junior races on the same afternoon at Brands Hatch, but both were beaten by Van Diemen. Meanwhile, Bernard Horwood was clocking up some reasonable results in the series, too.

Andrew Gilbert-Scott won the RAC Snetterton race on June 12th and Pratt the Oulton Townshend Thoreson race on June 25th. Graham de Zille won the BP Superfind round at Snetterton on July 3rd. Gilbert-Scott won at the Oulton Park RAC-sponsored race on July 23rd, placed second on August 7th but posted the fastest lap as compensation. With a win at Snettertom on August 21st, Gilbert-Scott comfortably led the championship from John Pratt.

Graham de Zille won the BP race at Snetterton on August 28th.

Gilbert-Scott clinched both the RAC and Townsend Thoresen series in the same weekend in mid-September; Graham de Zille taking the BP Superfind Championship the same weekend, too. All his cars had been run by Brian de Zille of Pegasus Motorsport of Quorn in Leicestershire, England. John Pratt from Dorset, England won the European Grand Prix support race – which was held at Brands Hatch – from Ross Cheever in a Van Diemen. Gilbert-Scott could only place seventh in the development car which proved a handful. It was the first time Formula Ford 1600 had been on a Grand Prix bill there.

The T642E was now introduced. It had a triangulated tubular steel spaceframe with the radiator front-mounted, and outboard Lola/AP disc brakes. The front suspension was by pullrods and wishbones with inboard coil spring/damper units, and the rear suspension was by top rockers with a single lower link and radius rod, inboard coil spring/damper units being fitted.

Peter Rose won the Thruxton BP Superfind event from Graham de Zille, with Lague placing fifth. Rogers had led but slipped back to third.

Andrew Gilbert-Scott won the Formula Ford Festival in a Reynard with 'Patch', whilst Andy Wallace in a Reynard was second and John Pratt, driving a T642E, placed third with a new lap record. Andrew Gilbert-Scott also won the Grovewood Award.

In Europe for 1983, the T642E of Harald Becker placed second to a Van Diemen in the Silver Lion FF1600 opening round at Zolder, but that same weekend saw three British titles decided in Lola's favour.

In the USA in 1983, Bob Lobenberg placed second and Jocko Cunningham fourth in the Road Atlanta SCCA Run-offs. R.K. Smith, in a Swift, won, but Lobenberg got his revenge by winning the Sports 2000 event.

The T670 of Dick Perry was fifth in the F4 Championship of 1983 with 58 points, Mike Whatley winning in his March on 100. Perry almost beat him at Thruxton in September but a late mistake dropped him back.

T680 – 1983 – FF 2000 – 2+ built

Announced at the start of the year as 'coming soon', the T680 was reannounced in *Autosport* in February 1983! Based on the T640-642 series, the T680 featured slim, ground effect sidepods grafted onto the spaceframe. The first car went to Wolber Motorsport, the Lola agent in Germany, and had undergone initial testing by Mike Blanchet at Silverstone and then Snetterton in mid-February. The price quoted in November 1982 was £8000 plus VAT for a rolling chassis.

Wolfgang Troost placed fifth in the German Championship at Hockenheim where the race was won by Volker Weidler, driving a PRS. He used a Gatmo motor and was third in the championship by September.

Bernard Horwood introduced the model at the Brands Hatch European Grand Prix support race on September 25th, the car being the 'works developement chassis' run by Cristal Racing. Unfortunately, Horwood was out after a first lap incident.

T700 – 1983 – Indy – 3+ built

At a visit to the Milwaukee CART race in 1982 with Carl Haas the week after Indy, Eric Broadley confirmed he had been working on an IndyCar project, but that it had been put on the back burner whilst the T600/T610 sports cars were sorted out. The programme was finally announced in *Autosport* in October 1982, whereby Mario Andretti was to drive the Budweiser car for the Newman/Haas team. Chief mechanics were to be Tony Dowe and Davy Evans, and soon afterwards Tony Cicale joined forces from the Van Diemen team.

The new T700 featured an aluminium honeycomb chassis, and had pullrod inboard front suspension, whilst that at the rear was mounted outboard. A carbon fibre rear wing

The T700 IndyCar prototype at the factory. (Courtesy LAT)

was employed and there were no anti-roll bars although a roll control link did the same job, only better! The body was built by Specialised Mouldings and the entire monocoque and sidepods were fabricated from pre-made flat panels, aluminium skins on aluminium honeycomb. The bodywork was made of GRP. Power was from the 2.65-litre Cosworth DFX via Hewland VG gearbox.

The on-board data-logging equipment was a novelty. Darrell Soppe and Tony Cicale were engaged to oversee the project for Carl Haas. The first car was airfreighted to the USA in February 1983, and first tested by Mario Andretti at Phoenix later that same month. No wind tunnel development work had been done by the factory. The T700 then posted a lap at 202mph at the Indianapolis racetrack with revised sidepods and suspension, pleasing the team. The Phoenix opener was rained off and Atlanta substituted, where Mario was fifth on April 17th. Gordon Johncock in a Wildcat won despite a wild pitlane spin. (He would soon be hospitalised for the duration of the season.) Mario qualified sixth in the back-up car after an all-nighter, having crashed the regular car in testing.

It was the Indianapolis 500 next and Andretti was unable to match his previous times in the prototype car with its replacement. Mario was down from 202mph to 199, and eventually qualified 11th at 199.4mph. Teo Fabi, in a March, was on pole with 207.4mph. Rookie Steve Krisiloff qualified n the last row in another T700 on 191.2mph, but had a driveshaft break after 42 laps. Mario retired at 80 laps as a consequence of becoming involved with a spinning Johnny Parsons and hitting the wall. Tom Sneva, in a March, went on to take the win.

Next was Milwaukee and Sneva won again after being disqualified for a skirt infringement but subsequently reinstated. All of this was irrelevant to Mario as a broken water pipe meant retirement. At Cleveland for round four, Mario made pole position thanks, in part, to his car now having a lighter underbody venturi in carbon fibre instead of aluminium. The carbon-fibre underbody had been the team's own modification, so saving 20 kilos and giving much cleaner airflow. Mario led the first 34 laps but spun off in the confusion of a yellow flag restart, damaging a sidepod and radiator in the process. Big Al Unser won in a Penske (which would prove significant).

For Michigan and round five, Mario was back in the pack. John Paul Jr in a VDS PC10 won after Rick Mears spun out of the lead on the last lap, Al Unser taking second and Mario third, coasting home out of fuel. The first win came at Elkhart Lake with father and son Unser third and second respectively. Tom Sneva was fourth on his Theodore's debut. Mario was on pole but led only the last four laps. Josele Garza, in a Penske PC10, had been the star, only to spin away the lead. Bobby Rahal then took over, only to run out of fuel. Mario Andretti had fallen back at the start with the lack of a clutch, and then experienced pop-off valve problems, but found himself well placed to take advantage as the others fell away.

Teo Fabi won round seven at Pocono, Mario managing only seventh after an early delay when he stalled whilst avoiding a Garza/Rahal tangle. Then at Riverside, Mario qualified third but retired with a deranged gear linkage when well poised. This would ultimately prove crucial in the final championship standing.

Mid-Ohio saw Fabi lead Mario home by just 26 seconds, with Bobby Rahal in third and Kevin Cogan sixth in a Theodore. Mario scooped the runner-up position in the last two laps as Bobby Rahal again hit late problems, the Lola's excellent fuel economy proving crucial. Mario followed this up with a fourth place at Michigan the next weekend in an understeering car. Las Vegas was round 11 and Mario won again. He had qualified third and finally took the lead with just five laps to go. Pole sitter John Paul Jr was second with Chip Ganassi in a Wildcat third. Mario's Lola had sported the latest sidepods and underbody. This race came down to a ten lap sprint finish following yellow flag periods. Mario had initially led from soon after the start, only for John Paul Jr to hustle past under braking. Mario did it to him later, pulling out a vital second at flagfall.

Then it was on to Laguna Seca where Teo Fabi won again. Mario placed second after having qualified sixth. Chip Ganassi was third again and Big Al had retired from fifth place in the last ten laps, so leaving the championship open to him, Teo or Mario ...

At the final race, held at Phoenix, pole man Teo Fabi won again, Mario finishing second again (from the front row), with Tom Sneva third and Big Al an easy fourth, although two laps down at the end. Chip Ganassi finished fifth. Mario led early on but had been unable to beat Fabi at the finish. Thus, Unser was champion with 151 points; Fabi second on 146 and Mario Andretti third with 133. Teo won four times, Mario and Sneva twice each, Al only once. Consistency ruled.

Eric Broadley, when interviewed, said in a company review that the car was started in October 1982 and was ready in January 1983. It had proved to be good on road courses, especially in the second half of season.

T760

In 1982, Geoff Byman kept up the good work with a fourth in a combined Formula Atlantic/Libre race at Castle Combe on April 12th, then a sixth at the Silverstone Formula Atlantic race the next month, and again in June. Using a Cosworth BDG, Bryman was fourth at Mallory on August Bank Holiday Monday, and then second to Dave Hoban in a March 78 in a Libre/FF2000 Challenge at Cadwell Park on September 26th, having led awhile. He finished fourth in the BRSCC Northern Libre points; the winner, Hoban in a March.

In 1983, Byman won the BRSCC Northern round at Cadwell Park in May, going flag to flag in the lead. He subsequently finished eighth in the Formula Atlantic series, Alo Lawler winning in an RT4.

T850

For 1982 the Docking-Spitzley team announced early on that it hoped to have revised F2 cars ready by March, suspension modifications being done by Neil Oatley. However, it soon became apparent the team would soon have its own chassis, called the DS1. These were the same chassis as the year before, modified – with help from Pat Symonds and Frank Dernie – for revised suspension and aerodynamics respectively. They were, however called Toleman-Hart DS1s.

They were intended for Thierry Tassin and Carlo Rossi and were to be Hart powered. The first race of the Formula Two championship of 1982 was at Silverstone where Tassin was disqualified from second place by an over-zealous scrutineer for a slight skirt infringement. Stefan Bellof won for Maurer with Satoru Nakajima in a March promoted to second, and Beppe Gabbiani, in a March, third. Roberto del Castello finished fourth in a BMW-powered Toleman T850.

Come the Hockenheim race, Tassin finished sixth in a Toleman DS1 as Bellof won again. Tolemen had, by then, accrued four points from two races and would not get any more. Indeed, Tassin and Del Castello managed to crash into each other at the first corner of Thruxton's round three of the championship, and Rossi's engine lasted only seven laps as Johnny Cecotto in a March took his first ever four wheel win. Despite Thierry Boutsen taking pole position by a full three seconds at the Nürburgring, still the problems mounted. A broken anti-roll bar, and then a deflated tyre put him down and then out with just two laps to go.

In a final indignity, both the Docking-Spitzley team cars were written off at Spa in June when they crashed in the wet at Eau Rouge after being third and sixth respectively. Tassin's car needed a new skin and Rossi's had to have a new tub. Both used the new 'old' TG280s at Donington for the next race while repairs were being done, but soon Del Castello was Toleman's only representative, being placed ninth at Enna. The return of the DS1s at Misano brought no joy and the season just faded away.

The Docking-Spitzley team had lacked finance and, without 'works support', foundered. The team had been helped along the way by Toleman's Pat Symonds and Frank Dernie of Williams, but the mountain had been just too big to climb, despite revised suspension and new aerodynamics for the Docking-Spitzley team. Corrado Fabi took the championship, winning by just one point from Johnny Cecotto; both had used Marches.

In 1983, Guido Dacco appeared at the Nürburgring in a T850. He qualified 19th but crashed out on the first lap after tangling with Fulvio Ballabio's Merzario. Next time out, at Vallelunga in May, he was sixth! This was due to a conservative non-stop run on Avons in a wet-dry race as the March/Maurer/Ralt scrap for victory took place ahead of him. Sadly, Guido could only qualify last at Pau and an accident ended his hopes after just 30 laps.

T870 – 1982 – F3 – 1+ built
This car was first tested by Mike Blanchet at Donington in mid-October 1982. The car's production was delayed due to IndyCar pressures, but finally ran properly for the first time in mid-July 1983, with Johnny Dumfries at the wheel at Snetterton. There were no major problems but Johnny Dumfries announced he would not race it until the car was properly sorted.

Development was postponed because the factory was under pressure with its IndyCar project.

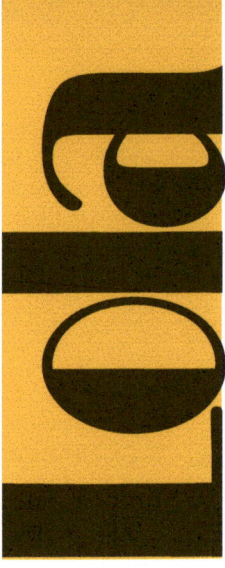

Lola

4
1984-1985

T332

In 1984, Tony Trimmer, driving John Jordan's car, won the British Open, (round four) at Silverstone on May 7th, having also won at Brands Hatch the previous day. At Silverstone he reduced John Lepp's seven-year-old club circuit outright record by 1.3 seconds! Trimmer also won round five of the championship at Silverstone on June 17th, as well as the Mallory Park race in July. Over the next 17-plus years, this became probably the most successful Lola/driver combo ever.

At Mosport In Canada, Jeremy Hill placed sixth in the first round of the Can-Am series, Michael Roe winning in a VDS.

1984

Horst Kroll was the main Frissbee exponent in 1984, in a (Lola-based) KR-3. He took second place at Brainerd and Atlanta, third at Mosport and Riverside, fourth at Mosport and Trois Rivières and Riverside, plus fifth at Lime Rock and three eighth places (as worst results). The Frissbee was reliable but was outrun by Roe in a VDS and Jim Crawford in the March 847.

T380

The ADA de Cadenet appeared at Thruxton for the Thundersports Round Five on July 8th 1984, driven by Raymond Taft and David Heynes. They qualified last but a reliable run netted third in class.

T490

In 1984, Keith Messer appeared at the British Grand Prix Support race at Brands Hatch with a stylishly rebodied T492, that had all-enclosing bodywork, as per the Aquila, Shrike and T590s.

T530

Also in 1984, Johns Foulston and Brindley won the second Thundersports race held at Brands Hatch on Easter Monday. They were fifth from pole position at Donington in mid-June. They took pole again at Brands Hatch on August Bank Holiday Monday, but retired during the race. However, they came back to win from pole again at Oulton Park the next weekend.

T594

In 1984 also Mike Blanchet and Mike Juggins used a Xerox-sponsored T594 with a Volkswagen engine in the Thundersports series. Head gasket problems meant a lost second place at Oulton Park on Good Friday, and the race was won by the T594C, with a 2.6-litre Mazda rotary engine, of Taylor/Lovett. The rotary engine was a Mazda 13B with 280bhp at 8800rpm, built up by Spike Winter of The Engine Shop at Maids Moreton, near Silverstone. Blanchet and Juggins did, however, place third overall at Brands Hatch on Easter Monday and were second in the fourth round of the series at Donington in June, with Tony Trevor and John Bright coming in third in a 2.0 T596.

Blanchet and Juggins were ninth at the next round at Thruxton in July, having started on the front row of the grid. Come the British Grand Prix Support event, they were fifth in a race won by Taylor and Lovett, who also won round eight at Brands Hatch on

HU600-5 was a T600 sold, first of all, to Chris Cord, who used it for occasional IMSA races in the early 1980s. Today, after a long sojourn with Chuck Kendall, the car is completely restored and going very fast in HSR races on the east coast of America.

August Bank Holiday Monday, having started third.

The Mazda-powered car was then second at Oulton Park the next weekend, having started from the pitlane. The VW car was fourth as Johns Brindley and Foulston won from pole in the ex-Tambay T530. 40-year-old Edvinsson came second at Falkenberg in July and second again at Knutstorp in August in the European Sports 2000 series to finish fourth in the championship. Thorkild Thyrring won seven out of eight races to dominate the championship; Charles Zwolsman was runner-up.

T600

The 1984 Daytona 24 Hours heralded in the new IMSA season, with the Porsche 962 (driven by the Andrettis) being the new IMSA yardstick. John Morton, Bob Lobenberg and Tony Garcia qualified tenth and finished 11th after 'incidents' in their T600, whilst Johns Kalagian, Lloyd and Mills (!) qualified 11th but were put out by an accident after only 27 laps. The Morton/Adamowicz/Garcia trio was seventh at the Sebring 12-hour race in Phil Conte's T600.

John Morton and Tony Adamowicz then teamed up to take fourth place at the Riverside Six Hours, despite a wheel bearing failure. Chuck Kendall and Jim Cook were fifth in their T600 as the Jaguars missed this race, preparing for Le Mans. Come the Laguna Seca race, T600s made fifth (Morton) sixth (Kalagian) and ninth (Kendall). John Morton and Richard Spénard were then fourth at the Mid-Ohio 500kms, finishing on the same lap as the winning Holbert/Bell 962.

In short, best T600 results of the IMSA season were: third in Miami (February 26th, Morton/Lobenberg), fourth and fifth in Riverside (as stated above), fifth and sixth in Laguna Seca (as stated above), fourth in Mid-Ohio (as stated above) and sixth in Michigan (Ray McIntyre/Mike Brockman, September 16th).

Becker was out again in his two-litre car, at the Norisring in late June 1984. He qualified 15th on the grid but did not feature in the race.

Chuck Kendall and Jim Cook decided to forego IMSA and chance their luck in late World Endurance Championship rounds. They qualified 19th at Mount Fuji on September 30th, and finished an amazing tenth on reliability in a race won by John Watson and Stefan Bellof in a Porsche. In Sandown Park, local man Peter Fitzgerald shared the driving with Kendall and Cook. They were out of luck, though, qualifying 15th, but suffering driveshaft failure after 95 laps.

T610

1984 saw John Bartlett buying the ex-Cooke-Woods car for Thundersports,

The Polimotor-powered Lola T616. (Courtesy Bob Roemer)

etc. Fitted with a Cosworth 3.3 DFL, this car was now closer to the original aerodynamic specification. Together with Steve Kempton and John Brindley, Bartlett qualified 27th at the Silverstone WEC round but they missed the cut by ten laps, doing only 138 because of throttle problems.

The WEC finale at Sandown had Bartlett paired with Richard Jones and David Borroughs. They were the penultimate qualifier of the 30 cars entered. The DFL engine was back in, but the car ran in C2. At the finish, they were unclassified, having done only 120 laps.

1984 – T616 – 1983 – GpC Junior – 4 built

This was virtually a scaled-down version of the T610. Among the differences were rearranged front aerodynamics and a Hewland FGB transaxle, as well as smaller wheels, 13x11in front, 13x14in rear.

The T616 was announced to the press in October 1983 and was intended for the new Group C Junior (or C2, as it came to be known), which was due to start in 1984. The first two cars had already been tested at Silverstone, prior to being shipped out to Jim Busby in America to be fitted with Mazda rotary engines. The T616 was to be run on BFG road-legal tyres! Probably just two more were laid down (one for Busby and another for Holzberg), with unspecified engines.

Three chassis in total were delivered to BF Goodrich and a fourth went to American, Matty Holzberg, who had designed an all-plastic Polimotor engine. This had a four cylinder, 2-litre capacity, ceramics-lined plastic cylinder head and aluminium cylinder liners. The Lola-Polimotor was driven in 1985 by Peter Argetsinger and Herm Johnson, its best results being third in Camel Lights class at Lime Rock and fourth in class at Elkhart Lake.

Soon after Christmas a Mazda-engined car was tested in preparation for the Daytona 24-Hour race, due to be held in February, and where the Andrettis would debut the Porsche 962: it went well before being put out by a variety of problems. Jim Busby, Rick Knoop and Boy Hayje qualified 17th and ran third for much of the night, only for the engine to blow up at dawn. Pete Halsmer/Dieter Quester/Ron Grable qualified 28th and finished 17th

The Polimotor engine. It featured piston skirts, connecting rods, timing gears and tappets made out of a plastic called Torlon. (Courtesy Bob Roemer)

Lola T616. This is believed to be the one car that won its class at Le Mans in 1984. (Author photo)

after delays caused by transmission problems. The race was won by the Kreepy Krauly March 83G of South African trio Sarel van der Merwe, Graham Duxbury and Tony Martin.

Best IMSA results of the season for the T616s were fifths at Miami (Halsmer/Hayje) and Watkins Glen Busby/Knoop).

In the World Endurance Championship, round one, Dieter Quester/Hayje qualified 18th at Monza but were not classified in the results, having lost an hour after Hayje hit the chicane armco. Busby and Knoop qualified 23rd and finished sixth, winning the C2 class behind a quartet of Porsches (led by Jacky Ickx and Jochen Mass) and a Rondeau C1.

The next championship outing for the T616 was the Le Mans 24 Hours where John Morton/John O'Steen/Yoshimi Katayama qualified 39th and finished tenth. Busby/Knoop/Hayje – whose team manager was Jim Tully –

Above & overleaf: Two Mazda rotary-powered T616s were entered in the 1984 Le Mans 24 Hours race. They ran on experimental T/A radial rubber intended for road use. Car number 68 (overleaf), driven by John O'Steen/John Morton/ Yoshio Katayama, won the C2 category and came tenth overall.

qualified 40th and finished 12th. They were split overall and in the class result by a Rondeau C2. The Lolas were first and third in C2. Busby and Knoop were eighth overall at the Mid-Ohio IMSA round and fifth at Watkins Glen in early July.

The third World Endurance Championship outing was at the Nürburgring the very next weekend, and Quester/Knoop and Busby/Halsmer qualified midfield but lost the C2 class win by seven laps to the Spice/Bellm/ Crang Tiga. Busby and Halsmer then qualified 27th at Fuji and were 13th and fourth in C2. Quester and Knoop started one place further back and finished 11th, and third in the C2 class, which was won by the Lotec BMW. The Mazda engines were very marginal on fuel so *sotto voce* ...

T642

During 1984, Peter Townsend won the P&O sponsored race at Oulton Park, held March 31st. Mark Blundell spun out, having been second earlier. Both drivers were in T644Es.

Mark then won at Snetterton on May 7th, and then the 'Champion of Snetterton' race one week later, with Doug Lague in the points, too. Blundell won the Dan-Air 'Star of Tomorrow' and the 'Star of Mallory Park' races in June. Peter Townsend still led the P&O Championship in his T640E.

Gerrit van Kouwen, in a T644E, won the Brands Hatch Townsend Thoresen round on June 10th, and Neil Cochrane in his T642E took the Knockhill race on July 1st. Van Kouwen won the RAC race at the Brands Hatch British Grand Prix support event, from third on the grid; the race was stopped after four laps following a big shunt. Yet while many switched to VDS in the D-A series, Phil Andrews upheld Lola honours.

Len Greeney and Eugene O'Brien were also stalwarts in their own series. Gerrit van Kouwen won the Townsend

Thoresen race at Brands Hatch at the end of September, which was the prelude to the big one. Van Kouwen won the Formula Ford Festival with a T644E from Uwe Schäfer in a Van Diemen and Bertrand Gachot in a Reynard. He was unbeaten through the heats, made fastest lap and set a new lap record. It was a resounding victory.

T710 – 1984 – IMSA GTP

This was the Corvette built for the GT Prototype class in collaboration with GM. It proved to be fast but fragile.

Featuring an alumimium honeycomb monocoque (said to be a refinement of the T600 tub) with a Group C central flat bottom and Kevlar/carbon fibre bodywork, the T710 had a centrally-located 120-litre fuel tank. It also had full-length side pontoons from pedal box to beyond the rear bulkhead. Despite its shorter air tunnels, Eric Broadley claimed the car could be tuned to produce twice the overall downforce of the T600. The front suspensiom was by pushrod with vertical dampers mounted centrally, and the rear wishbones had outboard springs/damper units. For braking, huge 13in AP ventilated discs were used. A structure of A-frames helped support the engine which drove through a 5-speed Hewland VG transaxle. Yet, the engine front plate was bolted directly to the chassis, too, so contributing to torsional rigidity. The body was styled by GM Technical Centre and had production Corvette cues. The bodywork was wind tunnel tested at Warren and Imperial College.

Overall length	188in
Overall width	79in
Overall height	41in
Wheelbase	106in
Front track	63in
Rear track	61in

A 209ci/3425cc twin plug turbocharged Chevrolet V6 of 700bhp was the chosen power unit, which was effectively a shortened 90-degree V8. Developed by Ryan Falconer, the engine featured an iron block and aluminium heads. There was a single Warner ISHI turbocharger, as per the IndyCars, with Bosch electronic fuel injection. Although the car was designed principally for IMSA GTP competition, its weight was claimed to be on the Group C minimum of 850kg and, for IMSA, it needed to be ballasted to 900kg.

The Corvette underwent shakedown tests by Jonathan Palmer at Goodwood and then at Silverstone, courtesy of Stefan Johansson. The prototype body had been shown at the Detroit Grand Prix in June 1983, mounted on an Interscope T600 chassis. The first real car was completed in February. There was then an inordinately long wait of six months before Mario Andretti was due to test the Corvette at Laguna Seca in late October. Problems with the engine precluded any further testing.

The Corvette GTP finally made its race debut in private hands at the 1985 Daytona 24 Hours. Now powered by one of Chevrolet's familiar 5.7-litre V8s, and carrying T711 identification, it was qualified 14th by Lew Price/Carson Baird/Terry Labonte/Billy Hagan. It retired from the race with transmission problems after an uneventful run.

Price carried on through the season, achieving some top ten finishes, but generally falling short of his expectations. The 'works' V6 turbo version was eventually entrusted to Rick Hendrick's team and appeared for the first time in Elkhart Lake in August. However, it was only after further lengthy testing that the car really made its mark, with versatile South-African, Sarel van der Merwe, taking pole position for the last IMSA race of the season at Daytona. Van der Merwe took the initiative in the race, but then lost his rear bodywork and wing, eventually retiring with handling problems. The car's promise had been obvious, though.

This form continued into 1986, when van der Merwe placed the car easily on pole for the Daytona 24 Hours. It has to be said, however, that few of the long-legged Porsches bothered to chase that honour, the crews preferring to prepare for the race. They were vindicated, too, when the Corvette GTP was withdrawn before the start, with chronic vibration problems that necessitated replacement of the engine and gearbox. A key factor in winning poles appeared to be the increase in power to some 800bhp.

At Miami the car was again on pole, having won a four-lap shoot-out. It led early in the race, but was put out when the turbo blew a hole in the exhaust system.

At Road Atlanta van der Merwe made it four out of four by taking yet another pole. This time that promise was fulfilled: after a fierce battle with the John Paul Jr/Whitney Ganz March-Buick, van der Merwe and Doc Bundy took a popular victory for the Corvette GTP.

The car was then destroyed in a Riverside shunt and subsequently superceded at Charlotte by a new version. This had an all-new underwing and the rear wing was attached by two wide-based supports, rather than being centrally supported over the transmission. This, together with a one-piece carbon fibre rear cowling, gave a more rigid rear end, inproving handling. The new car also had a tiny extra wing, mounted low, right behind the gearbox. The cooling systems were rearranged, too. In the Charlotte race the new car chased the leading Porsches, despite overheating problems, and finished fourth.

In June's Palm Beach Three Hours van der Merwe and Bundy were back to pole position and took their second victory of the season, again after a frantic battle. This time they beat Jochen Mass/Darin Brassfield in a Porsche by less than a tenth of a second.

Watkins Glen produced another pole and a competitive race, but disappointment, too, with a steering arm breakage.

In Portland the car shared the front row with Geoff Brabham's T810, and this was to be repeated at Road Atlanta, where the 'Vette had pole, as at Columbus, where the Nissan again had the edge. Despite yet one more pole at the season-closing Daytona race, luck was not with Rick Hendrick's team and the crew did not mount the podium in the remaining races, which left van der Merwe and Bundy tenth in the season's points.

In the 1987 Daytona 24 Hours the old team qualified third and ran competitively for its longest distance yet. Even so, it was only a third of the way through the 24 hours when a dropped valve ended hopes.

New rules restricting the Chevy turbo V6 to 3.0 litres at first seemed to hurt the car less than feared. It had ample horsepower, a fact emphasised by four pole positions that season. Lack of an effective engine management system made life difficult, though. The car's throttle lag made it tricky to drive and an extra pit-stop was often necessitated by poor fuel mileage.

Best result of the year was van der Merwe's single-handed second in Laguna Seca's sprint event. He shared third with Bundy at Mid-Ohio, Sears Point and San Antonio, but could not better tenth place in the championship.

The Hendricks team occasionally ran a second car. Cousins Michael and John Andretti out-qualified the regular pairing with third best time at Mid-Ohio, but were delayed in the race to finish 11th.

In the Columbus late season race a new chassis appeared (T86/12). This featured a Lotus-developed active ride suspension. In testing at Snetterton, Johnny Dumfries had earlier wrecked a car equipped with it. The drivers were impressed with the suspension – van der Merwe qualifying fourth and running third – until the active system went wrong

For 1988, Hendrick commissioned a new T88/11 from Lola, which was fitted with a 5-litre, normally aspirated Chevrolet V8. This was run in tandem with the V6 turbo, which now had a second-generation electronic management system by Delco. Elliot Forbes-Robinson moved across from Electramotive to share the driving with Sarel van der Merwe, while Bobby Rahal agreed to do half-a-dozen events for the team.

Hendrick increasingly concentrated on the new V8 machine, which sported a number of modifications, mostly carried out by the team. The most notable outward difference compared to previous versions was a short, truncated tail. Among other developments was a rising rate suspension.

By now, the momentum was no longer with Hendrick's Corvette programme. The team's only podium of the year was an inherited third at Watkins Glen, two laps behind the winning Nissan. There were to be no more front row starts, either.

Late in the season, another Corvette GTP joined the IMSA series. Run by the Peerless team, David Hobbs and Jack Baldwin debuted a new V8-engined car at Columbus, qualifying seventh and finishing a promising fourth, one place better than Hendrick's lead car. The Peerless car also featured the team's own developments, like changes to front suspension and undertray.

Peerless carried on in 1989, but was hopelessly uncompetitive. The Canadian pairing of Jacques Villeneuve (brother of Gilles) and Scott Goodyear was recruited in the spring, but the best they could extract from the ageing design was a few top 10 qualifying performances.

1990

Paul Canary's Eagle, which appeared at the 1990 Le Mans 24-Hour race, was an updated 1988 Corvette IMSA GTP previously driven by Jacques Villeneuve, Scott Goodyear, David Hobbs and Jack Baldwin. (It was the Peerless car discussed above.) It had an aluminium honeycomb tub, Hewland VGC tansaxle and AP discs. The car's rear end was extensively re-worked by the team from Santa Barbara, California.

According to *Road & Track*, a 9.6-litre/588ci version delivered 900bhp at 5500rpm. The engine was built by Joe Schubeck who built engines for dragsters. It was claimed that this engine had been designed by computers from scratch. It had an aluminium block, with capacity being adjustable between 9636 and 11,471 litres! The capacity for Le Mans was 10.2 litres and Haltech fuel injection was fitted.

Completing very few laps in practice, following a lot of problems with the scrutineers, the car was nowhere near the pace even to think of qualifying. A brave but ultimately sad effort.

T800 – 1984 – IndyCars

This car was principally designed by Nigel Bennett, who used to be Mario Andretti's race engineer when the latter won the World Championship with Lotus in 1978.

Moulded carbon fibre and Kevlar were utilized for the first time to form the top half of the monocoque. Carbon/Kevlar skins sandwiched the aluminium honeycomb. CART regulations precluded using this for the monocoque's lower half, which was similar to the T700 in construction. The T800 was substantially stiffer than its predecessor.

A notable advantage came from relocating the turbocharger half in, half out of the bellhousing between engine and gearbox, which not only reduced the height of the rear bodywork, improving aerodynamics, but also lowered the centre of gravity. A long-tail version of the car was designed for the superspeedways. This featured a totally different rear suspension, although it was claimed to be identical geometrically.

Round one of the 1984 Indycar Championship was at Long Beach and Michael Andretti won from pole position

The 1984 T800 IndyCar during a street race. (Courtesy LAT)

in the new T800. It was a great start to a great year for the model. Geoff Brabham, in a March, was second, Tom Sneva in another March was third and Jim Crawford in a Theodore fourth.

Round two was at Phoenix. This was won by Tom Sneva for Meyer's team. Mario qualified third and was running second when the fuel fail-safe failed, and Mario coasted into his pit garage, losing time. Later on a driveshaft also failed and he retired. The Indianapolis 500 was next and Mario qualified sixth after his engine failed at Turn four on the last lap of his run, leaving him to coast in. Tom Sneva was on pole position for the race. Danny Sullivan qualified 29th (17th best time) in a T800 after switching from Doug Shierson Racing's own Ian Reed designed DSR1. Tony Cicale was quoted as saying that the new Lola had 15-20% more torsional rigidity and was 125% better when twisted corner to corner.

In the race, Mario had an accident with Josele Garza in the pitlane, as he dived into the pits for fuel under a caution flag after a hundred and 53 laps, when well placed. This put Mario out. Garza, in a March, finished tenth, and Danny Sullivan went out after 57 laps when going well, having hit Guerrero who had slowed (as did someone ahead of him) for the Patrick Bedard accident. Roberto Guerrero subsequently survived a triple spin (the one which caused the Mario/Garza debacle) to come second to Rick Mears, two laps adrift.

Milwaukee was next and Tom Sneva won again, with Mario finishing eighth after qualifying third on the grid. The Lola suffered constant wheel nut problems, one wheel actually coming off, making the T800 a tricar for a whole lap. Portland was the next venue and saw Al Unser's first win. The early laps were, however, dominated by the Andretti and Sullivan Lolas, which had started on the front row. Mario was on pole but, in the race, he was forced out with a holed radiator. Danny Sullivan then led for the first time in his career, only for the gearbox to fail.

At Meadowlands, Mario was on pole position again and this time won a flag to flag victory. Danny Sullivan started seventh and finished second in a Lola 1-2. Geoff Brabham was third, having been second in Milwaukee, and the Lolas beat the rest of the field by a clear lap.

At Cleveland, it was Danny Sullivan's turn to win his first CART race, which also saw the Ford Cosworth DFX engine's 100th win. Danny Sullivan had been fifth on the grid, and Mario on pole position again, but he stopped after 45 laps with electric problems, leaving Bobby Rahal in a March to assume the lead, only for his pinion gear to break. Danny Sullivan won by two laps from Chip Ganassi and Michael Andretti.

At Michigan, polesitter Mario Andretti beat Tom Sneva by a length in a race of destruction to claim his first 500-mile race since 1969! But he still trailed in the championship. Danny Sullivan qualified 17th and finished in tenth place, whilst poor Chip Ganassi was injured in a crash. Elkhart Lake in Wisconsin was next and Andretti won again from pole to take the championship lead from Tom Sneva by one point (Sneva failed to finish when his engine let go). Danny Sullivan retired because of a fire caused by fuel venting problems, after he had been running with, and sometimes ahead of, Mario. Mario Andretti was third on the grid at Pocono with Danny Sullivan back in ninth place, but Sullivan won by 0.27secs from Rick Mears in a March, with Bobby Rahal's March another 0.5secs behind. Mario Andretti's engine blew and he dropped out. At Mid-Ohio, however, Andretti made it three wins from four starts. He turned a lap two full seconds ahead of Rick Mears in qualifying to emphasize his road racing supremacy. Danny Sullivan was fourth on the grid and finished third behind Bobby Rahal as Mario retook his championship lead.

Rick Mears was badly injured in a practice crash at Sanair where, this time, Bobby Rahal was on pole, ahead of Danny Sullivan, Roberto Guerrero and Mario Andretti. Danny Sullivan made no mistakes to win from Bobby Rahal, Mario Andretti finishing only seventh after a collision with a backmarker. Corrado Fabi, in another Lola, finished tenth, after being the innnocent victim of Rick Mears' crash.

Round 13 was at Michigan and Mario won again. Tom Sneva finished second to end a poor run of results. Danny Sullivan had dropped to ninth place at the end of the race. The race itself had started Sunday and finished on Monday, having been delayed by a bad accident which had befallen Derek Daly. Rain had started to fall while Daly's accident was being attended to. Mario had commanded most of the race after poleman, Johnny Rutherford, had handling problems while subbing for Rick Mears, but in the end he crashed out. It had been the eighth consecutive Lola win.

At Phoenix, the big news was that Corrado Fabi had out-qualified Mario Andretti! Teo Fabi was sixth with Mario seventh and Danny Sullivan tenth. The real surprise, however, was that Jacques Villeneuve was on pole in the Canadian Tyre March. Bobby Rahal surprised everyone in the end, with his first win of the year for the TrueSports team. Al Unser Jr pipped Michael Andretti for second place with Tom Sneva fourth. Mario had tangled with Gordy Johncock two thirds of the way through the race who had himself been battling with Pancho Carter (Mario had been about to lap these two). Mario had taken the high line but Gordy had moved up, too, and was forced out due to a broken steering arm. Danny Sullivan had crashed and Tom Sneva was now only four points adrift with two races left.

At Laguna Seca, Kenny Acheson deputised for Corrado Fabi (whose father had died) but crashed at the Corkscrew in practice due to a sticking throttle. Bobby Rahal won again but Mario Andretti was second from pole position. Danny Sullivan had started third and finished ninth, whilst Tom Sneva was tenth after having suffered gear selection problems. Mario Andretti had led the opening laps.

To take the championship, Tom Sneva now had to win the finale with Mario Andretti being outside the top ten. Tom Sneva fulfilled the first part of the equation, winning at Las Vegas. But Mario Andretti was second, only seven seconds behind, to claim the title. Bobby Rahal finished seventh. Danny Sullivan had been on pole with Mario alongside, but Danny Sullivan had crashed after 91 laps, hitting the wall. Tom Sneva had started fifth and Corrado Fabi started 14th but fire eliminated him after only 24 laps.

Post-season testing saw Danny Sullivan in a Penske, where he also tested an ex-Andretti T800 that Roger had presumably bought for comparison purposes.

Two views of the Lola T810 as a prototype outside the factory in 1985. This car ran in America in the IMSA series as a Nissan GTP ZX Turbo. (Courtesy LAT)

The Nissan GTP ZX Turbo was – underneath the Nissan-adorned skin – a Lola T810, which was developed very successfully in America by Don Devendorf's Electromotive team until it dominated IMSA racing in the late 1980s, ending the Porsche 962's long reign. (Courtesy Russ Blaise/IMSA Collection)

Mario	176pts
Sneva	163pts
Rahal	137pts
Sullivan+Mears	110pts

T810 – 1985 – Nissan GTP – 4 built
Commissioned by Californian Nissan agent Electramotive to run in IMSA GTP events, the T810 was designed by Eric Broadley and Clive Lark. In the US the car ran under the name of Nissan GTP ZX Turbo.

The use of a 3-litre turbocharged Nissan V6 engine meant that effective cooling was a design priority from the outset. The car's distinctive feature was big cooling ducts just forward of the windscreen, which collected air at the nose and fed it through tunnels running both sides of the cockpit to mid-mounted coolers: the engine's turbo intercooler and water radiator.

The monocoque was fabricated from flat aluminium honeycomb panels, but the floor had carbon fibre skins for increased rigidity. Honeycomb pontoons flanking the cockpit added strength.

The bodywork was glass pre-preg on aluminium and non-metallic Nomex honeycomb, depending on the complexity of shape in the area it was used. Some sources claim the chassis shared dimensions and suspension installation with the T710.

The Venturi-shaped underbody was of a sandwich structure, using glass pre-preg and carbon fibre strategically.

The engine was supported by a tubular steel frame, bolted to the bulkhead. The front suspension was inboard, with pushrods operating spring/damper units, which were

IMSA street fighting, 1989-style. San Antonio, Texas, September 3rd, and Geoff Brabham (race number 83) and Chip Robinson (race number 84) hit each other shortly after this photo was taken. They recovered well, with Robinson taking victory after Brabham's car broke towards the end of the race. (Courtesy David Allio/IMSA Collection)

crossed over the scuttle to make room for the cooling air channels. Conventional rear suspension was by outboard wishbones and coil/damper units. Brakes were 13in ventilated discs and AP four-pot calipers. A Weismann 5-speed gearbox was used initially.

The car's IMSA debut was at Laguna Seca in May, with Don Devendorf and Tony Adamovicz as drivers. Its potential was not realised in the first season, as Devendorf's car was twice written off when the suspension broke on superspeedway bankings, and it was also crashed badly in an incident at Elkhart Lake. In fact, the T810's best result in 1985 was achieved in a Japanese WEC event at Fuji, where Haruhito Yanagida and Aguri Suzuki took eighth place in a race boycoted by most Europeans, which was stopped because of torrential rain. This particular T810 was regularly raced in Japan.

The form only improved in the spring of 1986, when newly-signed driver pairing Elliott Forbes-Robinson and Geoff Brabham suddenly appeared on the front row of the grid for the Riverside Six Hours race. The pair had undertaken an extensive testing and development programme for Electramotive the preceding month, and this was paying dividends. Their race, however, was soon over, as Brabham crashed in the first hour.

The car's Weismann transverse transaxle had now been changed to Hewland's brand new VGC type.

Electramotive again resorted to testing in the middle of the summer, developing new bodywork for the nose, in the rear, and a new underwing, too. The team's aerodynamic-inclined thinking was drifting it away from the full-length venturi tunnel approach. By mid-86, two cars were being used which carried a lot of Electramotive ideas.

Electramotive came back with a bang. Geoff Brabham put the car on pole for Portland's sprint race, pipping the T710 Corvette, and would have won but for a last minute splash-and-dash pitstop for fuel. He dropped to third, but even that was by far the car's best result to date.

The pole-earning qualifying performance was no flash in the pan. The car again shared the front row with the Corvette at Road Atlanta, was in the third slot in Watkins Glen, and back to pole in Columbus with the 'Vette beside it. In the races, however, Electramotive was not in luck and further podiums eluded them for the rest of the season.

The T810's aerodynamics changed considerably during its time on the IMSA circuit. They were developed by Lola in conjunction with Yoshi Suzuka, who worked with Electramotive's own rolling road wind tunnel. The wedge-shaped front splitter had been removed early in the car's life. The underside aerodynamics evolved and the rear deck was shortened, plus the rear wing was mounted lower and further from the deck. By 1987 revisions had doubled the downforce the car was capable of at 200mph.

For 1987 the car's competitiveness was also helped by new rules restricting its turbocharged opposition to the same 3-litre capacity. Having missed Daytona, Geoff Brabham put the car on pole at Miami and, together with Elliott Forbes-Robinson, controlled the race from the front to score the car's first win in a convincing manner.

That the speed was there was obvious. Reliability remained a different matter, though. Even in Miami's three-hour race the oil-pressure gauge gave alarming signals, and thereafter the car finished only another three races during the season. Its problems were myriad and four more pole positions did not really reward the team's expectations as further podium finishes eluded them.

For 1988 the programme moved entirely in-house to Electramotive. Trevor Harris designed a new Nissan ZX Turbo, which virtually looked a replica of the T810 (team boss Don Devendorf said the plan was to fit everything under the old bodywork), but actually incorporated only a few parts from Lola, such as doors, roll cages, uprights and spindles. The torsional rigidity was said to be at least doubled. The car could no longer be considered a Lola, but it swept all before it! Partnered by John Morton in the longer races, Geoff Brabham scored nine wins from 12 contested, and took the championship title into the bargain.

In 1989 Brabham and new signing Chip Robinson bettered even that result with ten wins between them, including the Sebring 12 Hours with assistance from Arie Luyendyk. The only serious opposition for Brabham's second title came from Robinson, when they were in different cars. At the season's end,

Robinson was a close second in points and Nissan now claimed the Makes, title, too.

The Trevor Harris design went on winning in the early part of 1990, scoring a 1-2 at Sebring and a clutch of other victories before it was replaced by an entirely new model during the season.

Four of these prototypes were built by Lola, and Electramotive's own modified version continued winning right up to 1990 when it was replaced by its own Trevor Harris-designed car.

T900 – 1985 – Indy – 23 built

Introduced in December 1984, the T900 was stiffer with new aerodynamics to comply with the revised skirt rules. (It had a broadly similar chassis to that of the T800. The car was slightly longer and lighter.)

Glass pre-preg was used in the manufacture. Sandwich composite underbodies were now made by hot curing carbon fibre pre-preg on non-metallic Nomex honeycomb. Lola Composites Ltd., a new company founded by Eric Broadley and Barry Hobarth of Specialised Mouldings fame, designed and manufactured the composite body parts for the T900, as well as for other future top range models.

The suspension was by unequal length wishbones at both ends, pullrod operated inboard Monroe dampers were in use at the front, and the back had pushrod suspension.

Fifteen orders were confirmed and 23 cars were eventually built. The first car was shaken down by Mario Andretti at Phoenix pre-Xmas with help from Michael Andretti and John Paul Jr.

They reported favourably on the new IndyCar contender.

The success of the T800 gave Lola fresh IndyCar custom. Doug Shierson switched from March to a T900 for his new charge, 23-year-old Al Unser Jr. Other notable Lola users were Forsythe (Howdy Holmes) and Provimi Veal (Arie Luyendyk). Newman/Haas naturally stuck to Lolas for defending champion Mario Andretti; the team was now sponsored by Beatrice.

Andretti got the season off to a flying start by winning in Long Beach. He finished second in a trying Indy 500, having led strongly. He went on to win covincingly at Milwaukee and again, with some luck, two weeks later in Portland. Three wins and a second in four races! That, however, was as far as his luck ran.

Mario Andretti in the Beatrice-sponsored T900 in 1985. (Courtesy LAT)

After losing possible victories in Meadowlands (accident) and Cleveland (engine fire), Mario crashed heavily when a right front spindle broke with just eight laps of the Michigan 500 to go. He broke a collarbone and cracked a hip socket. These injuries were aggravated by two cracked ribs sustained in a motorboat accident just a couple of weeks earlier. His performance must have been compromised for some time, although he had returned after missing only the Elkhart Lake race, where Alan Jones deputised for him. Despite some gritty drives, Andretti's best result in the latter part of the season was a third in Phoenix, and he slumped to fifth in the final points standings.

Al Unser Jr took up where Mario left off in keeping Lola on the podium. He actually followed Andretti to a Lola 1-2 in Portland, before benefiting from Mario's misfortunes to win both Meadowlands and Cleveland. Those were to be his only victories of the season. He lost the championship by just one point to a driver who had won only a single race – his father, Al Sr!

In a historic showdown in Miami, Al Sr followed his son a couple of places adrift for most of the distance, but, with just six laps remaining, took over fourth place, and with Little Al running third that was enough to clinch the title.

Through the season Unser Jr had generally raced better than he had qualified, suggesting that his success was down to consistency rather than outright speed. Still, he had more wins and more podiums (second in Pocono and Phoenix, third in Sanair and Laguna Seca in addition to those already mentioned) than Al Sr and would actually have won the title had a Formula 1 type scoring system been used. Arie Luyendyk was Rookie of the Year in a debut season, which peaked with fifth in Cleveland. He was also best rookie at Indianapolis, finishing seventh.

Jim Crawford, too, was Lola-mounted, but did only seven races. His finest hour was the season opener at Long Beach, where he managed to come home fourth.

T950 – F3000

Lola was the first manufacturer to introduce a model for the new Formula 3000 category, which replaced Formula 2 in 1985.

A works Lola F3000 team was announced in December, 1984, to be operated by Jean Mosnier, former IRTS managing director, from new premises adjacent to the factory.

The new car was to use a developement of the Indy chassis, with Mark Williams (responsible for the T800) in charge of developement. Twelve cars were due (it was later suggested that only seven cars had actually been ordered and no more than four ever materialised), including one for Trivellato which never appeared. (Trivellato had currently lost its licence after comments made about CSAI intransigence over its protest at Capelli's rear wing fiasco.)

The car was first seen at the Beatrice Formula 1 project launch in London, in the winter of 1985. Much of the design was based on the successful T800 IndyCar, although the only common element to both cars was the composite monocoque top section. By now, this also formed the main bodywork profile. The lower half of the chassis was aluminium honeycomb, just as in the IndyCar.

Front suspension was by pushrods, whilst the rear arrangement had rocker arms, trailing links and narrow-based wishbones operating inboard Koni spring/damper units. Braking power was supplied by two twin-pot AP calipers at front and single four-pots at rear.

The Cosworth DFV engine was used as a stressed member and fed its power through a Hewland FGB gearbox.

With its IndyCar origins, the T950 was necessarily somewhat bulky in comparison with its, mainly Formula 2 derived, competition. The rear end had the 'coke-bottle' shape fashionable at that time for flat-bottomed single-seaters.

Despite extensive testing before the championship opener at Silverstone, the works team seemed completely unprepared. They brought just one car for Alain Ferté and managed to deliver another for Mario Hytten to drive for a customer team. Ferté was last in qualifying, but scrambled to eighth in a mostly wet race won by Mike Thackwell for Ralt. Hytten was ninth.

In the next two rounds Ferté managed sixth in qualifying, but both times 2 seconds off pole. It didn't get any better. Despite several modifications (including trying smaller sidepods), and changes of drivers through the season, the car's record shows only one measly sixth place for privateer Juan Fangio II at Spa, on a track that decimated the field with its crumbling new surface.

It was suggested that one of the T950's major shortcomings was the fact that as the Indy chassis had been designed to accommodate a much larger fuel cell than that required for F3000, there remained empty space between the engine and the cockpit, which badly compromised weight distribution.

Beatrice – FORCE – Lola-Hart – THL1

In December 1984 a company named Formula One Race Car Engineering, or FORCE, was started by former McLaren men Teddy Meyer and Tyler Alexander, together with Eric Broadley. The purpose of this company was to operate a Grand Prix team called Beatrice for Team Haas. Carl Haas was the new company's chairman.

A new Formula 1 car was designed for the team by John Baldwin and Neil Oatley. In charge of the car's aerodynamics was Ross Brawn. Eric Broadley was technical consultant. The THL1 was built in a new factory at Colnbrook. It had a carbon fibre composite monocoque with bulkheads of machined aluminium and carbon fibre. In contemporary F1 fashion, the chassis' upper surface formed body contours, without this need for additional panels, and the fuel cell behind the cockpit was an integral part of it.

Suspension was by wishbones at both ends, with pullrods working inboard spring/damper units. Outboard brakes were mounted within the wheels and had ventilated cast iron discs.

THL1 was powered by a turbocharged 4-cylinder (in-line) Hart 415T engine. A single Holset turbocharger was fitted behind the left-hand side radiator. The six-speed gearbox was of FORCE's own design. Hewland clusters were used in a magnesium casting.

Alan Jones was tempted back from retirement to drive. The car's debut at Monza was innocuous. As Jones said to Nigel Roebuck of *Autosport*: "At least we don't have to worry about the qualifiers (tyres) lasting – they seem to last longer than the engines ..." Jones took the penultimate place on the grid and retired early in the race due to overheating. After qualifying, Carl Haas

Right: Although Alan Jones tried his hardest, the Lola-Hart Beatrice THL2 was not a car that he could win with.

was heard to mutter to the car: "If you were a horse, we'd shoot you!"

A glimpse of promise was seen at the final race in Adelaide: Jones made a mercurial rise from 19th on the grid to seventh in 15 laps, but was soon out with engine trouble.

THL1, the Beatrice-Hart four-cylinder turbocharged F1 car of 1985, with Alan Jones in the cockpit. After a particularly disappointing debut, Carl Haas was heard to say to the car: "If you were a horse, we'd have to shoot you!"

FORCE – Lola-Hart – THL2 – 6 built

The THL2 appeared for the 1986 season. Looking very similar to its predecessor, it was both smaller and neater. It featured the new, eagerly-awaited Cosworth V6 turbo engine.

This was a very compact 120 degrees V6, equipped with two Garrett turbochargers. It had an advanced electronic management system, development of which had delayed the engine's introduction. Ford remained notably secretive about engine details.

Most of the redesign work was centered round the rear of the car, where an extended transmission housing was required to compensate for the shortness of the new engine's cylinder block. Pushrod suspension was introduced.

Delays in development of the Cosworth V6 turbo meant the team had to carry on for the first races of 1986 with THL1 and the unloved Hart, for which Brian Hart had designed a new cylinder block.

Patrick Tambay joined Alan Jones in the team, which lost Beatrice sponsorship, before the season began, although the signage remained on the cars. Neither driver could entice anything extraordinary out of the old cars.

The Ford-engined THL2 finally appeared at Imola for Jones, who was cautiously optimistic about it. Ironically, Tambay achieved the highest ever qualifying position for THL1 there, putting it 11th on the grid, whilst Jones, in THL2, was 21st. In the race Jones made rapid progress to lie ninth on lap 15, but then had a series of technical problems, which eventually dropped him out.

Tambay got his THL2 for Monte Carlo and improved to eighth on the grid. Forced to his T-car (also now a THL2) by an oil leak, he started the race steadily in ninth place. The race ended spectacularly when the Frenchman collided with Martin Brundle at Mirabeau.

It was Jones' turn to shine at Spa, where Tambay again was the better qualifier at tenth on the grid; very impressive, considering the team always qualified with its engines in race specification. While Tambay's race ended in a first corner pile-up, Jones benefited to run sixth by lap 3. Having been in the pits to change blistered tyres as early as lap 7, he was back into the top six by half distance. Close to the finish, however, he ran out of fuel.

Patrick Tambay was injured in a warm-up accident in Montreal, and his stand-in, Eddie Cheever, was impressive in Detroit, qualifying tenth and running well in the midfield until sidelined with a broken rear wheel drive peg.

Tambay was back for the French GP and again managed to run in the

Below & opposite: The Beatrice Ford THL2 was powered by a V6 cylinder twin-turbocharged Ford engine. Here is Alan Jones during testing of the car at Paul Ricard in 1986. Neither THL-1 nor THL-2 were the success that had been hoped for, although THL2 did show promise on occasion.

top six, but his race was spoiled by fifth gear jumping out and was eventually terminated by a seized brake caliper.

In France a new name joined the Haas team's line-up. Adrian Newey was tempted from March to step into Formula 1. His contract with Haas was said to be for three years.

At Brands Hatch it was Jones' turn to have the upper hand, but his race was stopped after 22 laps by a broken throttle linkage. Tambay again climbed into the top six, but retired with gearbox failure.

The first ever Hungarian GP gave the team its best chance yet. The Hungaroring's lack of notable straights allowed Tambay and Jones into seventh and tenth starting slots respectively. Tambay ran fourth for the first few laps and Jones climbed to fifth as the Frenchman started to slide down the field. A leaking brake caliper brought Jones to the pits after just ten laps. Although he carried on, the long stop spoiled his day. Tambay eventually finished seventh, having lost precious time stalling his engine after a spin.

The team finally opened its score in Austria. The fast Österreichring was not somewhere they expected to shine because of the engine's lack of top-end power. As Patrick Tambay summed up after qualifying, tongue in cheek: "The balance is very nice. All the corners are flat for us!" Both drivers qualified in the midfield but in a race of attrition the cars ran reliably. Jones was fourth and Tambay fifth, although both were lapped twice by winner Prost.

The Italian GP brought another point for Jones' steady drive to sixth. Heavy attrition was again a factor in this race.

Late season highlights included Tambay's eighth on grid for the Mexican GP, but his race ended in a first lap collision with René Arnoux's Ligier.

After rumours of Bernie Ecclestone being about to take over the team, it was announced in November that Haas was pulling out of Formula 1. Carl Haas cited Ford's decision to terminate its involvement as the principal reason for his move.

**T86/50 – 1986 – F3000 –
10 planned (at least 8 built)**
This car established the company in the new formula.

Ralph Bellamy joined from March to help with the new F3000 design, although Mark Williams was still involved. Carte blanche was given for the design, and completely new parts used. The result was more 85 March than Lola.

The monocoque was produced with carbon fibre skin on aluminium honeycomb. An aluminium honeycomb floor was bonded on and could be replaced in case of damage. Bulkheads were integral to the moulding.

The nosecone was of similar construction and its strength provided a useful impact absorbent. Suspension was by pullrods and short links in front, rockers at rear, operating inboard vertically mounted Koni gas/oil dampers. A cast bellhousing incorporated dry sump oil reservoir, concentric AP clutch mechanism, and an adaptor carrying suspension rockers. AP Racing open back calipers were used, allowing fitment of bigger discs. A modified five-speed Hewland FGB gearbox was specified.

The new car was a pacesetter in pre-season testing. The form was carried on into the first race, when Pascal Fabre put the works car on pole position at Silverstone. The race was spoiled by bad weather. It was first stopped after just two laps, and the restart was then red-flagged after another 22 tours. Fabre was not at the head of the field after either 'part', but won on aggregate by just over a second from Emanuele Pirro's March.

The season never lived up to that early promise, however. In the next race in Vallelunga, Fabre was second, but after that things started going downhill.

There was a resurgence mid-season, when the T86/50s appeared with revised rear suspension, which brought the roll centre above ground level. This had been drawn by freelancing Richard Divila at the instigation of Lola customer Gary Evans Motorsport. The works cars of Fabre and Alessandro Santin were third and second on the grid, but best Lola in the race was Olivier Grouillard's privateer entry in fourth.

Fabre managed to briefly lead the next two races at Enna and the Österreichring, but could salvage only a third from the former. His championship campaign was struggling and he missed the last two rounds altogether, due to lack of money, it was suspected. Fabre's results only put him seventh in the European Championship standings, and the series was won by Ivan Capelli in a March.

Grouillard's fourth place at Mugello was the best any driver managed in privateer Lolas, although it was equalled by Mike Thackwell at the opening Silverstone race in the same Hotz team car, and Tomas Kaiser at Enna in a BS Automotive example.

5
1986-1987

T86/00 – 1986 – Indy – 15 built

New IndyCar regulations restricting the height of venturis and size of wings on superspeedways forced designers to rethink. Lola came up with an entirely new design by Nigel Bennett, Bruce Ashmore and Eric Broadley.

Sidepod rear-treatment now developed into a semi-coke-bottle-shape, with shallow 'kickers' in front of the rear wheels. The lower chassis was again aluminium honeycomb with a carbon/Kevlar upper section bonded to it. Bulkheads were of aluminium honeycomb.

The engine installation was revised and included a redesigned bellhousing, allowing the turbocharger to be mounted lower, which improved airflow over the rear wing and lowered the centre of gravity. The engine was fully stressed and the transmission was now in Lola's own casing, on which the rear suspension mounted directly. Standard Hewland DGB internals were used in the gearbox.

The car was designed to be less critical to set up, and there was a change to pushrod front suspension and inboard coil spring/damper units at the rear. The uprights were cast magnesium alloy with stiffened hubs, and Lola rack-and-pinion steering was used. The brakes featured Brembo or AP calipers and 12.6in ventilated AP discs.

Lola guaranteed that cars delivered would be beneath the regulation minimum weight of 1550lb. Again, the previous year's success had brought more customers to Lola. While Mario Andretti, Al Unser Jr and Arie Luyendyk stayed on board, Galles Racing was now fielding three new Lolas for Geoff Brabham, Roberto Moreno and Pancho Carter. Simon Racing had them for patron Dick Simon and Raul Boesel and, among other converts, was veteran Gordy Johncock.

The season started promisingly enough with Mario Andretti on pole for the first round at Phoenix. That performance flattered to deceive, however, and Mario could not hold his own in the race, dropping back with flawed handling, which puzzled him.

Al Unser Jr was second on the grid and in the race at Long Beach, but, come the month of May and the Indy 500, Lola users were scratching their heads. Mario Andretti appeared to be the only Lola driver truly on the pace, but, after qualifying for the second row, he was forced to the back of the grid when he had to take the start in his spare car. Highest placed Lola in the race was Unser Jr in fifth.

It turned out that the 86/00 was not really a match for the latest March on superspeedways.

Mario Andretti bounced back to win by 7/100ths of a second from son Michael at Portland, but that was a lucky win as Michael had first been delayed by a pitstop to change a tyre damaged in the battle with Danny Sullivan, and then started to run out of fuel in the last few laps. It was the closest finish in IndyCar history – and it all happened on Father's Day!

A couple of third places in Cleveland and Toronto kept Mario in the hunt, and then he survived the rigours of 500 miles in Pocono to take a slightly

A cutaway drawing of the four-camshaft Chevrolet-Indy V8 of 1987. (Courtesy Bob Roemer)

surprising – if truly deserved – win. In fact, the results of this event defied the assumption that T86/00s were not that great on superspeedways, as Pancho Carter brought his Galles car to third and Raul Boesel and Unser Jr were fifth and sixth. Attrition played no small part in it all ...

Mario Andretti had jumped to the head of the points table, but, despite two more poles in Mid-Ohio and Laguna Seca, couldn't hold on to his lead as the remaining races brought no more podiums.

Unser Jr's only victory of the season in the final round at Miami dropped Mario to fifth in the championship as Little Al claimed fourth by one point. Bobby Rahal was champion in a March. Other notable scores for Lola were achieved by Geoff Brabham – third at Long Beach – and Pancho Carter, who took third at the Michigan 500, where Brabham, incidentally, was fourth in a Honda-engined T86/00.

During the season the T86/00 was developed, receiving new rear suspension geometry in the summer.

T86/90 – 1986 – Sports 2000

Wind tunnel testing contributed to this car having faired-in front wheels. The pre-preg underbody was a novelty in the revised tail section. The front suspension had detail changes, reinforced lower wishbones and strengthened uprights, aiding braking stability. The rear suspension was modified with lighter but stiffer uprights, allowing for raised lower suspension links. These now had a stronger mounting platform on specially cast gearbox side plates, which also stiffened the casing. The whole arrangement cleaned up airflow.

Lola's unique roll-control link replaced a conventional anti-roll bar at the rear.

F3000 develpoment delayed the car's appearance on British circuits, but Steve Knapp won the Pro Sports 2000 Championship with it in the US.

Lola-Cosworth – LC87 – Formula 1

When the Beatrice/Haas episode came to an end, Lola maintained its involvement with F1 through the new Larrousse-Calmels team. This was a new French team formed by Gérard Larrousse and his backer Didier Calmels, hence the chassis designation 'LC'.

Lola produced an F3000-based design by Eric Broadley and Ralph Bellamy. The monocoque was basically a T87/50, but extended behind the cockpit to accommodate the larger fuel capacity. The car's nosebox was also redesigned to conform with F1 regulations and, unlike the F3000 version, it had a partial engine cover.

Like T87/50, its springs were operated by pullrods at front. pushrods rear, and cast magnesium uprights were located by wide-based wishbones. The brakes featured SEP carbon discs. The 3.5-litre Cosworth DFZ engine drove through a modified Hewland FGB gearbox.

It was a simple, straightforward design, which offered a very sensible basis for a new team to get its act together in Formula 1. Eric Broadley was regularly seen in the pitlane, engineering the car.

Developments during the season included new front suspension plus a Magneti Marelli engine management system to improve responsiveness.

This was a time in Formula 1 when a team running an atmospherically aspirated engine no longer had any hope against the turbos, and so a Jim Clark Cup was created for which the atmo-teams could compete. In this 'second division' Larrousse had Tyrrell, March and AGS for opposition.

The team debuted with Philippe Alliot at the wheel at Imola for the second round of the series, the San Marino GP. He qualified 22nd (second atmo), and, having been delayed by Pascal Fabre's spin in the race, finished tenth overall and as second best non-turbo.

As the season wore on, the team did a thoroughly respectable job, often qualifying in the top 20 (with best grid slot of 15th in Hungary), and, more importantly, scoring odd points along the way.

Alliot managed to bring the car home sixth at Hockenheim, Jerez and Mexico City, obviously usually helped by high attrition among the leading runners. He also won the atmo-class on three occasions. His strongest race was at Jerez, where – starting 17th – he closely shadowed Jonathan Palmer's atmo-leading Tyrrell until the latter was taken out by René Arnoux. Alliot then proceded to take a strong sixth, was lapped, but only beaten by two Williams-Hondas, two McLaren-TAGs and a Lotus-Honda.

Much excitement was caused by inclusion in the team of Yannick Dalmas for the last three races of the season.

Lola-Cosworth LC87 Formula 1. Basically a development of the F3000 T87/50, the LC87 was Lola's F1 car of 1987. When the Beatrice/Haas episode came to an end, Lola maintained its involvement with F1 through the new Larrousse-Calmels team. This car featured the 3.5-litre Cosworth DFZ engine, which drove through a modified Hewland FGB gearbox. A simple, straightforward design, the LC87 offered a very sensible basis for a new team to get its act together in Formula 1. Philippe Alliot was the principal driver for the new team.

Mario Andretti again, this time in the T87/00, the version built for street racing. It differed from the T87/01, which was built specifically for oval circuits. (Courtesy Bob Roemer)

He out-qualified Alliot on his debut in Mexico, and in Adelaide's finale gave the team its best overall result of the year by bringing his car home fifth, even if he was three laps behind the winner, and beaten to atmo-honours by Palmer's Tyrrell.

Alliot finished the season third in the Jim Clark Cup (won by Palmer) and the team was second in the manufacturers Colin Chapman Cup, unable to offer a challenge to Tyrrell, which doubled its chances by running two cars throughout the season.

T87/00 – 1987 – Indy

TrueSports won the CART title with this car.

This was the first Lola to be designed using the full potential of the Prime Computer CAD/CAM system. The design was by Eric Broadley,

Mario Andretti in the Hanna-sponsored T87/01 at Indianapolis in 1987. (Courtesy Bob Roemer)

Nigel Bennett and Bruce Ashmore. Different versions for road circuits (T87/00) and ovals (T87/01) now had their own identities, though both had the same monocoque. The construction remained the same, with a carbon fibre/Kevlar top bonded to an aluminium honeycomb lower section, and bulkheads of aluminium honeycomb.

There was also a one eighth of an inch alloy floor panel for improved crash protection. The roll hoop's design was new, feeding impact loads into side skins of the monocoque rather than the top, thereby increasing driver protection. The centre of gravity was lowered by reducing fuel cell height by 2in and shifting the driving position, which was now more reclined. The whole car was narrower and slimmer than its predecessor.

Suspension geometry was slightly modified, but was still by unequal length wishbones with pushrods operating inboard mounted dampers.

The road circuit T87/00's track was the full 63in allowed by the regulations, but the T87/01's was 2in narrower in the interests of better air penetration on the speedways. T87/01's swept-forward front suspension made its wheelbase longer by 2in, too, to make it easier to drive. These were arguably some of the most stunningly beautiful single-seaters ever built.

Testing suggested that Lola had been successful in its quest to better rival March's downforce/drag ratio for improved performance on the superspeedways. Reigning champions TrueSports and Bobby Rahal had switched to Lola. Newman/Haas, of course, remained loyal to the product it represented in the States.

Whilst Mario Andretti stayed on board, the big difference for the new season was the team's switch to Ilmor-Chevrolet V8 engines. Haas' withdrawal from Formula 1 allowed Adrian Newey to concentrate fully on the CART effort.

Once again, Mario Andretti made a dream start to the season, winning Long Beach from pole. He was to plant the Haas-Lola on pole seven more times – including the Indy 500 – during the year, but scored just one more win at Elkhart Lake.

Engine reliability was a big factor in the team's frustrating season. Andretti finished only five of 15 races, his points tally only good enough for sixth in the championship.

It was particularly cruel that Mario did not win at Indy. Starting from pole, he held a cushion to the rest of the field, until the engine died less than 60 miles from the finish.

The 87/01 was clearly the best chassis at Indianapolis. Four Lolas qualified in the top six, and among these were less fancied runners A.J. Foyt and Dick Simon. Still, journeyman Simon was the only Lola runner to see the chequered flag, in sixth place.

Despite defending champion Bobby Rahal qualifying on pole only once, and leading just over half the number of laps Andretti did, he scored nearly twice as many points as Mario and managed to hold on to his title.

Rahal's TrueSports Lola was powered by the tried and trusted Cosworth DFX V8. After a slightly shaky start to the season, Rahal took the series lead with two consecutive victories; first in Portland and then at Meadowlands. From there, he added a string of podium finishes, not to mention a third win at Laguna Seca's penultimate round, which clinched the title.

Bobby Rahal also took home 225,000 USD for winning the Marlboro Challenge in Miami. This was a 100-mile invitation race for the season's ten most successful drivers.

Reliability was what TrueSports had been looking for, and that gave it the championship. It was also the first IndyCar team to run a test team with a separate car. Another notable CART result for Lola in 1987 was Derek Daly's third at Milwaukee's oval.

The results had done much to convince a number of March-running teams to switch to Lolas for the following season, a trend similar to that in the European-based F3000 series at the time.

T87/50 – 1987 – F3000 – 19 built
The T87/50 was a F3000 car with carbon fibre monocoque, a Mark Williams redesign of Ralph Bellamy's T86/50, and outwardly very similar to it. However, aerodynamic efficiency was much improved after a winter programme in the Cranfield wind tunnel.

Dramatically improved downforce was claimed. The sidepods had been redesigned. There were double wishbones all round, pullrod at the front, pushrod at the rear. New geometry was expected to give much better mechanical grip. Brakes were AP single

The T87/50 was Lola's Formula 3000 car of 1987, and was an improvement over the T86/50. However, it was not enough to stop Stefano Modena's March taking the title overall. Here is Andy Wallace at Le Mans.

T87/90 was a very successful Sports 2000 design by Andrew Broadley and Ralph Bellamy. Featuring all-round inboard dampers, it won many races. Here's one in action at Oulton Park in England in 1988.

caliper discs, and a modified Hewland FGB transaxle was in use.

Wheelbase	100in
Front track	66in
Rear track	61in

European cars were all powered by Cosworth DFVs, but some cars supplied to the Japanese F3000 series had Honda engines. Works drivers were Spaniard Luis Pérez-Sala and Canadian John Jones.

In his second season of F3000, Sala was in with a chance of the title throughout, helped by having Mark Williams to engineer his car. March driver Stefano Modena held the advantage from the start, and victories from pole for Sala at Donington and Le Mans failed to topple the Italian. Modena won the championship with Sala second in Lola's strongest F3000 campaign yet. Jones showed a lot of promise, but a good second at Pau remained his best result.

A particular Lola highlight was the dramatic Spa race, which started wet with all runners on wet weather tyres. Mark Blundell sensationally fought his way to the lead in a year-old T86/50. On a drying track he couldn't hold Michel Trollé's T87/50 at bay, but when the Frenchman dived into the pits for slicks, Blundell was left with a clear lead. To his misfortune, the race was red-flagged at that very moment, when an accident at Eau Rouge required attention. Results were declared from the end of the previous lap, giving victory to Trollé, with Blundell second; a Lola 1-2. Only half-points were awarded because of the early stoppage.

Julian Bailey was another race winner for Lola, taking the honours at Brands Hatch after a convincing showing in only his third F3000 race. Bailey had, in fact, done much of the car's testing in the winter.

The works effort was ably supported in F3000 by a couple of new teams. Jean-Paul Driot's high-profile – and works-supported – GBDA team ran Trollé, and journeyman Paul Belmondo. Of a number of drivers who ran for Mike Collier's GA Motorsport, Bailey was the most successful.

In a fairly evenly matched season between chassis suppliers Lola, March and Ralt, it is probably fair to say that a Lola was the car to have. Not until Enna's sixth race of the year did a Lola-mounted driver fail to qualify for a start – quite a record considering there were 12 Lolas out there, and an average of 7-8 non-qualifiers per event.

Japan's main single-seater championship had switched to F3000 rules for 1987. Geoff Lees went over to contest the championship for the Nova Engineering team in a Honda-powered Lola T87/50, and was conclusively the fastest participant, starting from pole position in seven of the nine races. Still, he only won two of them. Veteran Kazuyoshi Hoshino, who'd won the opening round in a March, switched to a similar Lola-Honda and took the title run by the Leyton House team.

T87/90 – 1987 – S2000
The design was by Andrew Broadley and Ralph Bellamy. The Prime Computer CAD/CAM system was used to achieve the best possible weight/stiffness ratio. Aerodynamics were improved by tidying up and reducing cooling drag, although front wheels were exposed again. Weight distribution was moved forward to improve front grip. Dampers were inboard, all-round. Steve Knapp once again won the Pro Sports 2000 Series in the States using a T87/90. Mike Wright won the 1989 British series with one.

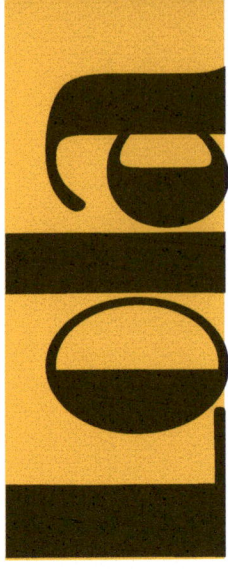

Lola

6
1988-1989

Right, top: Yannick Dalmas tried hard in 1988 for the Larrousse-Calmels team, but ended the season without a single point. It was not for want of trying, however, as this picture shows.

Right, below: The T88/00 IndyCar of 1998. (Courtesy LAT)

Lola-Cosworth – LC88 – Formula 1 – 5 built

For its second year in Formula 1 the Larrousse-Calmels team had a straightforward progression of the simple chassis used in 1987. The design was by Eric Broadley, Ralph Bellamy and Chris Murphy. Unusually for a contemporary F1, the Ford-Cosworth DFZ remained scantily clad, only partially hidden by the engine cover. The car appeared with a new nose from Imola's second race on to allow a lower mounting for the front wings. Pushrods now activated the front suspension shock absorbers, which were mounted on top of the tub's nose. By then, Ralph Bellamy had left the design team under somewhat acrimonious circumstances.

Philippe Alliot now had a full-time team-mate in Yannick Dalmas. The team achieved very little in a year punctuated by some heavy crashes for Alliot. Obvious potential was often shown in qualifying. Alliot started the Spanish GP from 12th on the grid, but there was not a single point to show at the end of the season.

The drivers' fates in Monte Carlo somehow summarise the whole season. Alliot started from the seventh row, with Dalmas four rows behind. Alliot retired after a spectacular coming together with Riccardo Patrese, who went on to depose Dalmas from sixth place just two laps before the finish. That was as close as Larrousse ever got to scoring during 1988.

The tub's strength was proved when Alliot miraculously walked away from an enormous crash in Mexico. Yannick Dalmas contacted Legionnaire's Disease late in the year and was replaced by Aguri Suzuki in Japan and Pierre-Henri Raphanel in Australia, the latter failing to qualify for the race.

Waiting for the new LC89, the team had to start the 1989 season with LC88-Bs, with Lamborghini V12 engines bolted to the back. In Rio Alliot just scraped into the last place on the grid, while Dalmas was the first non-qualifier.

T88/00 – 1988 – Indy – 29 built

This was an evolution of the previous year's model, designed by Bruce Ashmore and Clive Lark, with draughtsmen Keith Knott and Matthew Moore, Nigel Bennett having departed to Penske. Again, there were distinct versions for road circuits (T88/00) and superspeedways (T88/01). While the monocoque was similar in structure to Lola's previous IndyCars, frontal area had been reduced by further lowering the fuel cell and driving position.

At the back, the engine location package was changed to benefit from the compact size of the new engines. TrueSports liased with Lola to create a particularly low mounting for the new Judd engines. The cast magnesium bellhousing bolted to the engine cylinder heads, as well as the blocks, adding to the chassis' rigidity. Bruce Ashmore claimed the car was 50% stiffer torsionally between the wheelbase than had been the T87/00.

Lola's own gearbox incorporated a hypoid differential. Suspension was a development from 1987, with pushrods in the front and rockers at rear.

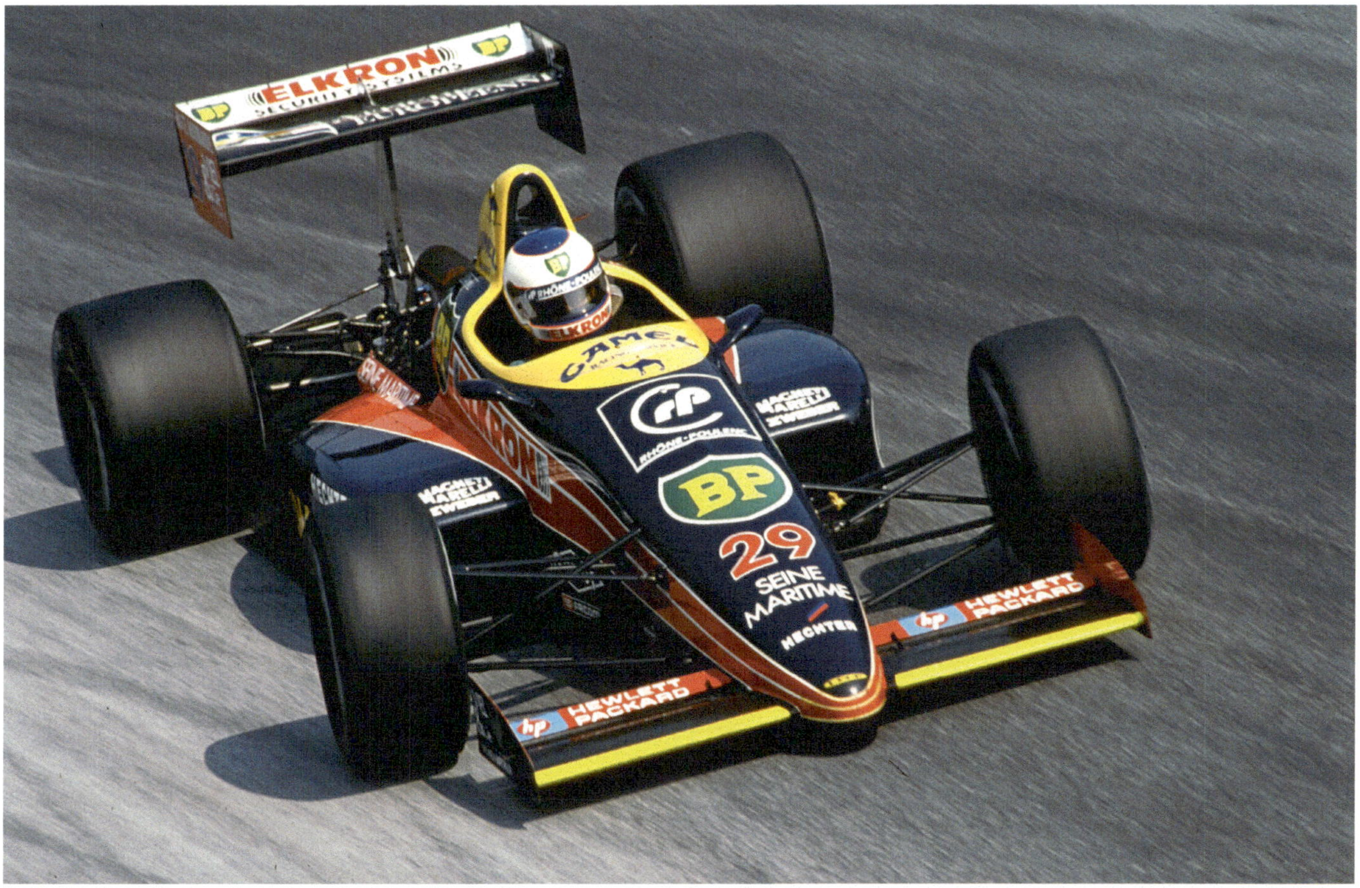
ELKRON
BP
29
SEINE
MARITIME
HECHTER
HEWLETT
PACKARD
hp

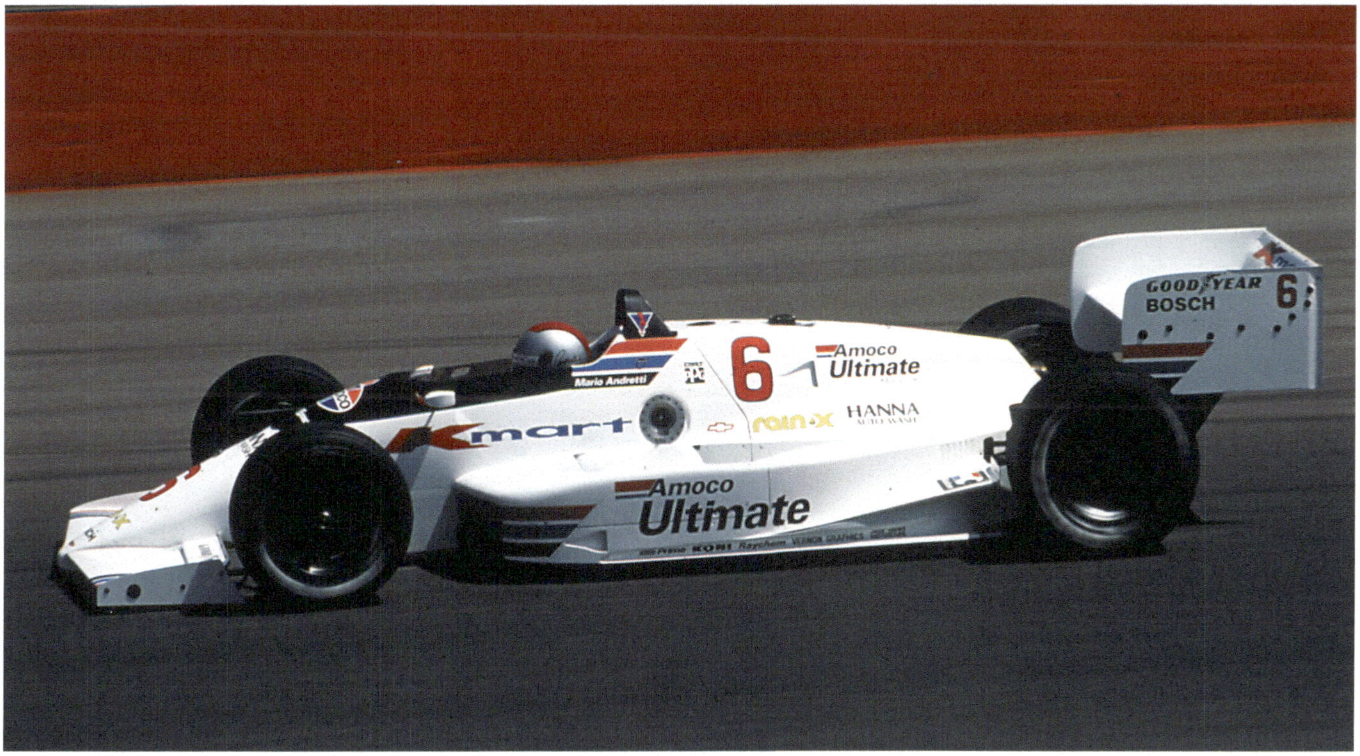
6
Amoco
Ultimate
HANNA
rain-x
Kmart
GOOD YEAR
BOSCH
Mario Andretti

T88/01 retained the swept front wishbones for a longer wheelbase, narrower rear track and different underbody and ducting, plus smaller wings, of course. Furthermore, the superspeedway version had rear wheelrims faired in to reduce drag.

The cars were equipped with Lola's new 'intelligent instrumentation' datalogging systems, which gave printouts of performance data, assisting set-up.

Defending champions TrueSports had made the switch to a Judd V8 engine for Bobby Rahal. Despite having been courted by Porsche, Mario Andretti carried on with Newman/Haas Lolas, now with Tony Cicale on board again, in place of the departed Adrian Newey.

Rahal and Andretti Sr were the strongest Lola-mounted contenders for the title as the season began, but other notable names were Roberto Guerrero, who had recovered from a huge testing accident in late 1987, Arie Luyendyk, A.J. Foyt and Derek Daly.

Mario Andretti once again opened his tally with a win, when he led Roberto Guerrero's Granatelli team car to a Lola 1-2 at the Phoenix oval. After that, however, Mario hit a bad patch with three retirements. He'd changed to the old T87/01 for Indy 500 for reasons which the team was unwilling to explain. The team was certainly competitive, qualifying fourth behind the all-Penske front row and being the only team to worry them in the early going, before gremlins struck.

Another Lola actually led at Indy after Mario had dropped back. Expatriate Scot, Jim Crawford, had badly injured his legs in qualifying for the previous year's race. Now, making his only appearance of the year in a Buick-engined T87/01, he jumped to the head of the field during a yellow flag period just before half-distance, and managed to hang on for some half-a-dozen laps. Crawford eventually lost a possible podium finish when he suffered a flat tyre and had to pit just a handful of laps from the finish. He ended up sixth.

Back in a T88/00, Andretti Sr won again at Cleveland, but after that a string of seconds and thirds put him fifth in the points.

For Bobby Rahal, the change of engine meant he needed to treat 1988 as a year of development. He did win one race, the Pocono 500, which also happened to be the only victory for any engine other than Chevrolet. Still, his consistency was rewarded once again, as he ended up third in the championship, four second places backing up that lone win.

Several leading drivers swapped to Lolas during the season, including Michael Andretti at Kraco and Emerson Fittipaldi at Patrick Racing. The latter used his T87/00 to win at Mid-Ohio and Elkhart Lake. With Rahal and Andretti Sr following him home at Elkhart Lake, Lola celebrated a 1-2-3 in Wisconsin.

Driving for Dick Simon, Arie Luyendyk impressed on several occasions, finishing second at Portland and battling for the lead in three races. Didier Theys was third for the same team at the Tamiami Park season closer.

Seven of the ten highest points scorers in the 1988 CART IndyCar World Series were in Lolas by the finish of the season. Ironically, the title went to Danny Sullivan, who had benefited from Penske's excellent PC17 model, penned by former Lola man Nigel Bennett.

Lolas also scored a 1-2-3 in Miami's Marlboro Challenge invitation race, where Michael Andretti was victorious.

T88/50 – 1988 F3000 – At least 25 made

Mark Williams strived to improve the already good package of T87/50. Comments from Japan, in particular, made him pay attention to the car's looks(!), as well as more functional aspects. Although the carbon fibre/honeycomb tub, with its replaceable aluminium honcycomb floor, remained much as before in construction, the new chassis was patterned in shape after the previous season's CART monocoque, which made it narrower at the front.

Front suspension was now by pushrods, which operated spring/damper units that crossed over the footwell. Access was through a large lid on the nose. The rear end pushrod arrangement was revised in detail only. New cast uprights were stronger.

AP four-piston brakes were used and the Hewland FGB box retained.

All cars competing in the FIA International Championship were again fitted with DFV engines, while several in the Japanese series had Mugens.

The T88/50 was a very sound design and won a lot of friends with the numerous drivers who took it to the tracks in 1988. Several of them achieved success, although works team leader, Mark Blundell, struggled after finishing second in the season opener at Jerez. In the final races he returned to form with new engineer, Duncan McRobbie, scoring another second at Dijon. In the championship he languished in sixth place, though.

GBDA again carried the torch for Lola, and Olivier Grouillard had two good late season wins at Le Mans and Zolder. He wound up second in the series.

The enigmatic GA Motorsport driver, Gregor Foitek, brought Lola another victory in the second race of the season at Vallelunga. The true measure of its F3000 chassis, however, was shown by the fact that gentleman driver, Jean-Denis Deletraz, managed to drive it to podium finishes – twice. Indeed, he crowned Lola's proudest moment on the F3000 circus by completing a 1-2-3 at Zolder behind Grouillard and Blundell.

Still, the F3000 Championship eluded the Huntingdon factory. This time it was denied by newcomer Reynard getting its act together with Roberto Moreno, who dominated the series with five victories.

The season's developments included revised rear suspension, which arrived for Monza's mid-summer race. This raised the rear roll centre. Also, to boost top speed, later in the summer Foitek tested a longer wheelbase, achieved by fitting a 7in bellhousing extension.

The Japanese Championship was rapidly gaining prestige, with ever more overseas drivers becoming involved. That series, too, was won by Reynard, with Aguri Suzuki taking the laurels. Kazuyoshi Hoshino finished second in a T88/50, Reynard driver, Emanuele Pirro, was third, and T87/50-mounted Masanori Sekiya fourth, all powered by Mugen-Honda engines. Takao Wada also managed to win a race with a T88/50.

Larrousse-Calmels – LC89 – Formula 1

Lola's F1 design team was now headed by Chris Murphy, but new Technical Director, Gérard Ducarouge, had some input in the new car, despite joining very late in 1988.

The carbon fibre/composite-chassised LC89 was built around Lamborghini's Mauro Forghieri-designed V12 engine and 6-speed transverse gearbox. It had a very narrow monocoque, which consisted of upper and lower halves bonded together. The wheelbase was 8in longer than its predecessor's. The engine had a Magneti Marelli management system, which was changed to Bosch during the season.

Suspension was double wishbones all round, operated via pushrods at the front and pullrods at the rear. Brakes had Brembo calipers and SEP carbon fibre discs and pads.

The car arrived for round 2 of the championship at Imola. It was very new and unsorted. Philippe Alliot qualified 20th with Yannick Dalmas 28th. Both were out of the race after the first lap with electronic troubles. Dalmas' season didn't get much better and it became apparent he had not fully recovered from the effects of Legionnaire's Disease. He was replaced in mid-season.

As usual, Alliot's season had its ups and downs. In the topsy-turvy opening laps of a wet Canadian GP he climbed from tenth on the grid to third by lap ten! Eight laps later he was down to 18th, but had clawed back to sixth when he crashed heavily at one-third distance. In his home race at Paul Ricard he qualified an heroic seventh and ran in the top six, until the Lamborghini engine started losing power and finally expired at half-distance. One week later he held fifth place at Silverstone, but felt the engine going and switched off.

The car had shown signs of promise; indeed, it was seen to ride the bumps of Mexico City better than any other chassis. Still, without a score in the first half of the season, the team was forced into pre-qualifying.

Eric Bernard appeared in France and Britain in place of Dalmas, but the seat was then taken over by Michele Alboreto for the rest of the year. He didn't achieve any tangible results in the car. Alliot, on the other hand, pressed on as had become his norm. At Monza he took the car to seventh on the grid and improved on that at Jerez, where he lined up fifth! Jerez finally gave the team a result, too, Alliot holding sixth in the early going, then dropping away, but managing to fight back to a lapped sixth by the end.

That was the team's highlight, in a year which had been trying off the track as well as on. Didier Calmels split from the operation when it was known he would be prosecuted for the murder of his wife. The team then carried on under Gérard Larrousse's name alone.

The T88/50 was Lola's Formula 3000 car, and won a lot of friends for its all-round good handling. Here, Damon Hill, distinguished by his highly-identifiable helmet (the design was inherited from his father, Graham), is seen with one of the cars.

Larrousse used the LC89 in slightly revised form for the first races of 1990, too. The aerodynamics had been tidied up and the monocoque modified to carry more fuel, considering the thirstiness of Lamborghini's V12.

In the Phoenix US GP street race, the Larrousse team humiliated Lotus, which now also used Lamborghini engines. Eric Bernard and his new permanent team-mate, Aguri Suzuki, out-qualified the Lotus drivers, who also had disastrously short races. Bernard and Suzuki were troubled with their brakes in the race, but Eric brought his car to the finish in eighth, while Suzuki had been just out of the points, when he was unable to restart after an innocent, brakes-induced off.

In Brazil, Bernard qualified a highly respectable 11th, but his race was soon over with a broken gearbox. The team still had the advantage over Lotus.

T89/00 -1989 – Indy

This was a second evolution of the successful T87/00. The design team was headed by Bruce Ashmore and Keith Knott.

The monocoque was lighter than before, with an even lower driver position. The revised fuel cell allowed a narrower cross-section for the rear

Monza 1988, and Mark Blundell's Formula 3000 T88/50 is seen here at the first chicane.

The LC89 was Lola's Formula One car for 1989, this time with a Lamborghini V12 and 6-speed gearbox. Here, Philippe Alliot leads Ivan Capelli on his way to sixth place in the Spanish Grand Prix at Jerez in October.

Mario Andretti was very successful in IndyCar racing, particularly with Lolas.

of the chassis. Pitch sensitivity was reduced with subtle re-profiling of the underbody. Stiffer suspension components were also introduced. The six-speed transmission was new.

Michael Andretti joined his father to form a dream team at Newman/Haas. The equipe was also strengthened by the presence of designer Bruce Ashmore to help with development.

Andretti Jr emerged as the most successful Lola driver in the 1989 CART/PPG IndyCar World Series. The scene was still dominated by Penske, for whom Emerson Fittipaldi won the title in a Patrick Racing-run car. Michael Andretti wound up third after leading no less than ten of the season's 15 races. Fact was, he only won two of them. The victories came in Toronto's street race and the Michigan 500, and he also led conclusively at Detroit, Meadowlands and Elkhart Lake, only to see his chances blown away. Neither of his two pole starts (Detroit and Cleveland) could be converted into victories. Two seconds and two thirds kept Andretti quite regularly on the podium, but he was still left trailing Fittipaldi and Rick Mears by some way in the points tally. Michael's drive in Michigan had been special, though. He overcame two stop-and-go penalties, plus a spin in the pitlane to emerge victorious.

For the first time in seven seasons with Newman/Haas, Mario Andretti failed to win a race! Nor did he claim a single pole position. He did lead four races, including the season-closing Laguna Seca event, where he did finish a fine second to Mears. Altogether, it was only good enough for sixth in the points table.

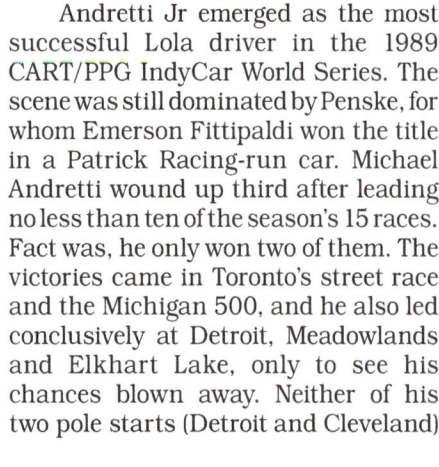
In 1989 Mario Andretti drove the T89/00, a development of the T87/00, together with this son, Michael, for the Newman/Haas team. Mario did not score but his son took two victories.

One place higher than Mario was Al Unser Jr, now in a Rick Galles-run Lola. His most famous moment of the season was the last lap crash, which lost him the Indy 500. Touching wheels with eventual winner Fittipaldi, Al spun into the wall. Despite the violent crash, he climbed out of the car to give Emerson the thumbs-up on his slowing down lap. Al was still classified second.

Even though victory slipped through their fingers, Indy was still a memorable success for Eric Broadley's marque, as 17 competitors in the top 20 drove Lolas! Raul Boesel, in a Judd-engined T89/01, was third and Mario Andretti fourth.

By Indy 500, Al Unser Jr had already scored a win from pole at Long Beach, albeit one which somewhat upset Mario Andretti, who found himself tapped out of the lead by Little Al a handful of laps from the finish. The Galles team seemed to lose momentum after Indy, though, and, despite leading on occasion, Unser Jr's best score for the rest of the year was second in Mid-Ohio. He did have the consolation of taking the money for winning the Marboro Challenge at Laguna Seca, however.

Bobby Rahal had switched to the Kraco team, where he took the wheel of a Cosworth DFS-engined Lola, while most other leading representatives of the Huntingdon manufacturer were powered by Chevy. Rahal scored a shrewd win in Meadowlands' wet race, having been second in Portland and third in Cleveland in the two previous races. Generally, Kraco suffered from mediocre reliability, however, and Rahal could manage ninth only in the series, just ahead of Provimi Veal's similarly mounted Arie Luyendyk. The Dutchman's best result was third in Portland.

Scott Pruett actually beat Rahal and Luyendyk in the World Series, placing eighth. He led Detroit's race in TrueSports' Judd-powered car on his way to second, and was third at Meadowlands.

T89/30 – 1989 – Nissan Group C or Nissan R89C

Nissan had negotiated with five different companies about the production of its 1989 Group C car, and eventually opted for Lola. The design concept was Eric Broadley's. Lola's CAD/CAM system was heavily used (as evidenced by excellent fitting of panels) in the design process by Andy Scriven, Clive Lark and Clive Cooper.

The R89C had a composite chassis of carbon fibre over Kevlar honeycomb, with Nomex honeycomb again being used in areas which were difficult to shape. Aluminium honeycomb was used in the larger flat areas such as the floor. Front, rear and dash bulkheads were integral. This was actually the first carbon/composite chassis by Lola for a sportscar. A steel roll cage was fitted within the monocoque.

The car's shape was influenced by engine and brake cooling needs and the Nissan styling department also had a hand in it. The bodywork was made of simple fibreglass, as this lent itself to modification, which was anticipated during the car's development. The rear wheels were enclosed, with winglets behind them. Horizontal skirts in sculpted recesses ran along the bottom sides of the car between the wheels. This was to improve airflow under the car. The rear wing was set at deck height for multi-functions, acting less as a wing and more as a deflector of air from underneath the car.

The front radiator was almost horizontally positioned, fed by central ducts in the nose. Hot air was vented upwards through an aperture on top of the nose. Ducts at the bottom of the windscreen fed cool air through tunnels flanking the cockpit to turbo intercoolers and oil coolers on both sides of the engine. With the exception of the length of the doors, the tunnels actually travelled inside the tub in the sponsons.

The fully-stressed, 3.5-litre, DOHC V8 engine had twin IHI turbos. The cylinder banks were at a 90 degree angle and had four valve heads. Nissan's ECCS-R-NDIS management system was used, and power output was said to be around 800bhp.

The 5-speed Hewland VGC transaxle with March Ramp differential was mated to a specially designed bellhousing/oil tank. The flanks of the gearbox case were machined smooth to form part of the diffuser wall.

Suspension was by double wishbones all round and coil spring/damper units were operated by pushrods. Front shock absorbers were mounted horizontally above the axle line; at the rear they were on top of the transmission. The clutch was a standard triple plate AP for Le Mans, but a carbon version was used for shorter

races. The 14in Brembo brakes had four-piston calipers.

The Le Mans specification car was tested at Snetterton and Nissan's Arizona track, and then Paul Ricard, where the sprint car, too, appeared. This had a more conventional two-tier rear wing, mounted higher, as well as larger volume diffuser tunnels.

The World Sports-Prototype Championship race programme was now handled by Nissan Motorsport Europe from Milton Keynes. Nissan hired young guns Mark Blundell and Julian Bailey as its driver pairing.

Race debut of the Nissan was at Dijon's WSC round. The crew qualified sixth, but the race was spoiled by two pitstops to replace the windscreen, which kept popping out because of flexing on the bumpy track. This led to the screen fixing being improved.

The car's main early problems were with brakes – before a switch to carbon for July's Brands Hatch race – and tyres, supplier Dunlop getting left behind in gearing-up for radial technology.

Le Mans witnessed a big onslaught from Nissan with three cars. Bailey and Blundell were joined by Martin Donnelly. The Japanese trio of Masahiro Hasemi, Kazuyoshi Hoshino and Toshio Suzuki drove the second car. The third car was entrusted to the Electramotive crew of Geoff Brabham, Chip Robinson and Arie Luyendyk.

It was discovered during practice that the low Le Mans specification wing had to be mounted higher to bring the centre of pressure further back.

The cars qualified roughly ten seconds off the pole-winning pace of the Sauber-Mercedes, but qualifying pace had never been a priority at Le Mans, anyway.

Julian Bailey set off at a scorching pace and was trying to wrest second place from John Nielsen's Jaguar at Mulsanne on the fifth lap. The cars came together and the resultant damage put the lead Nissan out of the race. The 'Japanese' car climbed to fourth after a steady start, but retired in the small hours of the morning, when its engine expired. Electramotive's trio then took up the challenge, holding fifth place in the morning, but sudden

In Europe, Nissan struggled with the Lola-built T89/30, occasionally scoring a good result but never achieving the same success as its American cousin.

oil pressure loss was a sign of serious engine damage, and their run came to an end, too.

Jarama next and it was tackled by Bailey and Blundell in a brand new chassis, which brought little reward as they struggled through to a delayed eighth. For the Brands Hatch WS-PC round the car was equipped with carbon brakes. To allow better cooling for the rear brakes the rear wheel covers disappeared. The car had a peculiar combination of Dunlop tyres with 17in crossplies at the front and 19in radials at the rear! This worked, though, and the drivers liked the handling.

The changes seemed to tap the car's potential, as Bailey qualified it fourth and charged to second in the race, before spinning into a gravel trap after just 19 laps.

That same weekend Masahiro Hasemi put one of the Le Mans cars on pole at Fuji for an All-Japan Sports Prototype Championship race. Tyre failure curtailed his race, however.

Martin Donnelly was the one to score the R89C's first victory. He was entered in a German SAT1 Supercup event on the Diepholz airfield circuit. He qualified second to Bob Wollek's Porsche, but managed to beat the mainly Porsche opposition in the sprint race.

Back in WS-PC Bailey was paired with Andrew Gilbert-Scott for the Nürburgring event. They qualified fourth and Gilbert-Scott managed to pass the Saubers in his opening stint to lead. Bailey then stretched their advantage to 30 seconds, but, in his second stint, had to back off to make his fuel allocation last the distance. This dropped them to third close to the finish. Bailey was ordered to stop before the finish line to wait for the last lap, which he did, but even then ran dry on that final tour and wasn't classified as a finisher.

Blundell was back for Donington, where the crew started from third on the grid and was involved in a four car battle for the lead during the early stages. Bailey pushed to the fore on lap 37 and the Nissan led the field for over 50 laps. During the second pitstop the crew suffered a 17 second penalty for fuelling too quickly during the first stop. A slow puncture then delayed them further, but they lost second place only three laps before the finish, Bailey hanging on to take third with a rooted tyre. They stayed on the same lap with the victorious Mercedes-badged Saubers.

At Spa the car was a handful as the crossply/radial tyre combination did not work in the wet practice. Still, from seventh on the grid, Bailey and Blundell were to inherit third in the dry race, when second-placed Jean-Louis Schlesser's Sauber-Mercedes ran out of fuel on the last lap.

The car again proved a handful on Mexico City's notoriously bumpy Hermanos Rodríguez circuit. It was a troubled outing, and the Nissan never got higher than fourth place. Delayed by fuel pressure problems and out of the points, Nissan Motorsport was left with fifth in the Team World Championship. Bailey and Blundell were joint 11th in the Drivers' series.

There was to be no joy in Japan, either, although Anders Olofsson led the early going in a late season race at Suzuka, but subsequently crashed. Julian Bailey had also taken in a SAT1 Supercup event at the Nürburgring, where a bad misfire restricted him to third.

T89/50 – 1989 – F3000

This car was advertised as the logical development of the T88/50, but was 70% new with an aerodynamically improved, stiffer tub. This tub could be fitted with Mugen, Cosworth or Judd engines. It had a Lola custom built, one-piece gearbox/oil tank, which was very narrow and designed to take advantage of the trend towards low sump engines. The unit held a Hewland Salisbury diff and FGB gears.

Bodywork and wings were revised. Alloy steel fabricated uprights were a lot stiffer than the magnesium castings they replaced. Suspension was again by pushrods all round, and the wishbones were now streamlined, as they were made of elliptical tubing.

There was a scare when the car failed its crash test. The forward inner aluminium skins of the footbox deformed beyond the degree accepted by the regulations. Lola was concerned it might have to sacrifice aerodynamic efficiency in reshaping the nose to comply with the rules. In fact, Lola managed to maintain the preferred aerodynamic configuration for the new replacement nosecones, which were soon delivered to customers who had already received their cars.

Former GBDA partner, Jean-Paul Driot, formed the new DAMS Team with René Arnoux. They got the deal to run

The T89/50 was the F3000 car of 1989. This was, however, the season that saw the meteoric rise of Jean Alesi, whose Reynard enabled him to win the title ahead of Lola-mounted Eric Comas (pictured).

Lola's works team in F3000. With drivers Eric Comas and Eric Bernard, they were strongly fancied for the championship pre-season. They got close. This was the year that made the career of Jean Alesi. A strong mid-season run gave the title to the Reynard-mounted Frenchman. Still, he only got it by having scored three wins as opposed to the two of second-placed Eric Comas, who ended up equal on points.

Comas came on strong too late, his last three outings yielding a second at Spa and convincing victories at Le Mans and Dijon. His team leader. Eric Bernard. finished third in the series, but probably had a better chance of winning it than Comas. Bernard took only one maximum score, winning at Jerez as he pleased, but there were others that got away from him. Pau he possibly threw away, and several other top placings just slipped through his fingers.

There were some particularly memorable Lola triumphs during the season. Jerez saw a DAMS front row, 1-2 race result and two fastest race laps scored by the same team's drivers. At Le Mans, Erics Comas, van de Poele (for GA Motorsport) and Bernard scored a 1-2-3. At Dijon's final round Lola had the front row and a clean sweep of the podium (Comas, Bernard and Andrew Gilbert-Scott for GA), plus fifth and seventh places. GA also flew the flag at Silverstone's opening round, where Philippe Favre took second place. Claudio Langes was second at Enna for future F1 team Forti Corse.

In Japan, Hitoshi Ogawa won the championship in a thrilling Suzuka finale from Ross Cheever and Reynard. Other race winners in T89/50s in Japan were Kazuyoshi Hoshino, Masahiro Hasemi and Takao Wada. In fact, Wada headed a Lola 1-2-3-4 at Sugo, where he was followed home by Akihiko Nakaya, Mauro Martini and Kunimitsu Takahashi.

T89/90 – 1989 – S2000

Basically similar to its predecessor, the T89/90 had revised front suspension geometry and adjustable tail flap.

Ian Flux scored a debut win with it at Brands Hatch in the autumn of 1988.

Chris Gilbert used a totally revamped version of the T89/90 in 1993. It was rebuilt around an aluminium honeycomb chassis designed by Mike Wright.

Lola built many successful Sports 2000 (S2000) cars. Here, a T89/90 approaches Paddock Bend at Brands Hatch.

Lola

7
1990-1992

Right, top: Eric Bernard in his Larrousse Lamborghini 90 leads Martin Donnelly in his Lotus at the British Grand Prix at Silverstone in July 1990.

Right, below: The British Grand Prix of 1990 again. While Bernard finished fourth, Aguri Suzuki completed a good weekend for the team with sixth.

Larrousse-Lamborghini-Lola 90 – Formula 1

Designed by Chris Murphy, this was a lighter development of the LC89. Not much was changed, as the previous car had already turned out to be one of the best handling of 1989. The wheelbase was slightly longer to allow for more fuel to be carried, and the car had new radiators, front wings and a revised engine airbox. The gearbox had re-designed internals and there was also a new exhaust system.

The new car arrived for the season's third race at Imola and, overall, Larrousse did a very good job with it in 1990. Despite having been forced into pre-qualifying through lack of results in the previous season, Larrousse's drivers, Eric Bernard and Aguri Suzuki, never missed getting onto the grid.

There were several highlights, starting with Monte Carlo. There, Bernard was a traffic-delayed 24th on the grid, but plugged on gamely in the race and took sixth from Gregor Foitek in a coming-together with the Onyx three laps from the finish. Foitek ended up on the sidelines and Bernard was the last classified runner, two laps behind winner Ayrton Senna, but it was a much needed point for Larrousse.

Mid-season saw the team's form come together, with a promising showing at Paul Ricard, finishing seventh and eighth in the French GP, just out of the points, but being lapped only once.

At Silverstone Bernard qualified an excellent eighth, with Suzuki an equally impressive ninth. In the race Bernard's Lamborghini engine was not pulling properly at first, but then cleared, and the Frenchman put in a charge. Blistering tyres gave him trouble later, but he still managed to wrest fourth from Nelson Piquet's Benetton-Ford two laps from the finish. Suzuki made it into the top six by quarter-distance. He got a puncture and pitted for it without losing position, eventually finishing sixth. With both cars in the points, this was the team's proudest day yet!

In the Hungarian GP Eric Bernard scored one more point, finishing sixth, despite brake problems. Again, as at Silverstone, he managed to stay on the winner's lap.

In the autumn it was Suzuki's turn to add to Larrousse's tally, when he drove to a very deserving sixth at Jerez in the Spanish GP. This was his first unlapped finish of the year.

The Japanese was to boost the team's fortunes further in the next race. Suzuka is a difficult circuit, where drivers who have extensive experience of it always seem to shine. Aguri qualified ninth, equalling his best grid position of the year. In the race he took sixth from Derek Warwick's Lotus on lap 7. Never out of the points thereafter, he raced splendidly to third, joining Benetton drivers, Nelson Piquet and Roberto Moreno, on the podium. Suzuki had crossed the line 22 seconds behind winner Piquet and 15 seconds in arrears of Moreno.

Larrousse's season had yielded 11 points, enough for sixth place in the Constructors' Championship: quite an accomplishment for a team emerging from pre-qualifying! Lotus, who was using similar Lamborghini V12 engines,

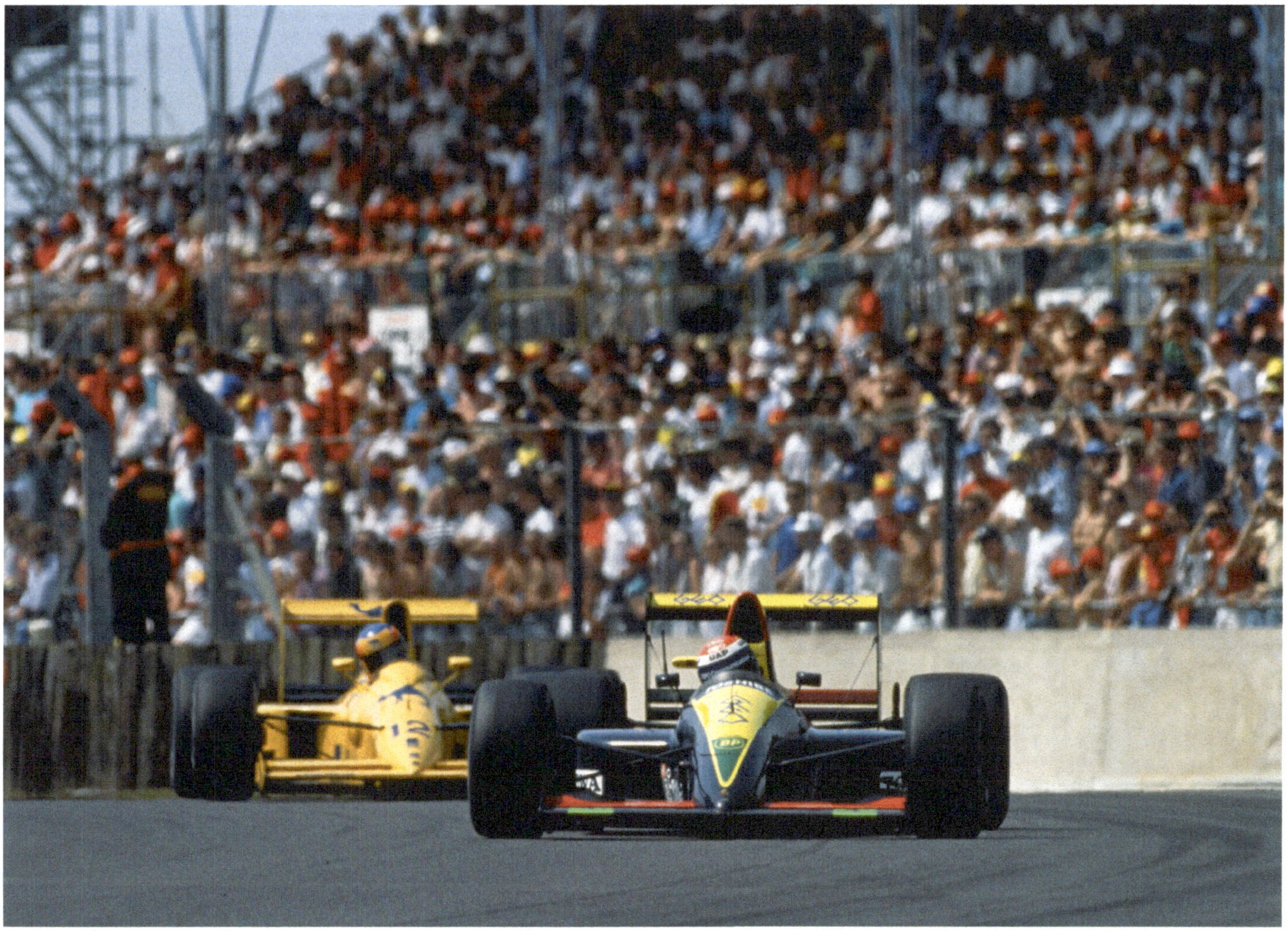

BP
SHOEI
Communications

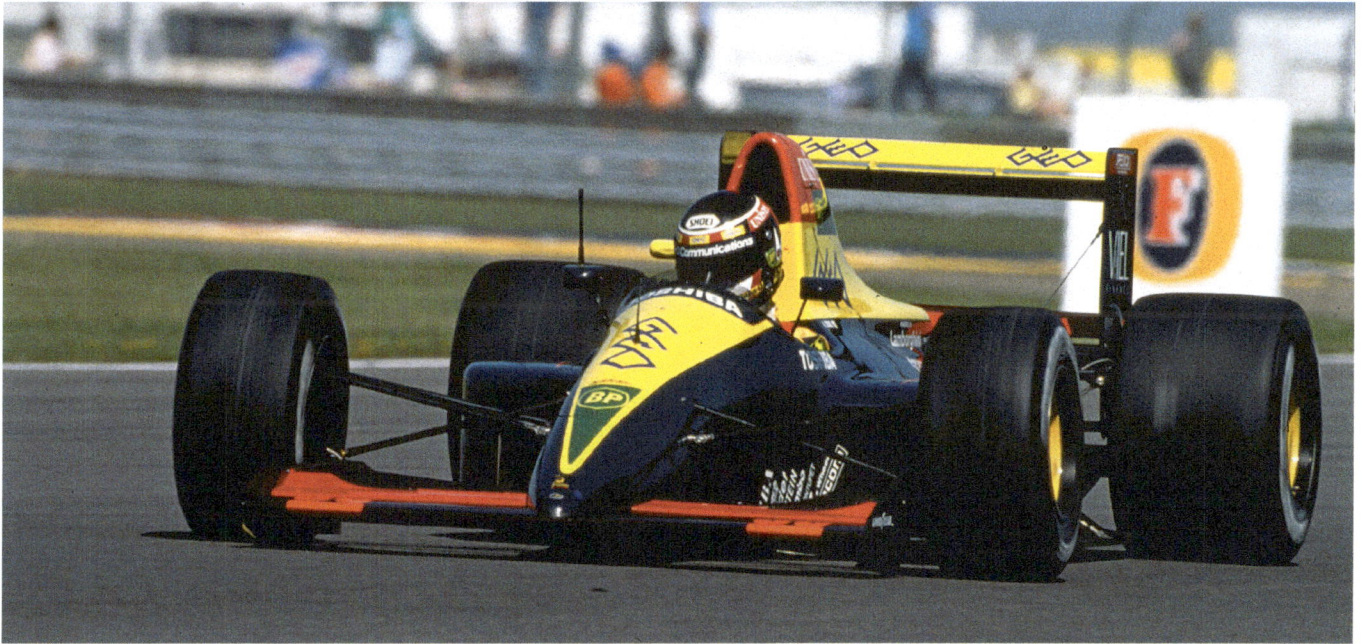

Always there or thereabouts, the Nissan R90CK was a fast and handsome beast, but could never quite come to grips with the Saubers and Jaguars in 1990.

had scored only three points. Still, it had been announced that Larrousse would lose the supply of the Italian engines for 1991.

T90/00 – 1990 – IndyCar

CART's safety-induced new rules pack led to this model having more outwardly obvious changes than any Lola IndyCar for some time. Again designed by Bruce Ashmore, the tub's lower section was still made of aluminium honeycomb, with a carbon/Kevlar upper half. The new regulations seated the driver no less than 10in further back in the chassis, which changed the car's proportions. The effect was emphasized by the Lola's longer, sharp, needle nose, which provided a crushable structure. The rules also reduced ground effect by further restricting underbodies, so clean and effective airflow to the wings was sought.

Particular attention was paid to the location of engine ancillaries, and to keeping the car's cross-section small. For the same reasons, the sidepods were lower than before with totally revised ducting. Lola replaced traditional water and oil radiators with smaller heat exchangers. The rear bodywork was lower, too, sweeping down beneath the upper rear wishbones and pushrods all the way to the wing. In place of the former long, swept windscreen, the front of the tub now directed the airstream all the way to the scuttle.

Pushrod operated springs were used front and rear.

Lola took a firm hold of the IndyCar market, as March only supplied chassis to the works Porsche and Alfa-Romeo efforts, which were to struggle during the season. Penske naturally offered strong opposition with three works entries, but numerically Lola was dominant.

So it proved results-wise, too: Lola won 12 of the 16 qualifying rounds of 1990 CART/PPG IndyCar World Series. And all but one of these wins were scored by two second generation drivers – Al Unser Jr and Michael Andretti.

Al Unser Jr was joined at Galles/Kraco Racing by Bobby Rahal, who finished second to Penske's Rick Mears in the season opener at Phoenix, with Al Jr third. Two weeks later, Little Al won from pole in Long Beach, his third victory in a row there.

At Indianapolis, the first surprise was Arie Luyendyk's place on the outside of the front row as the fastest Lola runner. A far greater upset was in store in the race. The Doug Shierson-run Dutchman stayed with the leaders to come through, when the fancied runners – including Al Unser Jr – hit trouble with blistering tyres. Luyendyk scored his first ever IndyCar win – at the Indy 500! Lola's success was completed by Bobby Rahal in second, Unser Jr in fourth and the evergreen A.J. Foyt in sixth.

One week on, Al Jr was back in the limelight, winning on the Milwaukee Mile.

Michael Andretti had been on the pace in the early races, losing Milwaukee to Unser Jr in the last couple of laps because of a dry fuel tank. He had only to wait until the Detroit street race, two weeks later, for his first victory, when he confidently set the pace from pole.

Portland gave Lola a 1-2-3, as Michael Andretti led home his Dad and Al Jr. In Cleveland, Unser looked in control, but lost out due to a pit fire, and the race slipped to Penske's Danny Sullivan. Bobby Rahal was the best Lola runner in second.

At the Meadowlands it was Michael Andretti's turn to win, again from pole position. In Toronto Little Al came from behind to win from Michael and Eddie Cheever in a Ganassi Lola. The Michigan 500, too, fell to Unser Jr, and Bobby Rahal completed a clean sweep for Galles/Kraco. Mario Andretti was third.

Denver was a new street venue for CART, but Al Jr maintained his winning streak. One week on, at another new street race, he extended it to four straight victories in Vancouver, after pole-sitter Michael Andretti lost the lead with a broken exhaust header. This was Unser's sixth win of the season and it turned out to be his last.

Michael Andretti took the next two races, both held on permanent road circuits. First he won from pole in Mid-Ohio, despite spinning in the rain. Lola got a clean sweep of the first four places, as Mario Andretti was second, Little Al third and Eddie Cheever, once more in a Lola, fourth.

Michael's fifth win of the season came at Elkhart Lake, but a fourth place finish for Unser meant the title was slipping from his reach.

Michael's home race in Nazareth sealed the championship for his rival. While the Penskes of Emerson Fittipaldi and Rick Mears took the first two places, the younger Andretti's fifth place was

not enough to keep him in the hunt. The best Lola finish was Rahal in third. The Laguna Seca final went to Sullivan's Penske, with champion Unser second and Michael third.

Unser's points total of 210 was a CART record. Michael Andretti was second, Bobby Rahal fourth, Mario Andretti seventh and Arie Luyendyk eighth. Mario Andretti endured a second season without a win, but did lead seven races.

During the season, some teams had carried out their own modifications on their Lolas. Galles/Kraco, for example, had their own running gear on their T90/00s, but, as Little Al pointed out after the season, the aerodynamic package and suspension geometry remained stock Lola.

All leading IndyCar Lolas were powered by Chevrolet engines in 1990, but TrueSports ran a modified T89/00 with Judd power. A couple of sixths by Raul Boesel was the best the team had to show for its efforts.

Lola also supplied chassis to Alfa-Romeo's Patrick Racing-run programme during the season. Roberto Guerrero managed a best result of fifth in the Michigan 500.

T90/30 – 1990 – Nissan Group C R90CK and R90CP

A refinement of the R89C, the 1990 version had a stiffer chassis structure with reduced internal dimensions, and right-angle joins replacing curved ones in the monocoque. The aerodynamics were modified. Outwardly, the car could be identified by a new nose.

There was also a subtly different engine cover, but this was almost unnoticeable.

Detail modifications had been carried out to the suspension for greater wheel movement. It was felt that, in the interests of maximising efficiency of underbody aerodynamics, R89C had gone slightly over the top in this. The gearbox had a new, one-piece casing, which allowed for wider tunnels underneath the car. There was a semi-dry sump modification to the box, too. AP Racing carbon brakes replaced the Brembo ones.

Engine specification was now VRH35Z. NME cars were to run Dunlop's latest radial tyres. The European version of the new car was dubbed R90CK.

The R90CP with revised bodywork developed by Electramotive (now NPTI, for Nissan Performance Technology Inc.) aerodynamicist Yoshi Suzuka, was to race in the Japanese series. The nose and tail sections were totally different to

When is a Nissan not a Nissan? Answer: when it's a Lola! The R90C Nissan was designed and built by Lola. A formidable Group C machine, this particular car still holds the lap record in qualifying for the 1990 Le Mans 24-Hour race. It was rumoured that the engine was developing some 1200 horsepower when Mark Blundell took it out on his Banzai qualifying lap.

those of the R90CK with a lower overall line and the 'nostrils' located further forward, adjacent to the headlights. The chassis were uprated R89Cs.

The R90CP debuted at Fuji's All-Japan Sports Prototype Championship round, where Masahiro Hasemi qualified it second, whilst the sister works car was slotted fourth by Hoshino, and the Le Mans Company's private R89C sixth. The works cars held their positions in the race which was won by the new works Toyota.

The WS-PC also opened in Japan, where Nissan was represented in the Suzuka race by the same cars that took the start at Fuji. Andrew Gilbert-Scott replaced an unwell Toshio Suzuki as Hoshino's partner. Hoshino qualified fifth, his '89-chassied – but R90CP-bodied, car now using carbon brakes for the first time in Japan. In the race the crew was forced into economy mode and eventually the car ended up stuck in the gravel after an off.

Masahiro Hasemi qualified ninth in the second works car, still sporting '89-style bodywork. On the first lap he was slightly delayed by a skirmish resulting from the tardy start of Jochen Mass in a Sauber-Mercedes, but steadily worked up the order. Co-driver, Anders Olofsson, climbed to fifth place, which eventually became third, as one of the Toyotas was called in for a stop-and-go penalty, and Martin Brundle's TWR Jaguar expired with engine failure just five laps from the finish. At the flag, Hasemi and Olofsson were one lap behind the two works Sauber-Mercs. The private R89C was not really on the pace and its race ended when Kenny Acheson was unceremoniously punted off.

The R90CK debuted in the first European WS-PC race of the season at Monza. Former Sauber team manager, Dave Price, had taken over from Keith Greene at NME, and the whole team had a fresh look to it. The team now fielded two cars for the season, with Gianfranco Brancatelli and Kenny Acheson joining Bailey and Blundell as drivers.

The cars qualified sixth and seventh at Monza. Blundell and Brancatelli benefited from a first lap shunt to run third for a while, but, in the last stints, the Nissans were down to fifth and sixth. Acheson/Bailey were delayed by a stop to attend to a loose front wheel, dropping to seventh. Blundell/Brancatelli, running out of fuel, did not make it to the finish, as the team had been caught out with telemetry troubles.

At Silverstone Blundell qualified fourth and Bailey seventh. This time the Nissans worked up a scrap for second place in the last driving stints, albeit a full lap behind the leading TWR Jaguar. Just ten laps from the finish Bailey's car suffered a broken rocker in the rear suspension, which put it out of the race. Blundell was once more forced to conserve fuel towards the finish, letting the second Jaguar past into second. He still ran dry. Julian managed to cross the finish line on the starter motor, but was not classified, as his last lap had taken too long to complete. A recurrence of the telemetry problems had let the team down again.

The drivers were not entirely happy with their understeering cars at Spa, where Blundell qualified fifth and Bailey tenth. On a wet but drying track the team's tyre strategy of starting on cut intermediates and pitting early for slicks proved a good one, moving the Nissans into second and third by the time of the first driver changes. In the middle stint Brancatelli started losing power and Blundell eventually brought their car to the finish a struggling tenth. Bailey and Acheson, too, lost some ground, but inherited third place when one of the Jaguars dropped out and held the position to the finish, staying on the same lap as Jochen Mass and Karl Wendlinger in the winning Sauber-Mercedes.

Nissan made a massive attack on Le Mans with no less than seven entries! NME had its usual two cars, with Martin Donnelly and Olivier Grouillard complementing the driving squad. NPTI had two similar R90CKs for Geoff Brabham/Chip Robinson/Derek Daly and Bob Earl/Michael Roe/Steve Millen.

One of the few Nissan/Lola R90Cs to escape the factory and be privately entered was this FromA sponsored car, which won the HSR races at Daytona and Sebring in 2001, driven by Charles Agg and Anders Oloffson. It took pole at Daytona a full two seconds faster than the polesitter of the 24 hours race.

NPTI had carried out an extensive test programme with the help of personnel from the abandoned Aston Martin Group C project, led by Ray Mallock. The cars had detail modifications, such as suspension adapted to the Goodyear tyres, which the team ran in place of NME's Dunlops. NISMO brought its own R90CP, the distinctively-bodied Japanese series regular, for Masahiro Hasemi/Kazuyoshi Hoshino/Toshio Suzuki. Team Le Mans also had the car it ran in Japan, an R89C for Takao Wada/Anders Olofsson/Maurizio Sandro Sala. The local Courage team fielded an R89C for Hervé Regout/Alain Cudini/Costas Los in addition to two cars of its own manufacture. The Nissan's rear suspension was modified, as the team used 17in instead of 18in Goodyear tyres.

The Le Mans circuit had been altered with two chicanes on the Mulsanne Straight, which made new demands on the cars. The R90CK's aerodynamics were closer to sprint specification, because top speed was no longer such a priority. NME and Nismo had taken the decision to run carbon-carbon brakes, while NPTI used iron discs with carbon-metallic pads.

Mark Blundell caused a stir in qualifying by putting Nissan on the pole with a margin of six seconds. For this purpose his engine was boosted to give over 1000bhp.

The Nismo car's aerodynamics obviously worked, as it recorded the highest straightline speed of all at 366kph. Hasemi placed it third on the grid, and with Brabham and Acheson securing the next slots, the front of the field had a distinctly Nissan look about it at the start.

However, Nissan's attack suffered its first setback before the race was even underway: Kenny Acheson was sidelined on the formation lap with crown wheel and pinion failure.

Julian Bailey, in the pole-winning car, led from the start, but gave way to Oscar Larrauri's Porsche on lap 4. These two were setting the pace, while Hasemi held off four TWR Jaguars in third. Mark Blundell, taking over from Bailey, retook the lead in the second hour, and the car stayed at the front until Gianfranco Brancatelli had a high-speed collision with the Toyota of Larrousse-Lola F1 driver, Aguri Suzuki, in the fifth hour. The Italian lost a lot of time crawling back to the pits with a puncture and damaged nose. Despite Bailey and Brancatelli working their way back to the lead lap, the crew's work was in vain. This Nissan retired with transmission failure in the small hours of the morning.

Brancatelli's delay left an NPTI car – with Geoff Brabham at the wheel – in the lead. A brake pad change in the sixth hour lost this crew almost a lap, but they were back out front after six hours, when Alain Ferté's leading Jaguar retired.

Brabham, Robinson and Daly all had their turn at the wheel, leading into the night, until another pad change dropped them to second behind the TWR Jaguar of John Nielsen/Price Cobb/Martin Brundle. They ran very close for a couple of hours until a telemetry glitch brought caution into Nissan's play and they backed off slightly.

The NPTI car was still in a strong second place in the morning, when a fuel leak in the bag tank first delayed them in the pits and then ended their run.

The NISMO entry had settled to a steady pace after the hectic early laps. It was delayed by a broken spring/damper mounting, and crawled to the finish with serious gearbox troubles, having lost second, third and fourth gears. Hasemi/Hoshino/Suzuki were still classified fifth in the lone R90CP, and might have been as high as second without their problems. The Nielsen/Cobb/Brundle Jaguar held on to the lead through the night and was out of reach to the Japanese crew.

None of the other Nissans really figured. Earl/Roe/Millen, in the second NPTI entry, were delayed by a water leak and eventually sidelined with gearbox problems, although Bob Earl had the distinction of setting the fastest lap. Wada/Olofsson/Sala also suffered gearbox problems, but their race ended with engine failure. The Courage-run Regout/Cudini/Los car suffered a catalogue of problems – including a gearbox rebuild, which took over an hour – but made the finish a lowly 22nd.

For the next WS-PC round NME reshuffled the driver pairings; Bailey and Blundell getting together again and new boys, Acheson and Brancatelli, sharing the other car. They qualified sixth and ninth, respectively. Acheson's race was spoiled by a spin on oil, which resulted in sufficient damage to put the handling off for the rest of the race. Bailey, on the other hand, had a strong start, climbing to third with genuine passing manoeuvres in the first five laps. There was not much he or Blundell could do about the two fleeing Sauber-Mercedes at the front, but they held their third place with ease, scoring a good podium finish for Nissan.

That same weekend, Hasemi and Olofsson took a victory from pole at Fuji, in the second round of the Japanese series. This result was slightly fortuitous, as Hitoshi Ogawa's Toyota broke its engine, when it seemed poised for victory. Hoshino/Suzuki, in the other NISMO car, were third and Wada/Nakako sixth in the private R89C.

At the Nürburgring's WS-PC race both NME Nissans had been fitted with small spoilers in the front corners to cure understeer. The cars qualified eighth and ninth, but the team unfortunately omitted to send Julian Bailey out in official qualifying, which meant he couldn't take part in the race. Blundell soldiered on for the full 2 hours 40 minutes duration, making it to fifth at the end, but three laps behind the victorious Sauber-Mercedes cars. Acheson/Brancatelli were slowed by their tyres losing pressure and a consequent puncture to finish ninth.

In Japan, Kazuyoshi Hoshino and Toshio Suzuki won for Nissan in the local series' most prestigious round, the Suzuka 1000kms. Their car had been switched to Bridgestone tyres and the Dunlop-shod sister car of Hasemi/Olofsson could not keep in touch.

Back in WS-PC, it was Kenny Acheson's turn to be the fastest qualifier of the NME drivers at Donington. He took fifth on the grid, bumping Bailey/Blundell into sixth. Bailey stormed to second at the start, but was unable to hang on. The pair fought with the Spice of Tim Harvey/Cor Euser for fourth, but dropped back with fading brakes and had to give way to Acheson/Brancatelli, too. The Nissans finished fifth and seventh on the road, but both benefited by one position, when the Jaguars were excluded for a refuelling infringement. The two Sauber-Mercedes were first and second once again.

In Montreal the Nissans were in good shape after an exclusive test. Blundell qualified second, benefiting from the use of qualifying tyres, for once, while Acheson had to be content with ninth. In a race punctuated by two pace-car periods, Blundell dropped back a little, but, during the second pace-car session, pitted for less fuel than the main opposition and was therefore well placed at the restart. With Bailey at the wheel, the Nissan actually took the lead soon after the pace-car pulled off. They were now forced to save fuel, however, and Bailey was powerless to fend off a charging Mauro Baldi's Sauber-Mercedes. Just two laps after Baldi had taken the lead the race was stopped when a manhole cover became detached and caused an accident involving three cars. Acheson had stayed in his car for the duration and was lying fifth, when the red flag came out. Half points were awarded because of the early stoppage.

On the other side of the globe, Masahiro Hasemi and Anders Olofsson clinched the All-Japan title for Nissan by winning at Sugo. Hoshino/Suzuki were fourth this time.

The drivers' title was to be decided at the last Fuji race. Hasemi and Hoshino claimed the front row of the grid. The two R90CPs set off to do battle on slicks with rain falling. Even the private R89C got in on the act, holding second for a while, but its transmission played up before half-distance. Anders Olofsson took the wheel from Hasemi, but spun on his first lap out of the pits and got stuck in a gravel bed, losing some ten laps ... Still Hoshino and Suzuki couldn't hold on to the lead and the Toyota of Roland Ratzenberger/Naoki Nagasaka was ahead when the race was stopped after an accident to Johnny Herbert's Porsche. Hoshino/Suzuki were second, about a minute behind, and Hasemi/Olofsson were classified fifth. This, amazingly, led to all four works Nissan drivers being equal on points, but Hasemi and Olofsson were champions as they'd had two wins to the other crew's one!

The last WS-PC round took place on the same weekend in Mexico City. Bailey and Acheson claimed fifth and seventh on the grid. Bailey followed the two Sauber-Mercs and the faster Jaguar early on, but pitted early to take a relatively light load of fuel, so emerged in the lead when the others had pitted also. The Mercs came steaming past and Blundell/Bailey then had to ease off to save fuel, but held on to third anyway, and eventually got second, when the fastest Mercedes was disqualified for having taken on too much fuel, just like the Jaguars at Donington. Brancatelli/Acheson suffered minor delays on their way to fifth, which became fourth.

Nissan finished third in the Makes Championship, not too distant from second-placed Jaguar. Bailey, Blundell and Acheson were ninth, tenth and 11th in the Drivers' standings.

It had been a season not without promise, but Nissan still decided not to continue in the World Series in 1991.

NPTI and NISMO carried on in their respective fields, however, and the 1991 Daytona 24 Hours saw the Californian team enter three ex-Le Mans R90CKs. The race allowed Group C entries, although it was estimated that these would have to run two seconds a lap quicker than IMSA opposition to compensate for longer pitstops. There was also a regulation that reserved the front row of the grid for IMSA cars ...

Therefore, NPTI's fastest car qualified by Derek Daly could only start from the third slot, despite recording a time that was one full second quicker than the pole-sitting Porsche. There was never any intention to run this particular car – effectively a spare – for longer than an hour or so in the race, unless problems hit the other two cars.

Arie Luyendyk, starting in the 'spare car', actually took the lead on lap 13. But it was just for show, as, after Luyendyk's 25 lap stint, the team used this entry for merely scrubbing in tyres for the other two cars. It subsequently dropped its pace, completing only 47 laps before being withdrawn.

The 'serious' Nissans worked themselves to the head of the field after a couple of hours running with Derek Daly and Steve Millen at the wheel. They held on for a while, but then settled into a pattern of trading the lead with the only TWR Jaguar in the race. All three pace-setters ran into trouble during the night, allowing a Porsche to lead.

The lead kept changing as the leading runners' fortunes see-sawed. As the sun was rising, Nissan lost one car when a CV joint broke, causing internal damage to the transaxle and breaking the engine mounts, too. The other car had still been battling for the lead, but was repeatedly delayed by repairs to bodywork that had been damaged, when Daly hit some debris after midnight. He could only struggle home second. Frank Jelinski/Henri Pescarolo/Hurley Haywood/'John Winter'/Bob Wollek were the winners in a Joest Racing Porsche 962. Bob Earl/Derek Daly/Chip Robinson/Geoff Brabham were 18 laps behind in the surviving Nissan.

For the rest of the IMSA programme, NPTI used its own NPT 90 models.

The proudest moment of Nissan's Group C involvement was yet to come, however. The 1992 Daytona 24 Hours was the scene of a concerted attack from the Japanese manufacturer. NPTI again qualified three R90Cs with the intention of running only two. These cars were run in the IMSA GTP category and therefore had to be fitted with downsized 3.0-litre engines. NISMO brought its R91CP in Group C trim, and Nova Engineering also had a R89C in Japanese specification.

The NISMO car was best equipped to go for a top grid slot, and Katsoyoshi Hoshino did set third fastest time to occupy the inside of the second row behind an Eagle-Toyota and a TWR Jaguar. Two NPTI cars were qualified fifth and sixth by Geoff Brabham and Chip Robinson, with equal times. Mauro Martini took the Nova car to eighth in qualifying, while Derek Daly put the 'reserve' NPTI entry in ninth. Eventually, this car replaced Geoff Brabham's, which sprang a fuel leak on race morning warm-up, so NPTI was down to two from the start.

Nissan took a convincing grip of the race from the very start, as Masahiro Hasemi seized the lead at the end of the first lap. Despite its longer pitstops the Japanese-crewed NISMO car then stretched its advantage.

Geoff Brabham climbed to second, but his brother Gary brought the other NPTI car's run to an end in the early evening. Exiting the pits on fresh, unscrubbed tyres, he slid into the end of the guardrail and wrote off the chassis. Only minutes earlier the same thing had happened to youngest brother David at the wheel of a TWR Jaguar, but he managed to continue!

The leading NISMO car was delayed after some seven hours' running, when fine sand blocked its radiators. It took some time to discover the cause of the

Damon Hill pulled off a last minute deal with the Middlebridge Racing Team to drive a Lola T90/50 in 1990. Despite being unprepared, he led several races, but was rewarded with only one second place over the season. Here he is at Brands Hatch in August 1990.

overheating, but after the sand had been removed the car ran faultlessly.

The remaining NPTI car's race came to an end just before midnight. Geoff Brabham/Chip Robinson/Bob Earl/Arie Luyendyk were out with a seized engine.

There were no problems for NISMO's R91CP, though. From midnight it extended its advantage and Masahiro Hasemi/Kazuyoshi Hoshino/Toshio Suzuki took an all-Japanese victory, beating by nine laps the second-placed TWR Jaguar of Davy Jones/Scott Pruett/David Brabham/Scott Goodyear. Anders Olofsson had been nominated for the winning car, but did not drive, thereby emphasizing the patriotic aspect of the effort. The tyres were the only non-Japanese element of the triumph, the team having swapped its Bridgestones for Goodyears for this race.

Mauro Martini/Volker Weidler/Jeff Krosnoff took the Nova R89C to eighth after suffering a variety of problems, including losing a wheel and braking trouble, which persisted despite a 40 minute stop to change the master cylinder.

T90/50 – 1990 – F3000

Mark Williams' new design at last had all-enveloping bodywork, like its main competition. This, and distinctive, tall sidepods, with what were often referred to as 'Benetton-style' air intakes, made it look quite different from the 1989 F3000 Lolas. The shape was a result of the on-going wind tunnel programme at the Cranfield Institute. The new car was also smaller and lighter.

The construction method for the carbon fibre monocoque was similar to that used for the Formula 1 Larrousse LC89. Upper and lower sections were separately cured in the oven and then bonded and riveted together.

The front suspension wishbone base was extended and pushrods operated the spring/damper units, which were longitudinally mounted on top of the footwell, with access through a hatch.

Stiffer fabricated steel uprights and different rocker pivot design were features of the rear suspension. Driveshafts had been redesigned to cope with higher loadings.

Both Cosworth and Mugen engines were used during the year, the works affiliated DAMS team banking on the Japanese units.

Allan McNish has been a most successful driver, winning in just about every category, including at Le Mans for Porsche. His progress to Formula 1 was not as smooth as expected, though. Here he is in 1990 at Pau in the Lola T90/50 Formula 3000 car with which he had considerable success.

The car had typical F3000 dimensions.

Wheelbase 103in
Front track 66in
Rear track................................. 61in

This turned out to be the car that finally gave Lola the International F3000 Championship title, DAMS driver Eric Comas taking the Championship in a convincing manner.

The events of the season's first race at Donington brought mixed feelings. Comas drove to victory from the front row, but his team-mate, Allan McNish, was involved in an horrendous accident, which killed a spectator. Amazingly, McNish bounced back, winning the next race at Silverstone from pole! Comas was second. The championship campaign was well and truly under way. The Pau street race turned into a demolition derby, won by Eric van de Poele's Reynard, but Comas took the next two rounds at Jerez and Monza.

Enna's speedbowl in Sicily witnessed another Lola victory when Gianni Morbidelli triumphed for the Italian Forti Corse team in a Cosworth-engined T90/50. Allan McNish was second and Gary Brabham, in a Middlebridge Racing T90/50, third, equalling his Monza result.

Brabham's team-mate, Damon Hill, was the unluckiest driver that year. He started the season virtually unprepared, having pulled off very much a last minute deal. Still, Damon led five races, but only scored points from one second place. He certainly made his mark, though.

Hockenheim was another Reynard benefit, but Comas stayed well clear at the top of the points table, finishing fourth.

McNish won at Brands Hatch from Hill's Cosworth-powered T90/50, but, at Birmingham, Andrea Chiesa took the highest Lola score in second for the new Paul Stewart Racing team. He'd also been second at the Donington race, where John Jones, in the team's other car, finished third.

Eric Comas was back to the top of the podium at Le Mans and rounded out his season with a second at Nogaro. Gianni Morbidelli took his second third place of the season, having first got to the podium as best Lola runner at Pau.

Comas' championship margin over closest rival, Eric van de Poele, was 21 points – or worth two wins and a fourth

111

The winner at the Brands Hatch F3000 race in 1990; Alan McNish in his Lola T90/50.

place. Reynard driver Eddie Irvine ended up third and Allan McNish fourth. Lola clearly had the upper hand on rival Reynard with seven wins and poles, as opposed to four and three.

The 1990 All-Japan F3000 Championship was the best yet. Overseas interest was growing fast and, in contrast to the control-tyre FIA series, Japan saw heavy involvement from competing tyre manufacturers Bridgestone, Dunlop and Yokohama.

The championship turned into a landslide success for Lola. Japan's superstar, Kazuyoshi Hoshino, won the title easily in a Cabin Racing-run T90/50 with six victories from ten races. He was Bridgestone's favoured man. Hitoshi Ogawa was second in the series, despite not winning a race;

five second places helped him to pip Mauro Martini, who won at Sugo. Other winners were Keiji Matsumoto, who took two victories, and Volker Weidler. All qualifying rounds went to Lola and the top seven in the championship were Lola-drivers, all powered by Mugen, with the exception of fifth-placed Ukyo Katayama, who had a Cosworth engine.

T90/90 – 1990 – Sports 2000
This model won the 1990 SCCA Sports 2000 series, Jay Hill winning three of eight races, giving Lola a clean sweep.

Larrousse-Lola L91 – Formula 1
Eric Broadley, Gérard Ducarouge and Michel Tetu designed a tidied-up version of the previous year's car. The nose was slightly raised, as several teams followed

the example of Tyrrell's pioneering 1990 car with varying degrees of caution. The front spring/damper units were more accessible on top of the front of the monocoque, and the two-part diffuser was a fairly original design.

Having lost the Lamborghini V12 engine, the cars were powered by Brian Hart-tended, Cosworth DFR V8 engines, to which the old transverse gearbox was mated. The gearbox oil-cooler was mounted in the rear wing support.

The car generally drew praise as a neat and effective design, but the team had other worries. Larrousse endured a nightmarish off-season, as the international sporting authority deprived it of points scored in 1990. This was as a consequence of the team registering under the Larrousse name,

16th June 1991, Mexico City. Aguri Suzuki drove the L91 for the team, and, at the US Grand Prix at Phoenix, pulled off a sixth place for a single point. The cars were now powered by the Cosworth DFR V8, with the old transverse gearbox, but it was the team's swan song

but using chassis made by Lola and not of its own manufacture. Larrousse also lost its main sponsor, ESPO. All of this had dire consequences on the team's financial state, and its very existence was threatened for much of 1991: for the first half of the season the team lived a hand-to-mouth existence.

In these circumstances, the US GP at Phoenix was something of a fairytale for Larrousse. Having qualified 21st, Aguri Suzuki had a brush with another car on lap 7, and pitted to change a wheel. It wasn't looking good, considering Eric Bernard was already out with engine failure. Suzuki, however, knuckled down and, as others retired, ran strongly to finish sixth and gain a valuable point for his beleaguered team.

This turned out to be a rare highlight in a difficult season. Eric Bernard produced some notable performances. He qualified an excellent 11th in Brazil, and had a possibly points-scoring drive spoiled by transmission breakage in Canada, where he dropped out of ninth place just before half-distance. In Mexico, Bernard raced strongly from 18th on the grid to finish sixth and bring Larrousse its second point of the season. This result was not down to luck, either, as the race did not have an unusually high rate of attrition.

The French GP at Magny-Cours looked promising, too, as Bernard had emerged from 23rd grid slot to challenge for seventh place, but transmission failures put both Larrousse entries out of the race around half-distance.

Eric Bernard's season came to a premature end when he suffered terrible leg injuries in a practice crash at the Japanese GP. Bertrand Gachot stood in for him in Australia's season finale. Aguri Suzuki seemed to lose heart somewhat as the season wore on, and failed to qualify four times.

The two points scored put Lola 11th in the Constructors' Championship, but this was the end of the co-operation between Lola and Larrousse as the team announced it would build its own cars in 1992. The last chapter

Mario Andretti in the T91/00 Lola at Phoenix International Raceway, Arizona.

in the Larrousse/Lola saga was the team's use of an old 90 chassis in testing Lamborghini's latest engine in winter 1992, before its new car had been completed.

T91/00 – 1991 – Indy – 40 built

Once more, the new IndyCar was designed by Bruce Ashmore. After the previous year's unprecedented success, he confined himself to refinement of the T90/00. The external shape remained virtually identical, but the cockpit was reshaped and steering rack raised to better accommodate taller drivers.

For the first time, the chassis was baked under proper climate control in an autoclave, instead of an oven. The lower aluminium honeycomb section of the monocoque was retained, even though CART regulations now allowed all-carbon tubs. Lola was still suspicious of the strength of full-carbon monocoques in second impacts, common on the fast oval tracks. Great attention was paid to detail finish in the bodywork to maximise aerodynamic performance. The suspension remained as before, but the rear uprights were vented.

The 1991 CART season belonged to Michael Andretti. Still teamed with his father at Newman/Haas, he won eight races and was eight times on pole position. He led all but one of the 17 races.

While Michael had a slow start to the season, his cousin John surprised everyone by winning the Surfers Paradise race in Australia for Jim Hall's and Count van der Straten's new Hall/VDS team. It was a somewhat lucky victory from ninth on the grid, but Mario's nephew had the presence of mind to conserve the brakes of his Lola-Chevy, while most front runners ran out of them on their first visit to the Australian venue. John inherited the lead from Rick Mears' Penske just three laps from the finish.

Al Unser Jr was dominant in Long Beach, leading Bobby Rahal to a 1-2 for the Galles/Kraco Lola-Chevies. Eddie Cheever, in Chip Ganassi's Lola, was third, confirming his early promise in Australia of a front row starting position.

Bobby Rahal had been second at Surfers Paradise, too, and completed a trio of runner-up placings at Phoenix, where it was Arie Luyendyk's turn to carry on Lola's winning streak. Chevy-powered like all leading Lolas, the Dutchman's car was now run by Vince Granatelli, with help from Mo Nunn.

The Indy 500, again, was something of a case apart. Buick-powered Lolas were staggeringly fast, and Gary Bettenhausen, in Menard's example, was quickest of all, but on the second weekend of qualifying that was not valid for pole, which had already gone to Rick Mears' Penske. A.J. Foyt took second on the grid with a run, which was widely suspected to have been boosted by rather more than the permitted turbo pressure ...

The race was a different story. It developed into a tough battle between Mears and Michael Andretti, with the latter leading much of the running.

At the end, the wily Mears outraced Michael in a couple of late race restarts. Andretti Jr had to be content with second and Luyendyk was third. None of the Buick-powered cars reached the finish.

Milwaukee, the next weekend, produced an historic Andretti 1-2-3! It was Mario, who was the best placed in the family after qualifying, in second. He led the first 30 laps, until Al Unser Jr took over. Little Al looked in control, but was stopped by electronical problems. The challenging Mears, too, was sidelined, and that left the way clear for Michael Andretti to score his first victory of the year. John followed him home in second, with Mario third.

Michael was on pole in Detroit, but the race was won by Penske's Emerson Fittipaldi. Bobby Rahal took yet another second place, while Arie Luyendyk was third.

Portland and Cleveland produced an identical top quartet: Michael Andretti won both times, Fittipaldi was second (from pole), Rahal third and Al Unser Jr fourth. Rahal then scored his only win of the season at the Meadowlands, with Unser now second.

At the halfway point of the series, Bobby Rahal's consistency was paying off with a handy points lead. He kept up the same level, driving to third in Toronto, but this time Michael Andretti was on the pole and won. Mario gave Newman/Haas a 1-2 with second place. The Canadian street race turned into a Lola walkover, as the Huntingdon firm's products filled all places in the top ten!

The year's second 500 mile race was next, and it was Rick Mears who took the honours again in Michigan. Despite a strong hold on the CART series, Lola missed out on both of the season's most prestigious races. Arie Luyendyk was Lola's best representative at Michigan in second, and Unser took third. Luyendyk drove a good race, coming from 20th on the grid to mix with the leaders, but a stop-and-go penalty took his chances of victory. Little Al took his second victory of 1991 in Denver, where Fittipaldi was second and Michael Andretti third.

At this point Michael stepped up his game. He won from pole in Vancouver and Mid-Ohio, and made it three wins in a row at Elkhart Lake. This last triumph at last got him to the top of the points table. Vancouver had been another good race for Lola, as Michael, Bobby Rahal and Unser Jr finished 1-2-3 in grid order. Mario Andretti completed the day with fourth. Elkhart Lake saw a tremendous duel between Michael and Little Al. Behind them, Mario, Rahal and Luyendyk made it a Lola 1-5.

The Andretti's home town race at Nazareth was another step closer to the title for Michael, who finished third, although Rahal narrowed the gap slightly by taking his sixth second place of the season. Arie Luyendyk took his second win of the season by avoiding the need for a last pitstop, and Lolas filled the top six.

At Laguna Seca, Michael Andretti crowned his first CART Championship in the best possible way. He planted his car on pole position, won the race, and took the Marlboro Challenge into the bargain!

Unser Jr's second place at Laguna Seca wasn't quite good enough for him to wrest second in the series from Rahal. Mario shared the podium with his jubilant son, having driven to third.

Lola won 14 out of 17 races in the 1991 CART Championship. Michael Andretti got 234 pts, Rahal 200, Al Unser 197, Mears 144, Fittipaldi 140, Luyendyk 134, etc.

T91/30 – 1991 – Nissan R91CP – Group C

For its 1991 campaign in the All-Japan Sports-Prototype Championship, NISMO used slightly modified versions of the R90CP. Now dubbed R91CP, the cars could only be outwardly distinguished by an airbox on the rear deck, and big, rear-view mirrors sticking out from the right-hand side upper corner of the windscreen. They were built in Japan.

At Fuji's opening round of the series Kazuyoshi Hoshino/Toshio Suzuki won from pole, despite trouble with a door, which had to be taped shut. Akihiko Nakaya/Volker Weidler were second in Nova Engineering's ex-NME R90CK, just over a second behind. Hideki Okada/Takao Wada, in a private R89C, were fourth.

The second race, too, was at Fuji, and culminated in a fierce scrap between Suzuki and Anders Olofsson in the sister NISMO car. Suzuki took another win with Hoshino, but beat Olofsson and Masahiro Hasemi by only 2.5 seconds after 1000kms of racing.

Still at Fuji for round three, Toyota got the better of Nissan, but Hoshino/Suzuki stayed at the top of the points table with second place. Hasemi destroyed his car in a crash caused by a puncture. He rolled over Takao Wada's Team Le Mans Nissan, which had already been shunted in the same place for a similar reason.

In the Suzuka 1000kms the leading Nissan spun off in Suzuki's hands after a suspected suspension failure, and the race went to Toyota. Nakaya/Weidler were second in Nova's R90CK and Hasemi/Olofsson third.

Sugo was the scene of another Toyota victory after Hoshino/Suzuki were severely delayed by a hub failure. Nakaya/Weidler had been the best Nissan crew in qualifying and took the lead at the start, but pitted with the left-hand door ajar. They still finished second, only seven seconds in arrears. Hasemi/Olofsson were third again.

Back at Fuji, Hoshino/Suzuki led most of the way to win a rain-affected race, which was interrupted by five pace-car periods and stopped early.

The Sugo finale was claimed by a visiting Jaguar XJR-14, run on this occasion by the Japanese Suntec F3000 team. Teo Fabi/David Brabham won from the Toyota of Hitoshi Ogawa/Masanori Sekiya. The latter pair came close to winning the championship, but Hoshino/Suzuki followed them to the flag in third, which was enough to give them the Drivers' title and Nissan the Manufacturers' title.

For 1992 the Nissans were further modified from the original Lola concept, although there were hardly any outwardly visible differences to the 91 models. The most important area of change was the front suspension.

NISMO carried on in the All-Japan Sports Prototype Championship, as did Nova Engineering, with the chassis that Lola had supplied in the middle of 1991. There was also a new Nissan entry from Team Take One, which had an ex-NISMO chassis in silver colours, carrying number 61 (like Sauber-Mercedes throughout 1989), and modified in the rear along the lines of a 1989 Sauber-Merc! Thomas Danielsson/Hideki Okada were the new team's drivers.

Toyota efforts had been directed towards the non-turbocharged SWC contender, so NISMO had it a bit easier in the championship, which, like any other sportscar series in 1992, had a depleted entry.

NISMO had had a fantastic start to the season, winning the Daytona 24 Hours. (See under T90/30.) Back home, the team won a tactical wet-dry series opener at Suzuka. Masahiro Hasemi was now joined by Jeff Krosnoff in the winning car. Hoshino shunted on the first lap and lost 18 laps in the aftermath. A very competitive second was the Nova car of Volker Weidler/Mauro Martini, which had actually led during the early wet phase.

Fuji next hosted a 1000kms race, where the leading Toyotas succumbed to transmission troubles and left the way clear for a Nissan clean sweep. Kazuyoshi Hoshino/Toshio Suzuki won, Danielsson/Okada took second in their 'Silver Arrow', Weidler/Martini were third and Hasemi collected fourth with Krosnoff and third driver Masahiko Kageyama, after losing several laps with an early visit to a gravel trap.

Fuji was also the scene for round three, and Hoshino/Suzuki won again, using their fuel allowance better than the chasing Toyota of Pierre-Henri Raphanel/Masanori Sekiya. Weidler/Martini were third, having led again.

At Sugo Hoshino/Suzuki simply drove off from the opposition to win by a lap. The other Nissans all had problems, but Hasemi was fourth with Kageyama, as Krosnoff had injured his leg.

It was back to Fuji next, where Toyota's TS010 atmo SWC challenger beat off the regulars in the hands of Geoff Lees and Jan Lammers. Hoshino/Suzuki were best of the turbos, however, and their second place put the championship titles out of reach of their rivals. Lees/Lammers won again at the Mine finale. Kazuyoshi Hoshino was partnered by Takao Wada on this occasion. They took second as the best turbo entry, which gave the Drivers' title to the evergreen Hoshino. Heinz-Harald Frentzen was Mauro Martini's new partner because of Volker Weidler's health problems, and the Nova pair capped their season with third.

The Japanese sports-prototype series collapsed after 1992, but there was a solitary swansong performance for two private Group C Nissans in 1993. Suzuka held its traditional 1000kms event as an invitation race for a mixed bunch of cars. The only Group C entries were the Nova Engineering R90CK for Martini/Frentzen and a NISMO R91CP for Toshio Suzuki/Takao Wada.

Mauro Martini took pole and the Nova car led for most of the race, but trouble with securing its re-designed doors caused extra pitstops and handed the win to Suzuki/Wada. The Nova car was not threatened for second.

Overleaf, main: After the domination of the T90/50, the T91/50's lack of success came as a shock to the Lola brigade. The championship was won by a Reynard. Here's Alan McNish at Nogaro in October 1991.

Overleaf, inset: After the previous year's success, Damon Hill grew frustrated with the T91/50 and switched to a Reynard. Before he did, however, he raced in the Lola at Vallelunga, as seen here.

T91/50 – 1991 – F3000 – 45 built

Mark Williams designed the successor to the all-conquering T90/50. The appearance was very similar, including high sidepods with 'Benetton-type' narrow openings for cooling. Yet Lola claimed the car to be 80% new.

In common with the new IndyCar, the T90/50 had a redesigned cockpit to make taller drivers more comfortable. This was a time when designers started applying new methods to improve underbody aerodynamics of theoretically 'flat bottom' cars. Lola's new F3000 had a much more complex design facing the tarmac, including a 'stepped' nose.

The engine cover was revised and had different air ducting and plenum chambers. This, together with changes to the cooling system to reduce pressure drop through the corners, was going to enhance engine performance.

The car had a new, one-piece gearbox/bellhousing, with a drain gallery and spray lubrication system to reduce transmission oil temperature.

The formula's change to Avon radial tyres in Europe was the cause of revised suspension geometry. Pushrods operated the spring/damper units on the nose and those flanking the bellhousing at the rear.

Rear uprights had been redesigned around a one-piece hub unit and tripod drive coupling.

The better braking traction of Avon's new radial tyres was the reason for using AP six-pot calipers in the front brakes, while the rear brakes still had four-pots.

Mugen (DAMS, Paul Stewart Racing) and Cosworth (Barclay Team EJR) engines were used in Europe, while Judd was tried by Geoff Lees in Japan.

It was a great mystery why, after dominating in 1990, Lola failed to win a single F3000 race in Europe with its new design. Lola's leading lights Allan McNish, Damon Hill and Marco Apicella were all considered pre-season favourites. Still, the only times a Lola was seen at the head of the field were at Brands Hatch, where Hill led briefly, and at Spa, where McNish's DAMS team-mate, Laurent Aiello, took pole position.

Marco Apicella, in his fifth season of F3000, took second places at Mugello and Enna for Paul Stewart Racing. He ended up the highest placed Lola driver in the series, in fifth. PSR worked its own modifications to the chassis during the season, such as lengthening the wheelbase.

Damon Hill was next in the points table. His Barclay Team EJR car was run by Middlebridge, as Eddie Jordan was concentrating on the company's F1 campaign. Ironically, Damon achieved his best result in the last race, when he'd ditched the Lola for a Reynard: he was third at Nogaro.

Hill's team-mate, Vincenzo Sospiri, stayed with the T91/50 throughout. He took it to a strong second at Hockenheim.

For DAMS, and Allan McNish in particular, the season was a disaster. The Scot even failed to qualify for two of the first three races. DAMS' best result was Aiello's third at Spa.

The championship was won by Christian Fittipaldi in a Pacific Racing Reynard-Mugen. He beat Alessandro Zanardi in a similar car to second and Emanuele Naspetti to third in a Cosworth-engined Reynard. Naspetti's four straight mid-season victories added insult to Lola's injury, as he'd had a T91/50 for the first three races and got nowhere with it, even failing to qualify at Jerez.

The T91/50's lack of pace was especially puzzling considering the FIA series had switched to radial tyres, of which Lola had acquired plenty of experience in Japan previously.

Indeed, T91/50 was to struggle somewhat even in Japan, where well-funded teams now commonly had the option of running different types, and even different makes, of car.

For the All-Japan F3000 Championship opener at Suzuka, only Kazuyoshi Hoshino and Thomas Danielsson had T91/50s. Older Lolas were good enough, however, as Ukyo Katayama won in a DFV-engined T90/50, and Hitoshi Ogawa was second in a Mugen-powered version.

This trend continued, as Akihiko Nakaya won the second round at the new Autopolis circuit from Hoshino, who raced his older car, and Mauro Martini. Lola took a clean sweep of the top six positions. In the next Fuji race, it was Hoshino's turn to keep the T90/50's winning streak going.

Eddie Irvine took a surprise victory on Yokohama rubber in the pouring rain of the Mine race. Then, in Suzuka, Katayama, in the DFV-powered T90/50, took his second win of the year. Ogawa was second and Volker Weidler gave

Heinz-Harald Frentzen was another who gave thanks for a good Lola chassis in his season in F3000 in 1991. Enna was the venue at which this photo was taken.

T91/50 its best Japanese result yet in third.

After the early summer break, Ross Cheever ended Lola's run of victories when he triumphed for Reynard at Sugo. Michael Schumacher followed Cheever to second in a Ralt, but third and fourth went to the T91/50s of Akihiko Nakaya and Thomas Danielsson.

Fuji was next, and Mauro Martini took his T91/50 to pole, but the race was again a T90/50 benefit. Hoshino won from Katayama, with Weidler third in the new model.

Ukyo Katayama then switched to the newer car and gave T91/50 its best finish yet with second at Suzuka. Ross Cheever won with Reynard and established himself as a serious threat to the championship aspirations of Lola's drivers. Danielsson and Nakaya were third and fourth with T91/50s.

Cheever won again at Suzuka in the penultimate qualifying round. From second to fifth places, Martini, Weidler, Jeff Krosnoff and Danielsson were now all in the new Lola chassis.

The championship was decided at Fuji in Ukyo Katayama's favour. He finished second in the race to Volker Weidler, who had the distinction of giving T91/50 its first Japanese victory. This gave Weidler third in the points, behind Ross Cheever. Apart from the American, Johnny Herbert was the only non-Lola driver in the series' top ten. The Ralt-mounted Herbert was tenth.

All top Lolas were Mugen-powered except for that of title winner Katayama, which had the Cosworth DFV.

Britain's domestic F3000 series saw an upturn in Lola's fortunes. This series, which didn't allow current chassis, had been dominated by Reynard, but now Swede, Fredrik Ekblom, took three late-season victories in a T90/50, and Julian Westwood won the last round in a similar car. The title, however, was posthumously won by Paul Warwick, who had been unbeatable in a Reynard until his fatal accident at Oulton Park. Ekblom was runner-up.

T91/90 – 1991 – Sports 2000 – 15+ built

T92/00 – 1992 – Indy – 22 ordered

Once more, Lola's IndyCar was mainly designed by Bruce Ashmore, and remained a logical development of the line. Unique among constructors for this category, Lola still based its carbon monocoque around an aluminium honeycomb 'bathtub'. Although there was less honeycomb and more carbon, specifically in the engine bay and below the fuel tank, Lola still felt the traditional lower structure was important in high-speed multiple impacts, even if this method was more costly than building an all-carbon tub.

Suspension for the T92/00 was all-new, with the spring/damper units on top of the tub. This gave more room inside the cockpit. The wishbones were repositioned with a resultant aerodynamic gain.

The gearbox had been lifted clear of the underbody, which improved aerodynamics significantly. The transmission also had a dry-sump system.

The car was to be produced with three different engines: Ilmor's Chevrolet V8 turbo, a Buick V6 turbo and Cosworth's new XB V8 turbo. Because of the individual needs these placed on the chassis, Lola had a different design team working on each installation. Designer Ashmore expected the XB package to be aerodynamically advantageous because of the unit's small size.

Lola remained well represented on the IndyCar scene, but it was fair to expect tougher opposition in 1992, as Galles-Kraco had produced its own chassis, joining Penske as the Huntingdon company's biggest competition.

Michael Andretti drove the Kmart-Havoline-sponsored T92/00 to finish second in the points behind Bobby Rahal. Michael led the Indianapolis 500 for all but 28 laps, but retired with fuel pump failure.

Bobby Rahal had bought Pat Patrick's team, which he was to run himself with Carl Hogan. They had the proven Chevrolet engines at the back of their Lolas. Newman/Haas, on the other hand, relied on the father and son Andretti duo, but were going to use the new Ford Cosworth XB engine.

At the Surfers Paradise race, Newman/Haas played safe by using 91 chassis with its untried engines. Michael Andretti led the race for longer than anyone else, but a broken exhaust header spoiled his run and the Penskes of Emerson Fittipaldi and Rick Mears took the first two places, with Rahal third in a T92/00.

Michael was still in the old car at Phoenix, but managed to put it on pole. Electrical problems delayed him for three laps at the start, however, and Rahal dominated the event to seize the points lead. Eddie Cheever finished second in Ganassi's Ford XB-powered T92/00.

Andretti Jr put his new car on pole at Long Beach. He dropped out of the lead with transmission failure and the race fell to the Galmer-Chevy of Danny Sullivan. Bobby Rahal extended his points advantage in second.

At Indianapolis Roberto Guerrero blasted to pole position with a record speed of 232.482mph. He was having a one-off outing in Kenny Bernstein's Buick-powered T92/00. John Travis, in charge of the Buick-Lolas, had done a great job in fitting the tall, single-cam V6 more neatly into the overall package, which was a pukka Indy design with no road course compromises.

The Indy grid looked promising enough from Lola's point of view. Eddie Cheever started second and his Ganassi team-mate, Arie Luyendyk, was fourth, with Mario Andretti on the outside of the front row. The first seven starters were in Lolas and, altogether, there were 27 of them among the 33-strong field.

And yet, they missed out on winning the race. Michael Andretti led for all but 28 laps, before stopping with a broken fuel pump 11 laps from the finish. When the ensuing yellow went out, it was a seven lap dash to the line between Al Unser Jr and Scott Goodyear in Derrick Walker's Ford-engined T92/00. Little Al held off the Canadian by half a car's length in the closest finish in history.

Third place went to Al Unser Sr, who had taken over John Menard's Lola-Buick entry for Nelson Piquet: the Brazilian F1 Champion had badly injured his legs in a practice crash.

Michael Andretti was strong again in Detroit, taking pole and leading most laps, but he collided with Paul Tracy, and Bobby Rahal took the win. Raul Boesel was second in a Dick Simon-run Lola-Chevy, with Michael third. He then won conclusively in Portland and Milwaukee, but Rahal followed him into second in the latter race, consolidating his points lead. Scott Brayton completed a Lola 1-2-3 at Milwaukee in Dick Simon's other car.

The next two races, at New Hampshire and Toronto, were also between Rahal and Andretti Jr: Rahal took victory on the oval and, in the Canadian street race, it was Michael's turn. New Hampshire witnessed another all-Lola podium, as Scott Goodyear finished third.

Scott Goodyear became only the second ever Canadian to win an IndyCar race at the next event, which was the Michigan 500, no less. This was rich reward for Goodyear, who had so narrowly been pipped to the post at Indianapolis. Penske's Paul Tracy, in fact, made it a Canadian 1-2, while third was Raul Boesel. The race had seen the first ever over 230mph front row, when Michael and Mario Andretti both broke the mark in qualifying.

Emerson Fittipaldi then won two events on the trot, at Cleveland and Elkhart Lake. Bobby Rahal and Michael Andretti took fourth/third and second/fourth respectively. A dominant victory from pole brought Andretti truly into the title battle with Rahal, when the latter crashed while running second.

There was no luck for either title contender at Mid-Ohio. Rahal crashed again and Michael's engine blew while he was leading. Fittipaldi and Tracy gave Penske a 1-2.

The Nazareth race culminated in a battle between Rahal and home town boy Michael, with Rahal snatching a narrow win.

At the Laguna Seca finale, Michael Andretti took pole and led every lap to win covincingly, but it wasn't enough, as Rahal managed to bring his poorly-handling car into a strong third. They were split by Mario Andretti in his best race of the season. Bobby Rahal was champion with 196 points to Michael Andretti's 192. Al Unser Jr lagged behind with 169.

Scott Goodyear was fifth in the final standings and Mario Andretti sixth.

Michael Andretti, again in his Lola T92/00, winning at Laguna Seca in October 1992. It was his last race before going to Europe to drive F1 with McLaren in 1993.

T92/10 – 1992 – Group C

The technical specification of the T92/10 was detailed in a press pack provided in relation to John Major's visit to the company in June 1991. Its design was mainly the work of Dutchman Wiet Huidekoper, conceived around Judd's GV10 engine, but with allowances for modifications to the engine package, bodywork and suspension.

Following the latest philosophies in Group C design, the car had a narrow but high-sided carbon monocoque with an integral composite roll-hoop. The chassis extended to a single-seater-type narrow nose structure, which was flanked by 'nostril' air intakes, leading air through ducts to the side radiators. The exit for cooling air was through openings in front of the rear wheels, similar to those of the Nissan Group C cars.

Access to the carbon-lined cockpit was through the windows, there being no doors, as such.

Huidekoper claimed his design to be particularly driver-friendly in that it would not let brake dust or engine heat into the cockpit.

A double rear wing was used, but it was stressed that great emphasis had been placed on getting downforce on the front.

The suspension was by unequal length wishbones front and rear, with pushrods operating inboard spring/damper units.

The six-speed longitudinal Lola gearbox shared its clusters with the 92/00 IndyCar, but had its own one-piece casing. A triple-plate carbon clutch and carbon disc brakes completed the

The T92/10 was Lola's last Group C car. Charles Zwolsman of Euro Racing ran the team and drove. Here is one at Sebring in 2000.

picture of extensive use of carbon fibre in the car's design.

Huidekoper left the company before T92/10's race debut and Eric Broadley took over technical control of the project.

Autosport announced in August 1991 that Charles Zwolman and his EuroRacing team were the officially nominated Lola team in the 1992 Sportscar World Championship. Three cars (two racers and a spare) were purchased at £350,000 each, and it was anticipated that testing would start in November using Judd engines but hoping to get Ford HBs to race with.

When the car appeared for Monza's opening round of the 1992 Sportscar World Championship, it sported small spoilers in the front corners.

EuroRacing had temporarily recruited Stefan Johansson, and he qualified the lead car in fifth, with Cor Euser taking the next place on the grid. Johansson, however, was over three and a half seconds off Peugeot's pole-winning pace. The cars had a serious stability problem, with the rear shock absorbers in particular.

Johansson and his driving partner, Jesús Pareja, did not make the start of the race, as their car got stuck in two gears on the assembly lap. Euser was paired with team patron Charles Zwolsman, who took the start. He suffered gearbox troubles from the off and the car was out at half distance.

In fact, the T92/10 had already made its racing debut the weekend before Monza, and that was more encouraging. Zwolsman drove at Mugello in an Interserie race and, having finished second to Manuel Reuter's Porsche 962 in the first heat, went on to win the second one, when the German's engine lost power.

The second SWC round was held at Silverstone, where the Lolas again qualified fifth and sixth. The problem with shock absorbers had been cured by fitting new dampers with an extra oil reservoir in the Euser/Zwolsman car. The damping system had been designed and built in Holland.

With the depleted sportscar racing entries of 1992, it only took the retirements in the race of both works Toyotas and the second works Peugeot to leave Stefan Johansson and Jesús Pareja to collect a promising third place. After two and a half hours' racing, they were six laps behind the winning Peugeot, but a place on the podium they got. Unfortunately, this was later docked, when a fuel sample taken from the car was found to have a specific gravity of below the required limit. This was deemed to be a genuine mistake by the fuel supplier. Engine failure cut the race short for Euser/Zwolsman. Only five cars were initially classified as finishers.

The Lola's gearbox problems had persisted through the early season. It appeared the box was not stiff enough, allowing the chassis to flex. Another snag was a fickle selector, which too often gave a wrong gear.

For Le Mans there was a new gearbox, which seemed to be an improvement. The Judd engine had a new cam, which reduced maximum revs by 2000rpm compared to sprint specification. The small spoilers were initially absent from the front corners and double headlights replaced the regular tiny ones.

EuroRacing brought in new drivers for the 24 hour classic. While Euser, Pareja and Zwolsman were going to team up in one car, the other was going to be handled by Heinz-Harald Frentzen and Japanese rent-a-drivers Shinji Kasuya and Hideshi Matsuda.

Cor Euser qualified ninth, some 16 seconds off the pole position time of Philippe Alliot's Peugeot, while Frentzen was three seconds slower; good enough for 12th.

The race illustrated that Lola's gearbox worries were not over, however. After being delayed by changing the nose in the pits, Euser was in for a gearbox change. The new one did not last into the night either, and the car was stranded out at the Indianapolis corner, stuck in two gears.

The T92/10 was Lola's attempt at building a competitive Group C car for the 3.5-litre Formula. This, basically Formula 1-engined series, was the last of the line as high costs and insufficient promotion killed the formula. While it lasted, the Lola was a decent private entrant car in the hands of Charles Zwolsman's team, but could not match the pace of the works Peugeots.

Frentzen again, this time in the Euro Racing Lola T92/00 Group C car. Here at Le Mans, Frentzen put in a stunning drive which impressed all who saw it.

Frentzen's car had picked up positions in the early going, but started suffering from gear selection problems after four hours. It, too, had the box changed a few hours later.

Charles Zwolsman swapped over to his team's surviving car, demoting Matsuda, who didn't get to drive at all. Frentzen put in some very quick laps at night, but persistent trouble with the car's fifth gear pinion, as well as Kasuya twice smashing its nose, dropped them out of touch with the top ten. The trio was still circulating at 4pm, however, and finished the race 13th.

At Donington the SWC entry slumped to ten. The cars were naturally back to sprint specification, but had the new stiffer gearboxes. Euser qualified fifth and a troubled Frentzen was seventh.

Euser/Pareja dropped out of the race with an electrical fire, but Heinz-Harald Frentzen with new pairing, Phil Andrews, brought the other car to fourth after one of the works Toyotas retired. The gap to the winning Peugeot was six laps.

For the Suzuka 1000kms EuroRacing shuffled its crews yet again. Cor Euser was joined in the lead car by Frentzen and Canadian David Tennyson. Hideshi Matsuda was back to share with Jesús Pareja. The Lolas lined up seventh and eighth on the grid, but ahead of them, in fifth, was the Nova team's Japanese series Nissan, which had been admitted to join the SWC for this race only.

In the race, the Mauro Martini/Jeff Krosnoff/Katsutomo Kaneishi took the Nissan to a respectable fourth place,

The new T92/50 Formula 3000 Lola of 1992. Outclassed by the Reynards to start with, it came good at the end of the season.

beating all of the regular SWC runners except for the two works Peugeots and the lone surviving works Toyota. It was, however, eight laps adrift of Derek Warwick/Yannick Dalmas in the winning Toyota. Three laps further behind was the Pareja/Matsuda Lola in fifth. The Euser car was out early with engine failure.

Financial problems forced EuroRacing to miss the series finale at Magny-Cours, which turned out to be the last ever Group C World Championship race, as high costs and lack of interest killed the category.

It was the end of the road for Euro Racing, too, as Charles Zwolsman got tangled up with charges of drug trafficking and money laundering a few months later.

After that, the T92/10 had a lower profile career in the Interseries, where Robbie Stirling won Division 1 with it as late as 1996, taking heat victories in Brands Hatch, Most, A1-Ring and Albacete. He was narrowly beaten to the overall Interseries title by Walter Lechner's Division 2 single-seater, which was based on an old Lola F3000, but had been converted by Horag to carry all-enveloping, Can-Am-style bodywork and was powered by an Audi engine.

T92/50 – 1992 -F3000

Designer Mark Williams concentrated on improving aerodynamic behaviour to make up for the shortcomings of the 91 car. The car featured a new underbody configuration, plus a new nose and front wing to improve stability. All-new composite bodywork was accentuated by lower and longer sidepods, as well as the fully sealed, F1-type engine airbox.

The gearbox had a revised oil tank. Suspension geometry was based on the results of extensive tests at the end of the previous season, but the car had a built-in facility to adjust roll-centre height and camber change for further aerodynamic and tyre development.

Front uprights now had a venting arrangement similar to the rear ones. Cosworth was the most common engine choice of customers in Europe, while Mugen remained dominant in Japan, although not to quite the same extent.

In the FIA F3000 International Championship Lola endured a second successive season of disappointment; no wins in the series for over two years until the final race of the season.

DAMS remained Lola's main team, although there had been some hesitation, before they committed to running T92/50s. Lead driver, Jean-Marc Gounon, opened his score with a good fourth in the first race at Silverstone after he'd spun and dropped to the tail of the field.

Ahead of Gounon were two Reynards, plus the Apomatox Lola of Olivier Panis, who finished third. In fact, it was the Apomatox cars which often emerged as the most successful Lola representatives. Emmanuel Collard gave the team fourth in Barcelona and at the Nürburgring, and third at Albacete, each time being the highest placed Lola driver.

It all came together for DAMS and Jean-Marc Gounon in the last two races, however. At Nogaro the cars had new rear suspension. Several Lolas had been modified during the season by opening a gap between the nosecone and the front wing. At the French circuit Gounon qualified third and finished the race second to Luca Badoer, who clinched the title with that result.

Then, at Magny-Cours the Apomatox cars of Collard and Panis occupied the second row of the grid with Gounon behind in sixth. Gounon made his customary blinding start and jumped to third, behind the Reynards of Badoer and Andrea Montermini. These two fought the lead tooth and nail until coming together. Both were forced to retire, which left the three Lolas of Gounon, Collard and Panis at the head of the field. Collard tried a move on Gounon, which went wrong and he dropped back, but it was still a great day for Lola as Gounon won, Panis finished second and Collard emerged fourth.

It wasn't enough to make a difference to the championship, though, and Gounon was Lola's highest placed driver in a shared sixth position.

Apomatox was the only Lola team to send its cars to an invitation F3000 race held in Buenos Aires in December. Collard finished second there, to Andrea Montermini's Reynard.

The All-Japan F3000 Championship started without any of the drivers using '92 model Lolas at Suzuka, although it would become compulsory to switch to contemporary chassis by the second round of the series. Ross Cheever took victory at Suzuka in his Reynard, with Kazuyoshi Hoshino and Volker Weidler second and third in Mugen-engined T91/50s.

The transition to T92/50s went fairly smoothly, even though first tests had raised fears that it might not. At Fuji's next race Paulo Carcasci won in a Reynard, but Thomas Danielsson brought his DFV-engined T92/50 into

Heinz-Harald Frentzen moved to the Japanese Formula 3000 series in late 1992 and made his mark with both T92/50 and T93/50.

second, Mauro Martini was third and Eddie Irvine fourth, both in Mugen-powered examples.

Suddenly there were 14 new Lolas on the grid.

The free tyre policy of the Japanese series caused a lot of chassis development to take place during the year, and T92/50s soon started appearing with modifications, including anhedral front wings.

Eddie Irvine took the first win for T92/50 at Mine in the Cerumo team car. With similar Mugen-powered cars completing the top three in the hands of Mauro Martini and Roland Ratzenberger, there remained little doubt that the new design was up to scratch in the hi-tech Japanese series. Volker Weidler provided further proof by winning the next race at Suzuka, an event marred by an accident in which Hitoshi Ogawa was killed. Weidler was then third in

Autopolis, beaten by Marco Apicella's winning Dome and Mauro Martini, but won again at Sugo to assume the series lead. After that, his career was sadly and abruptly cut short by tinnitus, a condition which causes constant ringing in the ears.

Weidler's Nova Engineering teammate Mauro Martini took up the challenge for the title, winning the next round, held in Fuji. Toshio Suzuki was second in a DFV-engined T92/50, as he had been in Sugo, and emerged as a championship threat when he won at Fuji three weeks later.

Roland Ratzenberger took his first win at Suzuka and Andrew Gilbert-Scott followed him home to give the Stellar team Lolas a 1-2. Lolas filled the top six, in fact, as Martini was third, Irvine fourth, Thomas Danielsson fifth and Frentzen, who had replaced Weidler, sixth.

Suzuki won the penultimate round of the series at Fuji, from Takuya Kurosawa's similarly DFV-powered T92/50 and Martini. This left the Italian at the top of the points table before Suzuka's finale, with Suzuki and Ross Cheever still posing a threat.

Martini and Suzuki were both shoved into retirement at Suzuka, but Ross Cheever could do no better than fourth, which left the Lola drivers first and second in the championship. The final race was won by Naoki Hattori in a Lola-Mugen. Kurosawa was second again and Frentzen third.

Lola

8
1993-1997

T93/00 – 1993 – Indy

Another IndyCar design from Bruce Ashmore. It had a longer, wider monocoque, as demanded by new regulations. The section in front of the pedals was longer, too. Despite an ever-increasing use of carbon fibre – full-length carbon undersides – the car still retained aluminium honeycomb panels surrounding the cockpit's lower parts.

The road course version had anhedral front wings, but the angle was not nearly as radical as in certain Formula 1 designs. Different versions of the chassis were made for Cosworth XB and other engine packages.

The front suspension arrangement was conventional, with wide-based wishbones and pushrods operating spring/damper units mounted horzontally in front of the scuttle. More

The new IndyCar for 1993: the T93/00 at its launch at the factory.

enterprising was the rear layout, which had to be adapted to different engine packages. The pushrods were attached to a central shaft over the gearbox, which acted as a torsion bar. The front arms of the upper wishbones mounted to a central casting, which shielded the turbocharger.

The car's transmission was re-engineered to give a smoother gearchange. Iron brake discs were still demanded by the regulations, but carbon-metallic pads were used.

1992 Formula 1 World Champion Nigel Mansell had found himself without a seat at the title-winning Williams team, and promptly made the decision to leave F1 to join the PPG IndyCar World Series instead. He signed to drive a new Lola-Ford T93/00 for Newman/Haas and spent the winter exhaustively testing on both ovals and road courses.

Mansell's move brought unprecedented world-wide exposure for the IndyCar series. In the Newman/Haas Lola he stepped into the most proven package of the series. The Ford XB engine was no longer an unknown quantity, whereas Chevrolet introduced a new 'C' power unit for 1993.

The season opened in Australia with the Surfers Paradise event, where Mansell fully lived up to the hype. He took a kerb-hopping pole to stir up the already keen expectations. Nigel lost places at the start and surrendered the first lap of the race to the Penskes of Emerson Fittipaldi and Paul Tracy, as well as Robby Gordon's A.J. Foyt-run Lola-Ford T92/00. After Tracy had dropped out with suspension failure, Mansell out-braked Gordon for second. He went on to take Fittipaldi for the lead on lap 16, but flat-spotted his tyres in the move, when the brakes locked.

It soon turned out Mansell had made his move under a yellow flag. He was shown a black flag to signify a stop-and-go penalty, didn't see it and decided to come in for fuel and tyres anyway, thereby minimising the effect of the penalty.

After the first round of pitstops Nigel was leading. He then brushed the wall and got a puncture. Pitting for this dropped him to fourth. Back to speed, he reeled in and passed team-mate Mario Andretti. When Fittipaldi and Gordon came in for their second stops, Mansell was back in the lead. He made a quick refuelling stop without losing the lead and managed to hold on despite having to conserve fuel and suffering from cramps and a sore Achilles tendon.

This was a classic Mansell performance. Fittipaldi and Gordon flanked him on the podium, while Andretti completed a jubilant day for Newman/Haas in fourth.

Phoenix was the scene of Mansell's eagerly-awaited oval debut. He attacked the track, breaking the lap record three times in practice, before crashing backwards into the wall at 170mph. Suffering back injuries, he was out of the race.

Mario Andretti rose to the occasion to lift the team's spirits. He started from second on the grid and, having dropped two laps down, avoided on-track drama, saw the leading Penskes of Tracy and Fittipaldi crash out and came through to claim an immensely popular victory. This made him the oldest ever IndyCar winner. Lolas filled the first eight places, with Raul Boesel second in Dick Simon's car and Jimmy Vasser third for Jim Hayhoe's team.

Despite still suffering from his back injury, Mansell bounced back in Long Beach and qualified on pole. In the race Paul Tracy was easily the quickest man, and took his first IndyCar win despite pitting for a puncture. Mansell had trouble keeping his car in gear late in the race and had to settle for third. Bobby Rahal was second in the ex-TrueSports chassis, which he'd taken to develop.

At Indy, Luyendyk got pole and Lola-Fords swept the front row, with Mario Andretti second and Raul Boesel third. Nigel Mansell professed himself 'frustrated' by the qualifying procedure and lined up eighth.

Mansell surprised the cognoscenti with his race showing at Indy. Having run in the leading group from the start, he emerged in the lead at one third distance. He then lost the position by overshooting his pit in a yellow flag pit stop.

After the last round of stops Mansell had worked his way to third, and charged round the outside of Emerson Fittipaldi and Mario Andretti to lead on a green flag restart. He lost his lead in a similar situation to Fittipaldi and Arie Luyendyk after the next yellow period.

There was to be one more yellow flag, and that was caused by Nigel smacking the wall after he'd got too wide in Turn Two chasing the leaders. His car was okay, though, and the last restart came with just five laps remaining. Fittipaldi had the situation under control and kept his Penske ahead to the finish. Luyendyk was second in Ganassi's Lola-Ford and Mansell got third.

Lola-Ford T93/00s filled second to seventh places, as Mansell was followed to the finish by Raul Boesel, who had led the early laps, Mario Andretti, who looked a potential winner for most of the afternoon, Scott Brayton and Scott Goodyear.

Nigel Mansell gave a further surprise just one week after Indy, when he won his first oval race at the Milwaukee Mile. He'd been in the picture throughout, and when Scott Goodyear, Paul Tracy and Robby Gordon hit trouble, the reigning World Champion was there to challenge and overtake Raul Boesel for the lead 18 laps before the end. A late yellow was not enough to help pole starter Boesel claim back the lead and he had to settle for second.

Mansell now had a handy points lead and, riding on the crest of a wave, he took pole for Detroit's street race. He crashed in the race, however. Danny Sullivan won in a Galles Lola-Chevrolet, and Raul Boesel's second place brought him to within three points of Mansell. Mario Andretti was third, as Lola filled the first eight places.

At Portland Mansell was yet again on pole. He led in the race, but, after sustained pressure from Emerson Fittipaldi's Penske, locked his brakes and slid up an escape road, dropping to third. Paul Tracy's late stop to change from wet to slick tyres let Mansell into second, but that was as high as he got.

The Penskes were clearly improving, and in Cleveland Paul Tracy won, with Emerson Fittipaldi completing the works team's perfect weekend. Nigel Mansell had led from third on the grid, but, when Tracy passed him on the 15th lap, he could not fight back. He eventually finished third.

The same trend continued in Toronto, where Tracy took a home win, with Fittipaldi again second. Danny Sullivan and Bobby Rahal fought a great battle for third, which was won by Sullivan. Rahal had forsaken the ex-TrueSports chassis and was now in a Chevy-powered Lola. Mansell was all at sea in Toronto. His practice was interrupted by crashes and, from ninth on the grid he never troubled the leaders, eventually retiring with engine failure. He also lost his points lead to Fittipaldi.

Of further concern to Lola, Newman/Haas and Mansell was designer Bruce Ashmore's departure to join Reynard for their imminent IndyCar project. Ashmore had been responsible for all Lola Indycars, since Nigel Bennett swapped to Penske in 1987. Carl Haas threatened to sue him for 'stolen trade secrets'. The feud was soon settled amicably, however.

On the track in the Michigan 500, Nigel bounced back like only he could. On the ultra-fast superspeedway the Newman/Haas cars set the pace from the outset. Mario Andretti qualified on pole with a 234.275mph lap that was the fastest ever recorded on a closed track. Mansell shared the front row with him. The race was all about them, too. Andretti led the early laps, but Mansell then took command and hung on to win, despite feeling ill towards the finish.

Mario was delayed when he spun whilst exiting his pit, but was only nine seconds behind his team-mate at the flag.

Everybody else had been lapped. Arie Luyendyk was third for Ganassi and it was Lolas all the way down to 12th on the results sheet! The Penskes had failed miserably in their home event.

New Hampshire's new oval was the scene of another brilliant Mansell showing. He qualified on pole again, but the Penskes were back in the picture in the race. Paul Tracy and Emerson Fittipaldi worked themselves to the head of the field, with Mansell on their tail as the race neared its finish. Four laps from the end – and on his birthday – Nigel squeezed through to win!

At Elkhart Lake Paul Tracy beat Mansell fair and square, despite injuring his ankle in Friday's qualifying. They occupied the front row, but from the pole Tracy simply disappeared in the race to win by half a minute. Mario Andretti followed Mansell in third until he was stopped by engine failure just three laps from the flag. Bobby Rahal inherited third in his Chevy-powered Lola.

Vancouver's street race gave a new twist to the story. Scott Goodyear qualified Derrick Walker's Lola-Ford on pole, Rahal lined up alongside him, and Mansell shared the second row with Tracy. After leading the early laps, Goodyear slipped back a little and later started losing gears, which dropped him to fourth at the finish. Tracy lost his chance when an alternator wire loosened, whilst Mansell – who'd complained of a lack of grip – stalled on a pit stop and struggled to sixth. All of which left the race to be battled

Nigel Mansell exploded onto the IndyCar circuit in 1993, after claiming the World Championship in F1 in 1992. Here's a dramatic shot of his pitstop on the way to winning at New Hampshire.

out between Al Unser Jr, whose Galmer team had returned to running Lola-Chevys, and Bobby Rahal. Little Al took his first win of the season with the help of slick pit work. Rahal finished second in his similar car and Stefan Johansson, in his private Penske, took third.

In Mid-Ohio Mansell was on the pole, but clashed on the opening lap, first with fellow front row man Tracy and then with Luyendyk. The first incident deranged the Lola's steering and the second knocked off its nose wings, so Nigel had to pit. He lost two laps and could only salvage one point after climbing to 12th. Emerson Fittipaldi won and closed to within striking distance in the points table. Robby Gordon finished second in A.J. Foyt's Lola-Ford and Scott Goodyear was third.

The penultimate round of the 1993 PPG IndyCar World Series was at Nazareth's little oval. Mansell showed he was by now undisputed master of the bullrings by taking another pole. Title rival Fittipaldi lined up alongside him. Mansell dropped behind the Penskes of Fittipaldi and Tracy at the start and soon lost another place to Raul Boesel. He worked himself to the lead just before the first pitstops, however, and dominated the race from then on. Tracy and Fittipaldi fell back with oversteering problems to finish third and fifth. For Fittipaldi, that was far enough to hand the title to Mansell with one round to go. Nigel won the race easily from Scott Goodyear.

The Laguna Seca finale was anti-climactic for Mansell's supporters. He qualified third and ran in the same

After Nigel Mansell had won the F1 Drivers' Championship in 1992, Williams did not re-sign him for the 1993 season, so Mansell went to America to drive a Lola T93/00 for the Newman/Haas team.

Nigel Mansell exhaustively tested the T93/00 at various oval and road tracks throughout America before the start of the season. Here he is on January 7th testing at Phoenix International Raceway for his first try on an oval circuit, still in a T92/00.

Nigel Mansell just about to go out for his first test with the Newman/Haas T92/00 at Phoenix on January 7th 1993.

"Our Nige's" first race for the Yanks. Surfers Paradise, Australia, March 21st, 1993: Mansell won it going away and finished the season as IndyCar Champion. Here he is with team boss and Lola importer, Carl Haas.

position for a while, but dropped back a couple of places and retired after a collision with a back-marker. Tracy and Fittipaldi walked off with a Penske 1-2, which placed them second and third in the championship, the Brazilian ahead of the Canadian. Tracy ended up winning as many races as Mansell, though. Arie Luyendyk followed the Penskes into third at Laguna.

A fresh new face tested a Chevy-powered T92/00 during the year at

Mansell at Indy. Despite never having raced there before, Mansell placed third at his first try and led for some laps.

For 1993 Lola built the BMS F1. Ferrari powered, it was a disappointment.

Michigan, Phoenix and Sebring under the guidance of the Forsythe Green team. At Michigan his times would have given tenth on the grid of the CART race. His name? Jacques Villeneuve.

T93/20 – 1993-96 – Indy Lights
This design was a spec chassis for the USA's IndyCar feeder category. It was based on the T93/50 F3000 design, but powered by a 425bhp 4.2-litre Buick V6. Andrew Broadley was in charge of the project. The new chassis represented a major technological step for the series, which had so far used cars based on the 1985 March F3000 design.

In the first race, at Phoenix, all but two of the competitors lapped faster than the existing lap record.

It was generally agreed that this car changed the fortunes of the Indy Lights series, which for years had been struggling to properly take off. A number of new teams joined in and the 1993 championship was won by Bryan Herta for Tasman Motorsports Group, which had been established by former TrueSports manager Steve Horne.

1994 saw former British Formula 3 racer Steve Robertson return to form and win the title from Brazil's André Ribeiro and Canadian teenager Greg Moore. Moore then went on to stamp his authority on the series in 1995. In Forsythe Racing's car, he won ten out of 12 races and was a most covincing champion.

The 1996 title also went to Canada and Forsythe, as David Empringham took the laurels, beating promising Brazilians Tony Kanaan and Gualter Salles.

T93/30 – 1993 – Lola BMS Ferrari Formula 1

Lola joined forces with the BMS Scuderia Italia Formula 1 team, which had been running Dallara chassis for the past few years. The car was to use a Ferrari V12 engine.

The design team was led by Eric Broadley and included Mark Williams, Duncan McRobbie and Andy Wall. They produced an entirely conventional carbon chassised F1 car.

Front suspension was via pushrods operating spring/damper units mounted horizontally in front of the scuttle via long rockers. Rear suspension needed a major rework in the pits at Kyalami before the first race to include more camber.

The project appeared to have sufficient funding, with sponsorship from Chesterfield, but the car had few of the contemporary frills of F1. It did have traction control developed by Marelli for Ferrari, but a semi-automatic gearbox and active suspension were promised later in the season. At first the car had a transverse sequential gearbox with Hewland internals.

Michele Alboreto and Luca Badoer were recruited as drivers.

Despite high hopes, the Lola-Ferrari was a project which simply never worked. In its debut race at Kyalami, both drivers had gearbox trouble and qualified on the back row of the grid. In the race, Alboreto went without a pitstop to run eighth (although there were only three cars behind him), but retired with engine failure. Badoer continued to suffer from gearbox problems and didn't make the finish either.

Already the car had received unkind remarks about its fairly substantial size.

In Brazil, Alboreto and Badoer got to the finish 11th and 12th, despite the former being bothered by his gearbox again. In the European GP at Donington Alboreto was 11th, again, but Badoer failed to qualify, and this became the norm for some time for both of the Scuderia Italia drivers, as the FIA had decided that the slowest participant should not be permitted to take the start.

At Imola it was Badoer who made the grid. He was seventh at the chequered flag, but lapped three times, and the only finisher classified behind him was Aguri Suzuki's Footwork, which had spent several laps in the pits. This was the team's best result of 1993.

There was some development during the year, and even talk of a completely new car before the season's end, but this did not materialise. The promised traction control arrived for the French GP at Magny-Cours, but had little noticeable affect on the team's fortunes.

For the German GP there was a new front suspension, and Ferrari supplied engines with pneumatic valves, but all this seemed to have little effect.

At Spa, Michele Alboreto scrabbled home 14th, and pronounced it the worst race of his life. At Monza pre-race testing seemed to help a bit. Alboreto managed to run in eighth – midfield – before retiring with engine failure.

It was no surprise that Lola and BMS announced an amicable split before the season was over and the team stayed away from the last races. Lola dug into the reasons behind the car's lack of pace and claimed the problem was insufficient acceleration from the engine/chassis combination, which would not allow enough downforce to be run, and vowed to be back in Formula 1 with its own team.

A book has been written about the gestation of this ill-fated car. It's entitled *The Modern Formula 1 Race Car*, and author Nigel Macknight was allowed to follow the car's conception from the planning stages.

T93/50 – 1993 – F3000

An evolution of the previous design, this had new sidepods with bigger radiator intake area and a new engine cover. The roll hoop was raised higher than the top of the airbox, again. Extra length allowed more space as the footbox was deeper.

A big step was the use of a Hewland TPT sequential shift transverse gearbox.

The suspension used Penske two-way spring units, mounted on the gearbox at the rear.

Even considering the disappointments of the last couple of seasons, it was surprising that Lola had no customers at all from amongst the teams competing in the FIA series. There was a plan to field a works effort later in the season, but it came to nought.

Paul Stewart Racing tried the T93/50 in an evaluation test at Silverstone after the European season was over. Vincenzo Sospiri and team patron Paul Stewart lapped quicker than they had managed with their Reynards, and felt that the cars were pretty equal.

Still, in 1993 the new F3000 Lolas were seen in competition only in the All-Japanese F3000 Championship.

Heinz-Harald Frentzen was the first driver to try the new car and confirmed its manufacturer's claims of increased stiffness. He tried works modifications, notably in suspension, in pre-season testing.

Only Nova Engineering, as Lola's Japanese importer (for drivers Mauro Martini and Heinz-Harald Frentzen), Roland Ratzenberger and Mika Salo used T93/50s for the opening round.

At Suzuka, Ross Cheever won for Reynard and was chased home by a swarm of Lola T92/50s, led by Kazuyoshi Hoshino's DFV-engined example. Eddie Irvine was third. Best T93/50 was Mika Salo's AD Racing car in 13th!

It was generally assumed that the T93/50 was 20-25kg overweight.

Kazuyoshi Hoshino won at Fuji in his DFV-powered T92/50; Apicella was second in Dome and Irvine third. Even Nova was running 92 cars. Ratzenberger had a 93 rear end grafted to a T92/50. Salo was the only driver in a new Lola and finished ninth.

At Mine the Nova drivers were back in their T93/50s, and, in a soaking wet race, Heinz-Harald Frentzen led, before a blown engine left the way clear for his team-mate Mauro Martini! The race had been stopped and restarted after Hoshino crashed heavily. On aggregate times Martini was quite a way ahead of second-placed Jeff Krosnoff, who still used the 92 Lola.

Suzuka, next, saw a return to previous form. Eddie Irvine won in the Cerumo team T92/50, and Hoshino and Danielsson were next in their DFV-powered 92 Lolas.

There was yet another new winner at Sugo, where Marco Apicella took the spoils in his Dome. Lolas had taken the top three places in qualifying, with Eddie Irvine on pole, but in the race Toshio Suzuki's fourth was the best they managed. Highest placed T93/50 was Mika Salo's in sixth.

Suzuki went one better to win at Fuji. Heinz-Harald Frentzen had put his T93/50 on pole in the mixed conditions of qualifying, but had to be content with second in the race. Roland Ratzenberger brought his 'bitza' T93/50 to third.

Ross Cheever became the first driver in the 1993 series to win for a second time, when he took the honours at Suzuka. Eddie Irvine still stuck to a T92/50, which he drove to second. Toshio Suzuki now had a T93/50 with '92 rear end and gearbox and he took third.

Fuji's penultimate round was a battle between Kazuyoshi Hoshino and Irvine, the Japanese veteran holding off the Irishman to win narrowly and assume the points lead. Thomas Danielsson claimed third aboard a DFV-engined T92/50, like the winner.

At Suzuka's finale, Kazuyoshi Hoshino, Eddie Irvine and Ross Cheever all had a chance at the title. Cheever put his Reynard on pole and led from the start, but was overtaken by Thomas Danielsson. Hoshino struggled and was never in the points, and eventually retired.

Danielsson held on to the finish in the DFV-powered T92/50 to take his first Japanese F3000 win.

Cheever stayed second and Andrew Gilbert-Scott was third in a Mugen-engined T92/50. Irvine came home fourth to push his points total to one over that of Hoshino's. The title went to the local veteran, though, as Irvine had to drop an earlier score and, on equal points, Hoshino took the verdict with two wins against Eddie's one! Cheever was just one point behind them.

Lola did take the top eight places at Suzuka, but the best T93/50 was only fifth, in the hands of Heinz-Harald Frentzen.

Late in the season, Dane Tom Kristensen tested an interim 93/94 car with revised suspension and aerodynamics.

T94/00 – 1994 – IndyCar

After the departure of Bruce Ashmore, a new 'no compromise' car was designed by Keith Knott and John Travis. This was the first Lola IndyCar to have a monocoque entirely manufactured of carbon fibre, without an aluminium honeycomb 'bathtub'.

T94/00 had a revised front wing, which went through the nose, taller sculpted sidepods and a lower engine cover with revised contours. The new nose was lower and had a 'hump' underneath, which wind tunnel research had shown to reduce pitch sensitivity and increase downforce. Significant gains in weight distribution had been achieved, with more of the weight between axles, helped by the adoption of a transverse gearbox, which had sequential shift. That also

Mika Salo was one of the first drivers in the All-Japan F3000 Championship to get his hands on a T93/50.

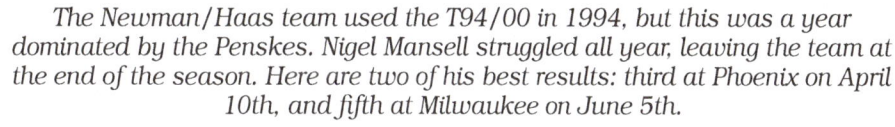

The Newman/Haas team used the T94/00 in 1994, but this was a year dominated by the Penskes. Nigel Mansell struggled all year, leaving the team at the end of the season. Here are two of his best results: third at Phoenix on April 10th, and fifth at Milwaukee on June 5th.

changed the concept of designing the underbody.

There was a lot of attention to detail, such as improved airflow around exhaust headers for better cooling, rationalised and shortened water pipes, and stiffened radiators. Rear suspension geometry was a concept used for the last few races of 1993, which gave better mechanical grip. The car had been designed to accept Ford, Ilmor or Honda engines.

Chevrolet had withdrawn from the IndyCar engine scene, which left manufacturer Ilmor to badge the power units under its own name. Ford had a new, high-revving engine, which was only available to preferred runners. Honda entered the scene with Bobby Rahal's team.

Nigel Mansell, naturally, had the benefit of Ford's new unit when he started his title defence by taking pole at Surfers Paradise. In the race he lost a duel with Michael Andretti's new Reynard-Ford, and then spun and stalled. Michael went on to win and Lola honour was salvaged by father Mario taking third.

Phoenix saw Mansell return to the scene of his 1993 accident. He crashed again in practice, taking rookie Jacques Villeneuve with him, and confessed to having been scared. He still qualified third and finished the race in the same position, beaten by the Penskes of Emerson Fittipaldi and the team's new signing Al Unser Jr.

Nigel couldn't keep up with the Penskes in the streets of Long Beach, either, but, after two of the three works cars hit trouble, he took second behind Unser Jr. Robbie Gordon finished third in Derrick Walker's Lola, which used the older Ford engine. Raul Boesel was fourth in Dick Simon's Lola-Ford and Mario Andretti fifth.

Raul Boesel excelled in Indy 500 qualifying, taking second place on the grid as fastest Lola runner. Nigel Mansell was seventh fastest, but somewhat humiliated by 45-year-old Lyn St James, who achieved the best ever starting position for a female driver at Indy. St James started one slot higher than Mansell in a Lola T94/00, which had a lower specification Ford engine.

Penske exploited Indy's equivalency rules and had a special 3.4-litre, single-cam V8 engine built by Ilmor for this race only. Badged Mercedes, it gave the team a clear edge, and Al Unser Jr won the 500 easily, with Jacques Villeneuve second for Reynard. Robby Gordon was the best of Lola's representatives, but was still only fifth.

Nigel Mansell's race deteriorated after a stop-go penalty, which dropped him from fourth to 14th. He crashed with backmarker Dennis Vitolo and left the track disgusted.

Milwaukee was a demonstration of Penske supremacy, as the team's cars finished 1-2-3. Mansell managed to finish fifth as best of the Lolas.

In Detroit Nigel put his car on the pole, but could not hold the Penskes in the race. Fighting with Emerson Fittipaldi in third, he hit Emmo from behind and limped to the pits to change the nose cone, but later retired with a broken throttle. Gordon's was the best Lola in third.

In Portland Unser beat Mansell narrowly for pole, but again Gordon was the best Lola driver in the race, passing Mansell on the last lap for fourth. Neither had the speed to trouble the Penskes, which made another clean sweep.

In Cleveland, Mansell alone took the fight to Roger Penske's squad. He was unable to do anything about Al Unser Jr, who won as he pleased, but he did beat Paul Tracy for second.

Gordon and Mansell occupied the front row of the grid in Toronto. Gordon led first, then Mansell, but after losing his lead to Michael Andretti, Nigel dropped back with a puncture, which also spoiled Gordon's race. Mansell later quit with handling trouble. Bobby Rahal finished second to Andretti Jr in his Lola-Honda.

The Michigan 500 once again produced a rogue result. From 12th and 26th on the grid, Scott Goodyear and Arie Luyendyk were first and second respectively for the Bernstein-King and Indy Regency equipes. More remarkably, Dominic Dobson completed a Lola 1-2-3 in PacWest's car. Mansell had been on pole and led the opening laps, until a stuck throttle brought him into the pits and a little while later put him out of the race. Goodyear had been two laps behind Al Unser Jr and Raul Boesel during the closing stages, but both dropped out with engine failure.

It was a familiar story at Mid-Ohio. The Penskes were simply untouchable and scored another 1-2-3. Mansell was best non-Penske in qualifying, but Gordon assumed the role in the race and finished fourth. Mansell complained that his car's handling had varied during the race, and came home a lacklustre seventh.

New Hampshire witnessed yet another Penske 1-2-3, with Raul Boesel fourth. Mansell was running second when, lapping Mario Andretti, he drove into his team-mate, which put paid to Newman/Haas' chances for the afternoon.

In Vancouver Al Unser Jr's victory took him to the threshold of the title. Robby Gordon had taken pole but, despite setting the early pace, was unable to challenge Little Al at the end, when he'd lost second gear. Nigel Mansell tried to overtake Emerson Fittipaldi for fourth place in the last corner, but ran into his side, taking both cars out of the race.

Jacques Villeneuve took his first IndyCar win at Elkhart Lake. Mansell was third on the grid, but hampered by a misfire in the race and out of the points. Boesel's sixth was the best any Lola managed to salvage.

Nazareth brought one more Penske 1-2-3, with Boesel fourth. Mansell qualified third, but faded away in the race, complaining of poor handling, and gave up before half-distance.

In Laguna Seca's finale it was Raul Boesel again who got closest to threatening Penske dominance: he was second behind Paul Tracy in the race. Nigel Mansell had qualified third, but, after a good early run, was delayed in the pits and dropped to eighth.

Al Unser Jr was the 1994 CART Champion. Robbie Gordon finished

As fast as Mansell rose, so he fell. After a miserable 1994 season in IndyCars, he left America at the end of 1994. At Vancouver in September, he was forced to retire at the last corner after a crash with Emerson Fittipaldi.

fifth and was highest placed of the Lola drivers. Mansell slumped to eighth in the points table and left the IndyCar scene apparently disillusioned. His two seasons of IndyCar racing had consisted of a meteoric rise and equally dramatic fall

Lola's only CART victory of the season had been Scott Goodyear's lucky triumph in the Michigan 500.

T94/50 – 1994 – F3000

Andrew Broadley headed the design team of Lola's new F3000 challenger. Its reprofiled, shorter, shapelier sidepods allowed by the new regulations were intended to make the car less pitch sensitive. Inside them, the radiators had been repositioned. The new tub was of a subtly different shape and narrower at the front with a slimmer nose. Detail changes were numerous.

The T94/50 weighed in at 530kg, thus needed 20kg of ballast to meet the 94 minimum weight. The sequential gearbox was revised and lighter than before.

Suspension was similar to that on the final version of T93/50, but front mountings were now outboard, not recessed in the tub. Koni shocks were adopted, in place of the Penskes previously used.

All the cars in Europe were powered by Cosworth AC engines, while Japan had Mugen and Judd units.

The car was raced in Europe by the Nordic Racing and Omegaland teams. Much was expected of F3000 winner Jordi Gené, in particular, but the best he could wrest from the T94/50 was a fourth place in Barcelona. His teammate Marc Goossens was sixth on that occasion, and later got a fifth at Hockenheim, but those were the only points scores.

The car was modified during the season. For the Enna race in July, there were aerodynamic mods, including a new front wing, different floor and improved cooling. An aerodynamicist was recruited from Williams to help cure the problems, but it was too late to see a change before the season ended.

The Japanese F3000 series was in decline, but still attracted top overseas drivers. Ross Cheever won the season's

The Indy Lights car, T93/20, was a successful design – powered by a 4.2-litre Buick V6 – which attracted new talent to the IndyCar series.

Main pic & inset right: The T95/30 was a development car for a forthcoming F1 Lola, which did not appear until the ill-fated 1997 car. Here it is in testing at Silverstone in 1995 with Allan McNish.

The T94/50, Lola's Formula 3000 car of 1994, did not match up to expectation, and quite a few Lola customers went back to using 1993 cars.

first race at Suzuka in his Reynard. Mika Salo, now DFV-powered, was the best Lola representative in third with a T93/50.

Suzuka also hosted the second round, where Andrew Gilbert-Scott took pole and won in Stellar Racing's bitza T93/50, which had a 92 rear-end, non-sequential gearbox and trick bodywork. Mauro Martini brought Nova's new T94/50 to second.

At Mine, Martini was on pole, but could not keep Marco Apicella's Dome back in the race. He then lost second gear and position to Gilbert-Scott and Takuya Kurosawa. Gilbert-Scott finished second, keeping the newer Lolas of Kurosawa and Martini behind him in third and fourth.

At Suzuka's next round the Lolas fared worse, with Kurosawa fourth and Martini fifth. Marco Apicella took another win in the Dome.

At Sugo, Kurosawa had his first victory, but had stepped back into a T93/50 to beat Andrew Gilbert-Scott. The new car still didn't win in the next race, at Fuji, when Gilbert-Scott took his second win of the season ahead of Mauro Martini's T94/50.

Back at Suzuka it was Ross Cheever's turn to take his second win of the year. Gilbert-Scott and Kurosawa, in third and fourth, again kept older Lolas to the fore.

Fuji gave Apicella win number three. Kurosawa was second and Kunimitsu Takahashi third in a T94/50.

Fuji was also the scene of the penultimate round, where Thomas Danielsson proved the new car fast in qualifying. In AD Racing's Judd-engined T94/50 he recorded a time good enough for pole, but it was disallowed as yellow flags had been out. Starting from second on the grid, the Swede stalled and fell back. Andrew Gilbert-Scott spiced up the championship battle by winning from Apicella. Martini and Kazuyoshi Hoshino, in third and fourth respectively; both had 94 Lolas.

The title fight was decided in the first corner of Suzuka's finale, when protagonists Apicella and Gilbert-Scott clashed. The race was ruined for both, which meant that the Italian Dome driver was champion. Naoki Hattori won the race in a Reynard, Kurosawa was second to share third place in the series with Cheever. Martini's third place got him equal fifth in points.

The T94/50, then, did not score a single win in 1994, although older models kept Lola in the hunt in Japan.

T95/00 1995 CART

A development of the old theme, the T95/00 had an extensively revised aerodynamic package, although very little of this was outwardly obvious. Sculpted recesses running along the bottom edges of the sidepods hadn't been seen before. The car also had a new monocoque and new rear suspension geometry.

In the 1995 CART series tyre manufacturer Goodyear had serious opposition from Firestone for the first time in over two decades. Another important change was the driving force at Newman/Haas: with Nigel Mansell gone and Mario Andretti retired, Lola's US importer was now represented by returnee Michael Andretti and Paul Tracy, who was contracted for one season from Penske. They still used Ford engines, while the Ilmors were now officially called Mercedes.

This time the season began on a street circuit in Miami. Michael Andretti was immediately at home in his old team, taking pole position. He led the race, but was pushed into the wall by a lapped car and broke the suspension. Jacques Villeneuve won a close race from fellow Reynard runner Maurício Gugelmin, with Bobby Rahal third in his Ilmor-Mercedes-engined Lola, and Scott Pruett fourth in his Patrick Racing Lola-Ford.

Andretti took the pole in Surfers Paradise, too. Again he led, but lost second gear and had to let Paul Tracy through. A clean sweep for Newman/Haas looked to be on the cards, but, under pressure from Bobby Rahal, Andretti hit a wall on the last lap. That let Rahal through to second, with Pruett again third.

In Phoenix victory slipped through Michael Andretti's fingers possibly because of communication problems with his pit. He led for most of the first half of the race and, with eight laps left, was running second behind Emerson Fittipaldi. Andretti then let Robby Gordon through without a fight, thinking the Reynard driver was a lap down. When Fittipaldi had to pit for a late splash-and-dash, Gordon won from Andretti by one second.

At Long Beach Andretti was once again to the fore. With Tracy he secured an all-Newman/Haas front row. Michael led the race for its first third, but Tracy dropped out from third after clashing with Gil de Ferran. Andretti was demoted by Al Unser Jr's Penske. Michael hung on, but twice slipped up an escape road when trying to pressure Little Al, and dropped down the order. Scott Pruett finished second to Unser.

Nazareth was another race that Michael Andretti led, but later crashed out from fourth. Eddie Cheever, in A.J. Foyt's Lola-Ford T95/00, had victory in the bag, but a computer error caused him to run out of fuel two laps from the finish. He still ended up best Lola runner, in fifth, but the win went to Emerson Fittipaldi's Penske.

The fastest cars in qualifying for Indy 500 were the big-boost Menard Lola-Buicks of Scott Brayton and Arie Luyendyk. These hump-backed cars occupied the first two places on the grid, but soon dropped back in the race. Michael Andretti started fourth and led confidently, yet again, until hitting the wall before half-distance. Late in the race, Scott Pruett duelled for the lead with Scott Goodyear's leading Reynard, but crashed on oil 15 laps from the finish. Jacques Villeneuve went on to snatch victory from Goodyear, when the latter was docked a four-lap penalty for passing the pace car. Reynard took a 1-2, as Christian Fittipaldi finished second. Bobby Rahal's was best Lola in third, after suffering a stop-go penalty.

On Milwaukee's one-mile oval Paul Tracy won after a terrific battle with Al Unser Jr; this pair lapped the rest of the field, which was led to the flag by Michael Andretti's understeering Lola.

In Detroit Robby Gordon started from pole and won a close race, with Scott Pruett third and Michael Andretti fourth.

Portland produced a disputed result, when the Penske of winner Al Unser was found to be underweight. After months of deliberation, he was allowed to keep the win, thereby denying Reynard-mounted Jimmy Vasser a first victory. Bobby Rahal was third and Michael Andretti fourth.

Jacques Villeneuve was back in winning form at Elkhart Lake, where

Indianapolis. All the drama of a pitstop at "The Brickyard" is captured in this fine shot of a Lola T95/00 being refuelled during the 1995 race.

he beat Paul Tracy by just 0.4 seconds. Tracy had been slightly delayed when he stalled on his first pit stop because of pain in his foot, which he'd injured in a karting accident.

Toronto produced another close finish. This time Michael Andretti won by 0.4 seconds from Bobby Rahal. Michael led most of the race and held off Rahal for the latter half. Jacques Villeneuve came in third, consolidating his points lead.

Cleveland's airfield race was a cracker. Michael Andretti was in the lead 13 laps from the finish, but slowed because of a broken valve spring, and saw Jacques Villeneuve head a Reynard 1-2-3. Bobby Rahal trailed them in to finish fourth.

The Michigan 500, too, was exciting. Going into the final lap, Scott Pruett's leading Lola-Ford was passed by Al Unser Jr, but Pruett re-took the lead around the outside of the final turn to win by less than half a car's length. Adrian Fernandez finished third in a Galles Lola-Mercedes. Pruett's victory was the first IndyCar triumph on Firestone tyres for 21 years.

Mid-Ohio was a scene of another dose of bad luck for Michael Andretti. Having worked his Lola into the lead, the engine dropped a valve just four laps from the chequered flag, handing victory to Al Unser Jr's Penske. Paul Tracy finished a close second.

At New Hampshire's short oval André Ribeiro made history by giving Honda its first IndyCar victory. Michael Andretti was unable to stay with the winning Reynard-Honda, but took second.

Al Unser Jr won in Vancouver to stay in the title chase. Michael Andretti led once more, but was sidelined by transmission failure. Lola's highest finisher was Bobby Rahal in fifth.

Laguna Seca saw Jacques Villeneuve crowned 1995 IndyCar Champion, although the race gave Reynard driver Gil de Ferran his first win. Paul Tracy raced to second and Michael Andretti to fourth from eighth and 12th on the grid respectively. Michael finished fourth in the series, too, beaten by Al Unser Jr in second and Bobby Rahal in third.

By 1996 a split had occurred between CART and the Indianapolis Motor Speedway. This most unfortunately led to the CART teams being absent from the Indy 500, which now became a round of IMS President Tony George's new creation, the Indy Racing League.

The IRL's first season was contested by former CART machinery, whilst new regulations demanded totally different cars from the beginning of 1997.

The level of competition in the Indy Racing League was very much below that of CART, although some names familiar from the latter series did swap. IRL got off to a somewhat shaky start at a new oval track in Disney World. This was won by Buzz Calkins in a Reynard, with promising former Sprint Car driver Tony Stewart less than a second behind in a Menard Lola-Buick T95/00. Michele Alboreto finished fourth in a Lola-Ford T94/00.

All IRL races took place on ovals, and next it was Arie Luyendyk, who won in a Reynard in Phoenix. This time Scott Sharp was second in a Lola-Ford T94/00.

Indy 500 suffered most from the rift with an entry just a pale shadow of the event's glorious past. In qualifying, the Menard Lola-Buick T95/00s of Scott Brayton, Tony Stewart and Davy Jones swept to the front row. Tragically, Brayton was then killed in practice before the race.

Menard did not quite manage to win the Indy 500, as Buddy Lazier triumphed in a Reynard. Davy Jones came in second, less than a second in arrears.

Curiously, the first IRL Championship was concluded by Indy 500, its third race. Scott Sharp and Buzz Clakins tied on points and, without a tie-break rule, ended up ex-aequo champions!

IRL's second season started in the autumn of 1996, but most confusingly went on into 1997, when the new cars became *de rigueur*. The 1996 rounds were tackled with old CART-type machinery, and in New Hampshire Scott Sharp took Lola's only IRL victory, beating reigning co-champion Buzz Calkins. Tony Stewart had dominated in Menard's car, but dropped out in the closing stages with electrical failure.

Las Vegas saw the last IRL event for the old cars. Richie Hearn's Reynard won, while Mexican Michel Jourdain Jr took second in a Lola-Ford T95/00.

T95/30 – 1995 development – Formula 1

This was a design by Julian Cooper intended to help Lola prepare for its next entry in Formula 1. Completed late in 1994, it did not strictly conform to 1995 F1 regulations, but the plan was to use it as a development hack for the definitive design.

The car had a carbonfibre monocoque, but aluminium honeycomb was also used. The shape was fairly conventional contemporary F1, with a narrow, high nose and high but squat sidepods. There was, however, no engine airbox. The rest of the design, too, was conventional.

Suspension was operated by pushrods and had Koni dampers located on top of the footwell at the front and over the gearbox at the rear. The brakes had AP calipers and Hitco carbon discs. There was a six-speed transverse gearbox, which had a semi-automatic sequential shift with TAG electronic management. Power was from a 3-litre Ford Cosworth ED V8 engine.

Allan McNish tested the car early in 1995, and it appeared in a racing car show in Paris, but when there wasn't sufficient reaction from potential sponsors for an F1 programme, the T93/30 was quietly shelved.

T95/50 – 1995 – F3000

After an extensive winter test programme, Lola introduced significant aerodynamic changes for its new F3000. While the monocoque and suspension remained essentially unchanged, the car looked very different from its predecessor, because of the adoption of a flatter, raised nose. The car also featured two small vertical deflectors, between the front wheels and sidepods, on each side. The sidepods, too, were different, as

Lola's F3000 car for 1995 revived its fortunes in this category. The T95/30 actually won a race; the first for Lola in this category since 1992!

was the sleeker engine cover. A lighter gearbox casing was an improvement, and the differential had undergone a series of modifications.

In Europe, all T95/50s were equipped with Cosworth AC engines, while the Japanese market again used mostly Mugens.

Testing gave evidence that Lola might be a serious threat to Reynard's supremacy in Europe. The main attack on the FIA series was handled by Nordic Racing again, whose number one driver, Marc Goossens, soon became notorious for his explosive starts and early charges. He picked up points by finishing fourth at Silverstone, fifth in Barcelona and then third in Pau's street race, where he caught the leading Reynards of Vincenzo Sospiri and Allan McNish towards the finish, but was unable to pass. Winner Sospiri stayed just over three seconds ahead and McNish beat the Belgian by only 0.8 seconds.

Promising teenager Marco Campos had graduated from Formula Opel with his Euroseries-winning team Draco, and was impressive – especially with quick qualifying performances in his T95/50. He took his first points by finishing fourth at Enna, where another of the new Lolas was sixth in the hands of Jérôme Policand.

At Hockenheim Goossens realised his and the car's potential. He jumped from third to first on the second lap and ran away from the opposition after that. He won by four seconds from the Reynard of Kenny Brack. This was the first FIA F3000 series victory for Lola since 1992.

On the daunting Spa circuit Goossens qualified second, but took the lead from Vincenzo Sospiri with a passing move at Eau Rouge. Sospiri returned the favour, however, on the next lap at the same place. Goossens was still on the Italian's tail with two laps to go, but clipped a kerb and slid into the barrier. Christophe Bouchut then inherited second place in another T95/50 run by the French Danielson Team.

His team-mate, Policand, was best placed Lola driver in Estoril, where he came home fourth, and Sospiri clinched the championship, despite finishing out of the points.

The Magny-Cours finale was marred by an accident which took the life of the promising Marco Campos. He interlocked wheels with another car and was thrown against the pit wall. Kenny Brack won his first F3000 race, but with Goossens in second despite a spin, these two tied for third in the championship.

In Japan, Mauro Martini once more raced the latest Lola for local importer Nova, but the customer teams mainly relied on older chassis. Toshio Suzuki won the championship, taking two race victories with a T94/50. The title was decided in a fairly chaotic

The Lola T96/00 was Lola's 1996 IndyCar. The Kmart-sponsored car of the Newman/Haas team was driven by Michael Andretti. He seemed to suffer bad luck during this season, finishing third at Detroit (this pic) and Mid-Ohio (overleaf).

This page: The teams were allowed to make virtually no changes to the 1996 Formula 3000 spec cars; even so, they usually kept them well covered for fear of rivals stealing their set-ups. Partially stripped cars were not a common sight.

Suzuka race, where the first five cars all crashed out.

Second in the series went to new Reynard star Toranosuke Takagi, with whom Tom Kristensen tied on points. The Dane won at Mine in a T94/50.

Andrew Gilbert-Scott was forced to abandon the trick bodywork on his T93/50, but scored one win at Fuji, where he headed a Lola 1-5.

The T95/50's best results in Japan were achieved by the evergreen Kazuyoshi Hoshino, who got the car to second place at best.

All Lola's 1995 successes in Japan were achieved with Mugen engines.

T96/00 – 1996 – CART

John Travis led the design of yet another evolution on Lola's CART theme. The regulations had been changed again, necessitating aerodynamic revisions at the rear in particular. The sidepods were taller than for some time, although, on the other hand, Ford's new XD engine was more compact than the XB had been, and the car's tight fit around it resulted in aerodynamic gains. Relocated oil and water pumps gave more scope for optimising airflow, too. Cars equipped with the older Ford XB, Honda or Mercedes engines had different underbody shapes. The engine cover was adorned by a vertical fin, now commonplace in rival CART designs, although not used on all circuits.

Michael Andretti was joined in Newman/Haas' Ford-engined Lolas by Christian Fittipaldi. The other leading Lolas were on Firestone tyres. Scott Pruett carried on in Patrick Racing's Lola-Ford, whilst Tasman Motorsports ran Lola-Hondas for André Ribeiro and Adrian Fernandez.

Miami's series opener now moved to the new Homestead oval, where Jimmy Vasser won in Ganassi's Reynard-Honda. Scott Pruett ran in the leading bunch, but, in trying to wrest second place, dropped to fourth.

Brazil had cause for celebration in the next race, when André Ribeiro triumphed at home in Rio. He ran with the leaders all the way in Tasman's Lola-Honda and emerged in the lead, when impressive rookie Greg Moore suffered electrical failure. Al Unser Jr took second for Penske and Pruett was third.

Jimmy Vasser won the next two races in Surfers Paradise and Long Beach. A strong second in Australia gave Scott Pruett the points lead temporarily, but that was the high point of his season as bad luck and mechanical problems wrecked his challenge from then on.

Michael Andretti's season went the opposite way. He had several collisions with fellow competitors in the early races, and was even put 'on probation' by CART's Chief Steward Wally Dallenbach. Michael bounced back in the best way possible, however, winning at home in Nazareth. He was running strongly in second, when leader Paul Tracy crashed in the pits. Michael then stayed in command for the latter half of the race, and got his championship campaign back on track.

Still, Jimmy Vasser was riding the crest of a wave and took his fourth victory in the next race. This was Michigan's US500, which had been put on the calendar as CART's flagship event after the loss to Tony George's Indy Racing League of Indy 500. Maurício Gugelmin was second in his PacWest Reynard, but third was reward to Roberto Moreno for a splendid performance. He took the position in Payton-Coyne's T96/00, which was powered by a two-year-old Ford XB. Moreno was one lap down after making a late fuel stop under green.

In Milwaukee Michael Andretti fought and won a classic duel with Al Unser Jr, which raged for much of the race. Michael passed Little Al to take the lead after a restart five laps from the finish. Having been on soft tyres, he felt he'd been saved by that late yellow flag period. Andretti's young team-mate, Christian Fittipaldi, started from third on the grid and battled with the leaders, but finished sixth.

Michael carried on the momentum in Detroit's Belle Isle, winning from Christian Fittipaldi to celebrate a Newman/Haas 1-2 in a partly wet race. Scott Pruett had been on pole, but fell back after he'd been demoted from the lead by Christian Fittipaldi on the second lap. Fittipaldi then led most of the race until he was pipped by team-mate Andretti just five laps before the finish. Gil de Ferran finished third in Detroit in Jim Hall's Reynard-Honda, and Adrian Fernandez was fourth.

Jimmy Vasser's Ganassi team-mate, Alex Zanardi, got his first win at Portland, where Gil de Ferran completed a Reynard 1-2. In a mixed conditions race, Christian Fittipaldi felt he'd made the right choice of staying on slicks throughout and took third.

On Cleveland's airstrips de Ferran won. Michael Andretti worked up from a poor grid position to lead, but dropped out of third with transmission failure.

The Tasman Lola of Adrian Fernandez emerged victorious in Toronto. He'd run third, but found himself in the lead after final pit stops. The Tasman Racing Lolas were particularly competitive in Toronto, as André Ribeiro had been on pole. Their joy was, however, overshadowed by a terrifying accident in the race, which took the life of Jeff Krosnoff.

In Michigan's second 500-mile race of the season, André Ribeiro made amends for not being able to capitalise on his pole in Toronto. He won after Alex Zanardi's dominant early showing had ended in a crash. This was an impressive result, considering Ribeiro had fallen back after changing a flat-spotted tyre under yellow during the early stages. Bryan Herta and Maurício Gugelmin kept Reynard on the podium with second and third respectively.

In Mid-Ohio Michael Andretti chased the Galles Reynards of Zanardi and Vasser, but simply could not match them. At the flag he was 3.4 seconds behind the victorious Italian, in third.

In Elkhart Lake Michael inherited a lucky win from Al Unser Jr's Penske, which blew its engine less than half a lap from the finish. Christian Fittipaldi had also been in the thick of the lead battle, but his engine went five laps before the finish. Bobby Rahal was second in his Reynard-Mercedes.

Michael had some luck in Vancouver, too. When poleman Zanardi tripped up with a backmarker, Andretti inherited the lead. He ran hard, chased by Bobby Rahal, who could get close but not threaten to pass. Michael was better in traffic and kept his lead to the finish. Christian Fittipaldi was third.

Andretti still had a chance of the championship going into the last race in Laguna Seca. Jimmy Vasser, who hadn't won a race since late May, did enough by securing fourth place and landed the title. The race was memorable for Alex Zanardi's spectacular passing move into the Corkscrew, which demoted Bryan Herta to second. Scott Pruett got his best result for months by coming home third.

Zanardi finished the season on equal points with Michael Andretti, but the latter was runner-up, as he'd won five races during the season – more than any other driver. Christian Fittipaldi finished fifth in the series. Remarkably, Penske failed to win a single race.

T96/50 – 1996-98 – F3000 specification car

Motor racing's international federation, the FIA, changed Formula 3000 into a single chassis category from the beginning of 1996. Lola got the contract to supply the cars, which were all to be powered by a 3-litre, Zytek-Judd V8 engine. This gave out some 450bhp.

The intention was to produce a car of somewhat lower specification than before, but strong and easy to service. The resulting T96/50 was said to have some 40% less downforce than the preceding F3000 design, but was more rigid. It was built to the new regulation minimum weight of 625kg with driver on board.

The monocoque was made of carbon fibre/aluminium honeycomb composite. The 'survival cell' conformed to F1 safety norms, and was considerably larger than during the earlier formula.

The car's looks were characterized by a raised nose, lateral F1-style head protection blending into a bulky engine cover, and high sidepods. It had a three-element rear wing, which could be run with just two elements when high downforce was not a priority.

Suspension was, naturally enough, by double wishbones front and rear, with spring/damper units operated by

A T96/50 driven by 1997 F3000 champion Ricardo Zonta.

pushrods. At the front, the adjustable Koni gas dampers (similar to those used by Tyrrell in F1) were placed longitudinally over the footwell, and at the rear they resided at an angle on top of the Lola-made gearbox.

This was a five-speed transverse unit with sequential shift. The aluminium alloy casing also housed a Salisbury differential, oil tank and starting motor.

The four-pot brakes had ventilated cast iron discs.

13x10.50in Avon tyres were specified for the front and 13x15in for the rear.

The drivers found this an entertaining car to drive. It produced some close and entertaining races, but the 1996 Championship was unfortunately decided by disqualification, when Kenny Brack's defence of his lead in the Hockenheim finale was considered too forceful by the stewards. The Swede knocked his pursuer, Jörg Müller, out of the event, when the latter dived for the lead, which would have given him the title. Anyway, Brack was promptly shown the black flag and Müller took the championship with two race wins to his credit, against Brack's three. Marc Goossens was third in the series and newcomer Ricardo Zonta fourth, both of them also winning two races.

The T96/50 was also adopted for use in a Mexican F3000 series, fitted with a Chrysler V6 engine. The 1996 championship was won by Jaime Cordero from Briton Derek Higgins.

In 1997 the number of cars in the FIA F3000 series was higher than for some time, and the same could be said of the quality of the drivers. Pre-season favourite, Riccardo Zonta, had joined the crack Super Nova team, and recovered from a nightmarish early season to take the title. He was disqualified from a season-opening Silverstone victory on a technicality and then retired from the next two events, but went on to score three other wins to put the championship beyond doubt before the last race.

That was won by his closest challenger Juan Pablo Montoya, who closed the gap to just 1.5 points, having also taken three victories during the season. Other race winners during 1997 were Jason Watt, Jamie Davies, Soheil Ayari and Tom Kristensen, who took top score at Silverstone after Zonta's exclusion.

The 1997 Mexican F3000 Championship was won by Jimmy Morales with Derek Higgins second again.

There was also an attempt to run a British F3000 series in 1997, but, after the first round attracted only three entries, the idea was shelved. The lone Brands Hatch race was won by Dino Morelli.

T96/51 & T96/52 – 1996 – Formula Nippon

While Europe went for a one-make series with the FIA F3000 Championship in 1996, Japan kept its series open for cars of the old F3000 category, and renamed it Formula Nippon.

Lola produced a development of T95/50 for this category. There were few differences, but the 96 tub was more rigid, and separate versions were made for different makes of tyre, hence the two codes for the same series of car.

Kazuyoshi Hoshino won Suzuka's Formula Nippon opening round in his Mugen-powered T96/52 from Shinji Nakano's Dome. The emerging overseas stars of the series were Reynard-mounted Ralf Schumacher, and Norberto Fontana in a Lola-Mugen T96/51. Toranosuke Takagi, in another Reynard, was the best new domestic hope. Fontana managed to win once in Fuji, but this, and Hoshino's Suzuka success, remained the only Lola victories in the 1996 series. Ralf Schumacher claimed the championship title; Naoki Hattori was second, also with Reynard, and Hoshino was Lola's most successful representative in third.

T97/00 – 1997 – CART

Yet more restrictive regulations caused all 1997 CART chassis to look quite similar. Outwardly, there was little new in the T97/00.

John Travis had left Lola in spring 1996 to draw Penske's next chassis, and the CART design team was now led by Ben Bowlby, who claimed the car to be the most user-friendly IndyCar ever. It was the first chassis for this category on which the complete rear end – including cooling ancillaries – could be removed F1-style.

The new regulations resulted in a bigger cockpit, as well as higher and thicker head protection. Great attention had been paid to making the car's overall shape more slippery. The chassis' underside was totally redesigned. The nose of the road course version was now raised slightly above the new front wing, which was attached to it by small supports on each side.

Lola's CART challenge was blunted even before the season started. Its Haas US franchise had been terminated, which led to Newman/Haas running the new Swift chassis. The Patrick and Green teams had bought Lolas, but both defected to running Reynards after pre-season testing. This left Tasman Motorsports as Lola's main customer, fielding Honda-powered T97/00s for André Ribeiro and Adrian Fernandez.

The season started on a truly depressing note. At Homestead all six Lolas present qualified among the nine slowest entries. In the race, Richie Hearn, in Della Penna Racing's Lola-Ford, finished 11th, which was a disappointment after he'd set promising times in testing. Still, all the other Lolas were even further back, and to add insult to injury Michael Andretti won the race on the debut of Newman/Haas' brand new Swift.

In Sebring testing, a reprofiled front wing and stiffened rear bulkhead seemed at least a partial cure to T97/00's problems.

At Surfers Paradise André Ribeiro managed to bring his car sixth to the chequered flag. This race, too, was won by a Lola defector as Scott Pruett took the laurels in Patrick Racing's Reynard-Ford. There was no further improvement, however, and during the high season Lolas were occasionally seen in the top ten, but never the top six.

Before the Cleveland race, a virtually all-new rear end was introduced, with different transmission casing and rear uprights. This hardly seemed to help, as the four Lolas present qualified among the slowest five. André Ribeiro now had a Reynard, but his Tasman team-mate, Adrian Fernandez, soldiered on with his T97/00.

Lola's T97/00 was not a good car. Most teams had by now forsaken Lola and bought Swifts and Reynards. Despite this, a T97/00 did place third at the last race of 1997, at Fontana in California.

Some honour was restored in the season's last race on the new California Speedway in Fontana. Adrian Fernandez had a new underwing, which gave his Lola a better balance. In a 500 mile race he brought the Tasman car home third, one lap behind winner Mark Blundell and Jimmy Vasser, who were in Mercedes- and Honda-powered Reynards respectively.

Still, it was very little, very late, leaving the company with a collapsed IndyCar market.

T97/20 – 1997-2000 – Indy Lights specification car

This was the first Indy Lights car to be designed from scratch for the IndyCar feeder series. Although based on the F3000 T96/50 design to some extent, the car's specification was dictated by the series organiser, and it differed quite a lot from its European counterpart. The monocoque was made of carbon fibre and aluminium honeycomb composite. The aerodynamic specification gave considerably more downforce than did that of the new F3000.

The slim, slightly raised nose and discreet but effective driver protection around the cockpit aperture gave this new Indy Lights chassis a distinctive and appealing look. Performance was very similar to that of the preceding T93/20, but safety had been emphasized with greater structural integrity and a strengthened footbox, which had a double bulkhead. The gearbox was a conventional, longitudinal Hewland with five speeds.

The cars were still powered by a 4.2-litre Buick V6, giving 425bhp, although the design could be fitted with a V8. The weight was 650kg without a driver on board.

The 1997 Indy Lights Championship developed into a battle between three highly promising Brazilians. The previous year's runner-up, Tony Kanaan, took the title from his Tasman Motorsports teammate Hélio Castroneves, with Cristiano da Matta third.

The T97/20 Indy Lights car at Laguna Seca in 1997. (Courtesy LAT)

T97/30 – 1997 – Formula 1

In late autumn 1996, Lola made the decision to go Formula 1 racing for the first time with its own team. Sponsorship was secured from MasterCard in an innovative scheme, whereby the money was intended to be sourced from revenue created by a club for MasterCard holders. Membership of the club would give access to certain aspects of F1. Ideally, Lola should have joined the F1 circus in 1998, but the MasterCard deal meant it had to be on the grid for the first race of 1997, which only allowed nine weeks for building the car.

A company separate from Lola Cars was established for the venture. This enterprise was called Lola Formula 1.

The initial design of T97/30 was laid out by Eric Broadley, although there was input from Chris Murphy, among others. The design was based on the T95/30 tub, which had been tested by Allan McNish in the winter of 1995. The solutions were cautious and conventional, leaving a lot of scope for development.

Built around a carbonfibre monocoque, the car had a high nose – like every other F1 car of 1997 – and tall sidepods, which gave it quite bulky looks. It also featured turning vanes between the front suspension and radiator openings. The rear suspension wishbones were mounted high, out of the diffuser air flow. The exhausts also blew over the diffuser, which had no central tunnel, as this space was filled by the compulsory deformable structure. In the cockpit, the instruments were integrated in the steering wheel. A semi-automatic transverse gearbox was used, which had six speeds.

The power source was Cosworth's Zetec R V8, effectively the same engine as that which had helped Michael Schumacher to the 1994 World Championship in a Benetton. The plan was, however, to replace it with an Al Melling-designed V10, possibly before the end of the 1997 season. This was to have dimensions very close to those of the Zetec, so the initial use of a V8 had reputedly not affected the design.

The team was contracted to run on Bridgestone tyres, the Japanese manufacturer entering F1 after an extensive test programme.

Amid widespread perplexity about Lola's decision to enter Formula 1 at such short notice, and with a car that had barely seen the inside of a wind tunnel, Eric Broadley commented: "We're doing F1 because it's there and we're ready!" Lola vowed to challenge for the championship in four years' time.

For its F1 programme Lola signed Vincenzo Sospiri and Ricardo Rosset, the same pair of drivers that had beaten Marc Goossens to the 1995 FIA F3000 Championship in Super Nova Reynards. There was very little time to test before the Australian GP, which opened the season. The team managed only a systems check at the Santa Pod drag strip, plus eight laps at Silverstone. Downchange problems with the semi-auto gearbox were experienced.

In Melbourne, there was a rude, if widely anticipated – shock. The team's quicker driver, Sospiri, was over 11 seconds slower than the pole position time, and nowhere near qualifying within the 107% rule. Sospiri said the car lacked downforce, but had too much drag!

After Australia, the suspension geometry was modified and the sidepods were reprofiled. These now had a far more concave shape in the rear 'coke bottle' section, where large holes had been opened, too.

If Melbourne had been a shock, there was a bigger one in store for team members when they arrived in Brazil for the second race. Eric Broadley had decided to cut his losses and pull the plug on the programme …

Lola claimed more of the funding from MasterCard was needed up front, and when this was not possible, the F1 operation was terminated to protect mother company Lola Cars. Even so, Lola Cars went into administration in May over debts said to be around 3 million GBP, the sum owed to it by Lola Formula 1.

The last hurrah. The T97/30 was Lola's F1 car of 1997, and a combination of insufficient financing and a chassis and engine which was not on the pace forced the company into temporary liquidation.

Disaster. Although sponsored via an innovative scheme by Mastercard, the Lola T97/30 was a failure, lapping many seconds slower than the competition in F1. Here it is at its launch (above), and at its first race in Melbourne, Australia, on March 9th, 1997 (below). Shortly afterward, the company folded because of debts incurred from this debacle.

T97/51 – 1997 – Formula Nippon

The T97/51 was still very much like the T95/50 from which it was derived. It became the brightest light in Lola's last year under Eric Broadley's direction.

Spaniard Pedro de la Rosa drove for Lola's Japanese importer Nova, and marched to the championship in a convincing manner. In his second season in the category, de la Rosa won six out of the ten races, equalling the series record of Kazuyoshi Hoshino, who bid farewell to single-seaters in 1997. De la Rosa ended up with nearly three times the points tally of his closest pursuer, Takuya Kurosawa, who drove a 96-model Lola. Kurosawa took a single victory at Fuji. Both drivers used the ubiquitous Mugen engine.

Despite its resounding success with the latest Lola, Nova Engineering decided to order a new Formula Nippon design from G-Force for the 1998 campaign.

APPENDIX & BIBLIOGRAPHY

April 16th 2000: Scott Dixon wins at Long Beach in the Indy Lights Lola, a car built in 1997.

Events of note, which do not appear in main text

1990 – Export Award for Smaller Businesses (Indy win, fastest lap at Le Mans, plus five million GBP exports to Japan in the past year).

1991 – Eric Broadley received an MBE in the New Year honours list. John Major opened the new Tech Centre, with the words: "An illustration of what dreamers can achieve!"

1992 – Lola Motor Racing Management subsidiary established.
Activities:
    To raise budget for F1 programme.
    Sponsorship management for customer teams.
    Driver management (Bryan Herta on board).

1992 – "Zero" project: Lola and Zytek unite to build electric racing car.

Bibliography

Research sources used by Esa Illoinen:
Autosport
Autosprint (I)
Road & Track
Le Mans Yearbooks
Endurance Racing 1982-1990 (Ian Briggs)
Motor Racing Directory 1979 & 1981 (Mike Kettlewell)
Directory of World Sportscars (Michael Cotton)
Super Sports (Ian Bamsey)
World Sportscar Racing Annuals 1989-1993 (Ullrich Upietz)
IMSA Yearbooks
Aston Martin Race Cars
(Paul Chudecki)
Build to Win (Keith Noakes)
The Anatomy and Development of the Sports Prototype (Ian Bamsey)
A-Z of Formula Racing Cars (David Hodges)
Autocourse annuals
Automobile Sport annuals

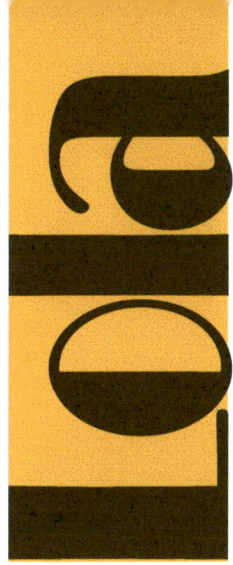

INDEX

A1-Ring 131
Absalom, Hugh 14
Acheson, Kenny 20, 39, 40, 41, 68, 106-109
Ackerley, Andy 19
ACO 11, 13, 24
ACR 24
AD Racing 147, 154
ADA 43, 58
Adam, Bill 46
Adamowicz, Tony 59
Adams, Jim 37, 44-46, 49
Adams, Nick 14
Adelaide 7, 13, 76, 85
Aero 20
AGS 83
Aiello, Laurent 117
Aintree 30
Akin, Bob 35
Albacete 131, 132
Alboreto, Michele 40, 93, 146, 158
Alesi, Jean 100
Alexander, Tyler 75
Alfa (Romeo) 14, 104, 105
Alford, Chris 14, 32
Allam, Jeff 44
Allen, Michael 9, 42
Alliot, Philippe 22, 83, 84, 85, 90, 93, 95, 126, 129
Allison 7, 8
Alsup, Bill 20, 25
Andretti, John 66
Andretti, Mario 16, 18, 25, 28, 54-56, 59, 65, 66, 68, 70, 73, 74, 81, 83, 85, 86, 92, 96, 97, 104, 105, 115, 123, 124, 136, 137, 150, 155
Andretti, Michael 51, 52, 59, 66, 68, 73, 81, 92, 96, 114, 115
Andrews, Phil 129
AP 34, 53, 64, 66, 72, 75, 80, 81, 86, 92, 98, 104, 105, 114, 115, 117, 123, 125, 149, 150, 155, 157, 158, 165, 166, 168
Apicella, Marco 117, 134, 147, 154, 155
Apomatox 132
Aquila 58
Argetsinger, Peter 60
Argo 20, 39
Arizona 98
Armstrong Dampers 31
Armstrong, Sherman 25
Arnoux, René 79, 83, 99
ASCAR 25
Ashmore, Bruce 81, 86, 90, 94, 96, 104, 114, 121, 122, 135, 137, 147
Aston Martin 11, 12, 34, 44, 48, 107
Audi 131
Auger, David 25
Auriga 51
Australian GP 14, 23, 170
Autopolis 117, 134
Autosport 14, 19, 24, 30, 32, 34, 51, 53, 54, 75, 126
Avon Tyres 57, 117, 167
Ayari, Soheil 168

Badoer, Luca 132, 146
Bailey, Julian 19, 51, 52, 88, 98, 99, 106-109
Bailey, Len 11, 37
Baird, Carson 65
Baldi, Mauro 108
Baldwin, Jack 66
Baldwin, John 75
Ballabio, Fulvio 56
Barcelona 132, 151, 159
Barclay Team EJR 117
Barnard, John 17, 18
Barth, Jürgen 13, 24
Bartlett, John 48, 49, 59, 60
BBS 34
Beasley, John 13
Beatrice 73-78, 83, 84
Becker, Harald 53
Becker, Karl-Heinz 45, 47, 59

Bedard, Patrick 67
Bell, Derek 7, 11, 35-37, 59
Bellamy, Ralph 80, 83, 86, 88-90
Bellasi 24
Bellof, Stefan 56, 59
Belmondo, Paul 88
Belso, Tom 42
Benetton 102, 110, 117, 170
Bennett, Colin 49
Bennett, Derek 23
Bennett, Nigel 66, 81, 86, 90, 92, 137
Bernard, Eric 93, 94, 100, 102, 113
Bernstein, Kenny 123
Bernstein-King Team 150
Bettenhausen, Gary 17, 25, 114
BFG 60
Bigelow, Tom 17, 18, 25
Bignotti, George 15
Bilstein 34, 44
'Birmingham Mail & Post' FF1600 series 52
Birrane, Martin 24, 43
Blanchet, Mike 19, 20, 22, 31-33, 39, 44, 51, 53, 57, 58
Blundell, Mark 63, 88, 93, 94, 98, 99, 106-109, 169
BMS Scuderia Italia 146
BMW 8, 35, 37, 40, 45, 47, 56, 63
Boesel, Raoul 81, 83, 97, 105, 123, 136-138, 150
Booth, John 52
Borgudd, Slim 20
Borroughs, David 49, 60
Bosch, & F1 64, 93
Bouchut, Christophe 159
Bousquet, Jean-Louis 20
Boutsen, Thierry 40, 41, 56
Boutwood, Peter 43
Bowlby, Ben 168
BP 49
Brabham, David 110, 116
Brabham, Gary 110
Brabham, Geoff 9-11, 26, 28-30, 34, 42, 65, 67, 72, 81, 83, 98, 106, 107, 109, 110
Brack, Kenny 159, 167
Bradley, Frank 31
Brainerd 10, 23, 28, 46, 58
Brambilla, Vittorio 24
Brancatelli, Gianfranco 106-109
Brands Hatch 13, 14, 16, 18, 19, 24, 25, 30-33, 37, 43, 44, 45, 49, 51-53, 58, 63, 64, 79, 88, 98-101, 110, 111, 112, 117, 131, 168
Brassfield, Darin 65
Brawn, Ross 75
Brayton, Michael 9
Brayton, Scott 123, 137, 155, 158
Brazil 94, 113, 146, 165, 170
Brembo 81, 93, 98, 105
Bridgestone 108, 110, 112, 170
Briedenbach, Don 7
Briggs, Ian 32
Bright, John 45, 46, 49, 58
Brindley, John 14, 25, 33, 43, 48, 49, 58, 59, 60

BRM 29
Broadley, Andrew 88, 89, 145, 151
Broadley, Eric 11, 19, 20, 31, 33, 47, 54, 56, 64, 70, 73, 75, 81, 83, 85, 90, 97, 112, 126, 146, 170, 171
Brockman, Mike 59
Brown, Garvin 23, 28
Brown, Warwick 7-9, 13
Brundle, Martin 31, 77, 106, 107
Brunn, Siggi 24, 35
Bryan, Jimmy 15
Budweiser 54
Buenos Aires 132
Buick 92, 114, 115, 122, 123, 145, 152, 158, 169
Bullimore, Chris 30
Bundy, Doc 65, 66
Busby, Jim 23, 60-63
Busch 9, 10
Button, Dave 31
Byman, Geoff 56
Byrne, Rory 40, 41
Byrne, Tommy 32

Cabin Racing 112
CAC 28-30
Cadwell Park 20, 56
Calder 14, 23
Calkins, Buzz 158
Calmels, Didier 83, 93
Can-Am 8-10, 23, 25, 26, 29, 39, 42, 43, 49, 56, 58, 131
Canada 113
Canadian GP 9, 93
Canary, Paul 66
Candy, Vivian 24
Cannon, John 7
Capelli 75
Capelli, Ivan 80
Caplan, Herb 10
Capoferri 24
Carcasci, Paolo 132
CART 16-19, 19, 53, 66, 85, 86, 92, 96, 104, 105, 114, 115, 145, 150, 151, 155, 158, 165, 168
Carter, Pancho 16, 68, 81, 83
Castle Combe 53, 56
Castroneves, Hélio 169
Cecotto, Johnny 56
Chaparral 15, 17-19, 25, 34
Chapman, Colin 85
Charlotte 8, 10, 46, 65
Cheever, Eddie 78, 104, 114, 123, 155
Cheever, Ross 53, 100, 121, 132, 134, 147, 151, 154, 155
Chevalley, Andre 24
Chevrolet 8, 22, 26, 27, 29, 34, 44, 46, 47, 64-66, 82, 86, 88, 92, 105, 122, 123, 136, 137, 149
Chevron 7, 8, 20, 23, 25, 28
Chiesa, Andrea 111
Church, John 39
Cicale, Tony 29, 30, 54, 55, 67, 92
Clark, Jim 83, 85
Classic & Sports Car 26
Cleveland 55, 68, 74, 81, 92, 96, 97, 104, 115, 123, 137, 150, 157, 165, 168

Cobb, Price 107
Cochrane, Neil 63
Cocks, Les 43
Cogan, Kevin 55
Cohen-Olivar, Max 49
Cole, Nick 31, 32
College Station 15, 16
Collier, Mike 88
Colnbrook 75
Colt 15
Columbus 65, 66, 72
Colville, Martin 43
Comas, Eric 100, 111
Connor, Mike 42
Conte, Phil 59
Cooke, Jim 59
Cooke-Woods 35, 37, 49, 59
Cooper, Clive 97
Cooper, Garrie 7
Cooper, John 11, 13
Cooper, Julian 158
Cooper, Rob 31, 32
Cord, Chris 37, 45, 46
Corvette 23, 64-66, 72
Costanzo, Alfredo 7, 13, 23
Cosworth 13, 15, 17, 24, 34-36, 44, 47-49, 55, 56, 60, 68, 75, 77, 83, 84, 86, 88, 90, 97, 99, 111-113, 117, 121-123, 132, 135, 151, 158, 159, 170
Cotton, John 25
Courage Team 107, 108
Coyne, David 32
Coyote 15, 16
Craft, Chris 11, 13, 37
Cranfield 86
Cranfield Institute 110
Crang, Neil 63
Crawford, Chris 43
Crawford, Jim 40, 42-44, 58, 67, 74, 92
Cristal Racing 53
Crossle 19, 25, 32
CSAI 75
Cudini, Alain 107, 108
Cunningham, Jocko 53

Da Matta, Cristiano 169
Dacco, Guido 56
Dallara 146
Dallas 43
Dallenbach, Wally 19, 165
Dalmas, Yannick 83, 90, 93, 131
Daly, Derek 68, 86, 92, 106, 107, 109
DAMS Team 99, 110, 111, 117, 132
Daniels, Jack 23
Danielson Team 159
Danielsson, Thomas 116, 117, 121, 132, 134, 147, 154
Datsun 38, 46
Davies, Jamie 168
Dawson, Ian 34
Daytona 11, 24, 37, 38, 44-47, 59, 61, 65, 72, 107, 109, 116
De Angelis, Elio 20
De Cadenet, Alain 9, 11-13, 24, 43, 58
De Dryver, Bernard 43
De Ferran, Gil 155, 158, 165
De Fierlant, Hughes 11
De la Rosa, Pedro 171

173

De Villota, Emilio 34-37
De Zille, Brian 53
De Zille, Graham 53
Del Castello, Roberto 56
Delco 66
Deletraz, Jean-Denis 93
Della Penna 168
Delta 31, 32, 43
Denver 104, 115
Depailler, Patrick 8
Dernie, Frank 56
Detroit 65, 78, 96, 97, 104, 115, 123, 137, 150, 155, 161, 165
Devendorf, Don 46, 72
Dickens, Stanley 33
Dickinson, Tony 25
Dickson, Larry 17
Diepholz 99
Dijon 93, 98, 100
Disney World 158
Divila, Richard 80
Dobson, Dominic 150
Docking, Alan 40
Docking-Spitzley team 40, 56
Dome 134, 147, 154, 168
Donington 19, 32, 33, 40, 44, 47, 52, 53, 56-58, 88, 99, 108, 109, 111, 129, 146
Donnelly, Martin 98, 99, 102, 106
Dowe, Tony 29, 54
Downe, Viscount 11
Dowsett, Tony 44
Draco Team 159
Driot, Jean-Paul 88, 99
Ducarouge, Gérard 93, 112
Duckhams 11
Dumfries, Johnny 57, 66
Dunlop 19, 30, 31, 35, 98, 99, 105, 107, 108, 112
Duret, François 43
Duxbury, Graham 62
Dykstra, Lee 9, 10

Eagle 16, 17, 66
Eagle-Toyota 109
Earl, Bob 106, 107, 109, 110
Eau Rouge 56, 88, 159
Ecclestone, Bernie 79
Edge, Ray 19
Edmonton 30
Edvinsson, Hans 33, 44, 59
Edwards, Guy 34-37, 47-50
Ekblom, Fredrik 121
Electramotive 46, 66, 70, 72, 73, 98, 105
Elfin 7, 10, 11, 13, 14, 23
Elgaard, Peter 32, 43
Elgh, Eje 40
Elkhart Lake 9, 10, 28, 29, 37, 42, 46, 49, 55, 60, 65, 68, 72, 74, 86, 92, 96, 104, 115, 123, 137, 150, 155, 166
Empringham, David 145
Engine Shop, The 58
Enna 36, 40, 56, 80, 89, 100, 111, 117, 120, 151, 159
Ensign 13, 42
ESPO 113
Estoril 159
EuroRacing Team 33, 126, 129, 131
Euser, Cor 43, 44, 108, 126, 129, 131
Evans, Bob 13

Evans, Davy 54
Evans, Tim 10

Fabi, Corrado 56, 68
Fabi, Teo 29, 30, 40, 55, 56, 68, 116
Fabre, Pascal 80, 83
Facetti, Carlo 36
Falconer, Ryan 64
Falkenberg 44, 59
Fangio, Juan II 75
Farmer, Geoff 33
Faure, Nick 13, 24, 49
Faure, Philippe 100
Fernandez, Adrian 157, 165, 166, 168, 169
Ferrari 11, 36, 42, 145, 146
Ferté, Alain 75, 107
Field, Ted 37, 44, 46
Finotto, Martino 36
Firestone 155, 157, 165
Fittipaldi, Christian 117, 155, 165, 166
Fittipaldi, Emerson 92, 96, 97, 104, 115, 123, 136-138, 143, 149-151, 155
Fitzgerald, Peter 59
Fitzpatrick, John 13, 37, 39, 46
Flux, Ian 100
Foitek, Gregor 93, 102
Follmer, George 8-10
Fontana Speedway 169
Fontana, Norberto 168
Footwork 146
Forbes-Robinson, Elliott 10, 11, 28, 29, 66, 72
FORCE 75
Ford 33, 34, 77-79, 90, 102, 124, 126, 136-138, 149, 150, 155, 157, 158, 165, 168
Ford C100 37, 43, 44, 47, 49
Ford Mustang 46
Forghieri, Mauro 93
Formula 3000 74, 87, 94, 111, 130, 133, 154, 164, 166
Formula 5000 7
Formula Ford 18, 19, 31-33, 51-53, 64
Formula One 13, 79, 80, 83
Formula Opel 159
Forsythe Green Team 145
Forsythe Racing 73, 145
Forti Corse 100, 111
Foulston, John 27, 43, 58, 59
Fox, Syd 14, 19, 25
Foyt, A.J. 15-18, 86, 92, 104, 114, 136, 138, 155
Francia, Giorgio 35, 36
Francisci, Claudio 24
Freeman, Bill 28
French GP 78, 102, 113
Frentzen, Heinz-Harald 116, 120, 126, 129, 133, 134, 147
Friselle, Brad 9
Frissbee 9, 23, 28-30, 42, 58
Fuji 49, 63, 72, 99, 106, 108, 115-117, 121, 132, 134, 147, 154, 165, 168, 171

GA 88, 93, 100
Gabbiani, Beppe 56
Gachot, Bertrand 64, 113
Gaillard, Patrick 20, 24
Galica, Divina 25
Galles 23

Galles Racing 42, 81, 83, 97
Galles, Rick 42
Galles/Kraco Team 104, 105, 114, 122, 137, 157, 166
Galmer-Chevy 123, 138
Ganassi, Chip 55, 56, 68, 104, 114, 123, 137, 165
Ganley, Howden 8
Ganz, Whitney 65
Garcia, Juan Fernandez 35
Garcia, Tony 59
Garretson, Bob 35, 37
Garrett 77
Gartner, Jo 40
Gary Evans Motorsport 80
Garza, Josele 55, 67
Gatmo 53
GBDA 88, 93, 99
Gehlhausen, Spike 16
Gené, Jordi 151
George, Tony 158, 165
German GP 146
Giacomelli, Bruno 14, 23
Gilbert, Chris 100
Gilbert-Scott, Andrew 51-53, 99, 100, 106, 134, 147, 154, 165
Gillen, Kevin 30
Gilliard, Tony 19
Gimax 36
Girling 26
Goodwood 65
Goodyear 35, 107, 110, 155
Goodyear, Scott 66, 110, 123, 125, 137, 138, 143, 150, 151, 154, 155
Goossens, Marc 151, 159, 167, 170
Gordon, Robby 136, 137, 139, 150, 151, 155
Gorne, Rick 19
Gounon, Jean-Marc 132
Gove, Gary 28, 29
Grable, Ron 61
Granatelli Team 92
Granatelli, Vince 114
Green Team 168
Green, Barry 28
Greene, Keith 11, 13, 106
Greeney, Len 63
Gretton, Rod 14
Grohs, Harald 35, 37, 45, 46
Grouillard, Olivier 80, 93, 106
Group C 12, 34, 45, 47, 48, 59, 60, 64, 97, 105, 106, 109, 115, 116, 125, 127, 129, 131
Guerrero, Roberto 19, 20, 39, 40, 67, 68, 92, 105, 123
Gugelmin, Maurício 51, 52, 155, 165, 166
Gulf GR7 6
Gunn, John 8, 9
Guthrie, Janet 17, 18

Haas, Carl 7-10, 17, 36, 37, 51, 53, 55, 75, 76, 79, 137, 144
Hagan, Billy 65
Hall & Fowler 43
Hall, Jim 8, 15, 17, 114, 165
Hall, Peter 43
Hall/Haas 114
Halliday, Don 25
Halsmer, Pete 61-63
Haltech 66
Hamilton, Alan 8

Hamilton, Robin 11
Harris, Trevor 9, 28, 30, 42, 72, 73
Harrower, Ian 43
Hart 420R 25, 40, 75, 77
Hart, Brian 77, 112
Harvey, Tim 108
Hasemi, Masahiro 98-100, 106-110, 116
Hattori, Naoki 134, 155, 168
Hawkins, Mike 30
Hayhoe, Jim 136
Hayje, Boy 61, 62
Haywood, Hurley 13, 23, 46, 109
Hazell, Jeff 48
Hazelwood, Mike 8
Hearn, Richie 158, 168
Heavens, Roger 20
Hendricks, Rick 66
Henneman 31
Henneman, Maarten 19
Henton, Brian 25, 40
Hepworth 29
Herbert, Johnny 108, 121
Herd, Robin 29
Hermanos Rodríguez Circuit 99
Herta, Bryan 145, 166
Hewland 7, 15, 26, 34, 44, 47, 55, 60, 64, 66, 72, 75, 80, 81, 83, 84, 88, 92, 97, 99, 146
Heyer, Hans 13
Heynes, David 58
Higgins, Derek 167
Hill, Damon 94, 111, 117
Hill, Graham 18
Hill, Jay 112
Hill, Jeremy 58
Hill, Mick 8
Hilton, London 34
Hitco 158
Hoban, Dave 56
Hobarth, Barry 73
Hobbs, David 23, 35, 37, 44, 46, 66
Hockenheim 40, 53, 56, 83, 111, 117, 151, 159, 167
Hogan 8-10
Hogan, Carl 123
Holbert, Al 8-10, 28-30, 42, 47, 59
Holland 126
Holland, Keith 7
Holmes, Howdy 10, 17, 25, 73
Holset 75
Holzberg, Marty 60
Homestead 165, 168
Honda 40, 83, 88, 89, 93, 149, 150, 157, 165, 168, 169
Horne, Steve 30, 145
Horwood, Bernard 53
Hoshino, Kazuyoshi 40, 89, 93, 98, 100, 106-110, 112, 115-117, 121, 132, 147, 154, 165, 169, 171
Hotz Team 80
Hubert, Alain 20, 22
Huidekoper, Wiet 125, 126
Humberstone, Alan 32
Hungarian GP 79, 102
Hungaroring 79
Hungary 83
Huntingdon 93, 97, 115, 122
Hytten, Mario 75

Ickx, Jacky 9-11, 13, 23, 28, 36, 62
IHI 97
Ilmor 86, 122, 149, 150, 155
Image 31
Imola 77, 83, 90, 93, 102, 146
Imperial College 33, 64
IMSA 33, 34, 59, 62-66, 69, 70, 72, 109
Indianapolis 14, 15, 17, 25, 55, 67, 74, 86, 93, 97, 104, 114, 122, 123, 126, 129, 150, 157, 158
Indy Racing League 158, 165
Indy Regency Team 150
IndyCar 15, 16, 18, 53, 54, 57, 64, 67, 73, 75, 81, 104, 105, 122, 123, 135-138, 145, 147, 149-152, 157, 158, 161, 168, 169
Iglesias, Placido 18, 19, 22
Interscope 16, 34, 36, 37, 45, 46, 65
Interseries 126, 131
Intrepid 23, 28, 29
Irvine, Eddie 112, 117, 133, 134, 147
Italian GP 79

Jacklin, David 43
Jaguar 59, 98
Jaguar XJR-14 116
Jaguar XJR-S 46
Japan 72, 89, 90, 92, 99, 100, 106, 108, 112, 115-117, 132, 151, 155, 165, 168
Japanese GP 113
Jarama 99
Jarier, Jean-Pierre 8
Jaussaud, Jean-Pierre 49
Jelinski, Frank 109
Jerez 83, 93, 100, 102, 111, 117
Joest 109
Joest, Reinhold 35
Johansson, Stefan 20, 39, 40, 65, 126, 138
Johncock, Gordon (Gordy) 8, 15-19, 55, 68, 81
Johnson, Herm 20, 60
Jones, Alan 8-11, 14, 23, 74-78
Jones, Davy 110, 158
Jones, John 88, 111
Jones, Parnelli 9
Jones, Richard 24, 49, 60
Jordan, John 58
Jordon, Eddie 35, 44, 117
Jourdain, Michel 158
Judd 90, 92, 97, 99, 105, 117, 125, 126, 151, 154, 166
Juggins, Mike 58
Jyllandsringen 33, 43

Kageyama, Masahiko 116
Kaiser, Tomas 80
Kalagian, John 42, 46, 47, 59
Kanaan, Tony 145, 169
Kaneishi, Katsutomo 129
Karlskoga 44
Kasuya, Shinji 126, 129
Katayama, Ukyo 112, 117, 121
Katayama, Yoshimi 62
Keegan, Rupert 47-49
Kempton, Steve 31, 48, 49, 60
Kendall, Chuck 59
Kennedy, David 23, 29, 44

Kent-Cooke, Ralph 37, 44-47, 49
Kevlar 64, 66, 81, 86, 97, 104
Khan, Ian 30
Kinser, Sheldon 17
Klausler, Tom 8, 23, 28, 30
Kluit, Ron 19, 32
Knapp, Steve 83, 89
Knockhill 63
Knoop, Rick 61-63
Knott, Keith 90, 94, 147
Knutstorp 59
Koni 75, 80, 151, 158, 167
Krab, Fred 31
Kraco 92, 97
Kreepy Krauly 62
Kremer Brothers, Manfred & Erwin 24, 37
Krisiloff, Steve 15, 16, 55
Kristensen, Tom 147, 165, 168
Kroll, Horst 23, 42, 58
Krosnoff, Jeff 110, 116, 121, 129, 147, 166
Kunzman, Lee 17
Kurosawa, Takuya 134, 154, 155, 171
Kyalami 146

La Chinita 31
Labonte, Terry 65
Lague, Doug 53, 63
Laguna Seca 8-10, 29, 30, 36, 37, 42, 45, 46, 55, 59, 65, 68, 72, 74, 83, 86, 96, 97, 105, 115, 123, 125, 138, 143, 145, 150, 158, 166, 170
Lamborghini 90, 93, 94, 102, 112, 114
Lammers, Jan 116
Lancia 47, 48
Lancia, Beta Monte Carlo 24, 35, 37
Langes, Claudio 100
Lark, Clive 70, 90, 97
Larrauri, Oscar 107
Larrousse 102, 104, 107, 110, 112-114
Larrousse, Gérard 83, 93
Larrousse-Calmels Team 83, 84, 90, 93, 94
Las Vegas 23, 30, 42, 55, 68, 158
Lawler, Alo 22, 56
Lazier, Buddy 158
Le Mans 11-13, 24, 33-37, 43, 47-49, 59, 62, 63, 66, 87, 88, 93, 97-100, 106, 107, 109, 111, 116, 126, 147
Lechner, Walter 131
Lee-Davey, Tim 30
Lees, Geoff 10, 11, 13, 26, 40, 41, 89, 116, 117
Leffler, Greg 25
Lepp, John 58
Leslie, David 19, 32
Leven, Bruce 46
Lewis, Randy 23, 29, 30
Leyton House 89
Lightning 15, 16, 18
Ligier 10
Lime Rock 42, 43, 46, 58, 60
Lindstrom, Leif 44
Lloyd, John 47, 59
Lobenberg, Bob 44, 46, 53, 59
Lockheed 14, 26, 30, 31, 33, 34

Lombardi, Lella 35, 36
Londono, Ricardo 28
Long Beach 66, 73, 74, 81, 83, 86, 97, 104, 114, 123, 136, 149, 155, 165
Longhorn 19, 25
Longines 24
Los, Costas 107, 108
Lotec 63
Lotus 28, 66, 102
Lotus-Honda 83, 94
Lovely, Pete 29
Lovett, Peter 13, 44, 58
Ludwig, Klaus 37, 46
Luyendyk, Arie 20, 72-74, 81, 92, 97, 98, 104, 105, 109, 110, 114, 115, 123, 136-138, 143, 150, 155, 158
Lydden 31, 32, 43

Macey, Paul 30
Macknight, Nigel 146
Magneti Marelli 83, 93
Magny-Cours 22, 113, 131, 132, 146, 159
Maids Moreton 58
Mainz 47
Major, John 125
Mallock, Ray 11, 13, 107
Mallory Park 14, 19, 22, 31, 32, 52, 56, 58, 63
Mandel, Leon 23
Mann, Basil 32
Mansell, Nigel 20, 22, 39, 136-138, 140, 141, 143, 145, 149-151, 155
Mantorp Park 33, 40
March 7, 20, 25, 29, 30, 39, 40, 42-44, 47, 53, 55, 56, 58, 62, 65, 67, 68, 73, 79, 80, 81, 83, 86-88, 89, 97, 104, 145
Marchant & Cox 43
Marelli 146
Marlboro 86, 92, 115
Marston, Bob 31, 33
Martin, Jean-Michel 24
Martin, Philippe 24
Martin, Tony 62
Martini 22
Martini, Mauro 100, 109, 110, 116, 117, 121, 129, 133, 134, 147, 154, 155, 159, 165
Martlet 30
Mass, Jochen 35, 62, 65, 106
Mastercard 171
Matsuda, Hideshi 126, 129, 131
Matsumoto 40
Matsumoto, Keiji 112
Maurer 40, 56
Mazda 43, 44, 58-61, 63
McCall, Alan 17
McCluskey, Roger 17, 18
McCormack 7
McCrea, Mike 30
McElreath, Jim 17
McIntyre, Ray 59
McKee, Bob 8
McKitterick, Skeeter 23
McLaren 7, 8, 16-18, 75, 125
McLaren-TAG 83
McNish, Allan 111, 112, 117, 152, 158, 159, 169, 170
McRae, Graham 7, 29
McRobbie, Duncan 93, 146

Meadowlands 67, 74, 86, 96, 97, 104, 115
Mears, Rick 16-19, 25, 55, 67, 68, 96, 104, 114, 115, 123
Meister, Howard 37
Melbourne 170
Melling, Al 170
Menard, John 114, 123, 155, 158
Mercedes 150, 155, 157, 165, 166, 169
Merl, Volker 35
Merzario 56
Messer, Keith 58
Mexican GP 79
Mexico 25, 168
Mexico City 83, 85, 90, 93, 99, 108, 113
Meyer, Bob 43
Meyer, Teddy 67, 75
Miami 46, 59, 62, 65, 72, 74, 83, 86, 92, 155, 165
Miaskiewicz, Rick 42
Michigan 16-18, 25, 55, 59, 68, 74, 83, 96, 104, 105, 115, 123, 137, 145, 150, 151, 157, 165, 166
Middlebridge Racing 111, 117
Mid-Ohio 8, 23, 28, 29, 42, 46, 55, 59, 63, 66, 68, 83, 92, 97, 104, 115, 123, 138, 150, 157, 161, 166
Migault, François 12, 13, 24, 49
Millen, Steve 106, 107, 109
Mills, John 46, 59
Milton Keynes 98
Milwaukee 16-18, 25, 53, 55, 67, 68, 73, 86, 104, 115, 123, 137, 150, 155, 165
Minardi 40
Mine 116, 117, 133, 147, 154, 165
Minister 51, 53
Mirabeau 77
Mirage 8, 9
Misano 40, 56
Modena, Stefano 88
Momo 24
Monaco 20, 22
Monk, Dr Charles 42, 43
Monroe 73
Monte Carlo 77, 90, 102
Montermini, Andrea 132
Montoya, Juan Pablo 168
Montreal 9, 78, 108
Monza 24, 35, 37, 47, 62, 75, 93, 106, 111, 126, 146
Moore, Greg 145, 165
Moore, Matthew 90
Morales, Jimmy 168
Moran, Rocky 9, 23, 29
Morbidelli, Gianni 111
Morelli, Dino 168
Moreno, Roberto 81, 93, 102, 165
Moresch 36
Moretti, Gianpiero 23, 37
Morgan, Dave 51
Morgan, Peter 19
Morgan, Richard 14, 32, 44
Morris Minor 43
Morris, Rick 52
Morton, John 9, 23, 28, 30, 42, 59, 62, 72
Mosley, Mike 17

Mosnier, Jean 75
Mosport 9, 10, 15, 16, 23, 28-30, 37, 39, 42, 43, 46, 58
Most 131
Mount Fuji 59
Mountain View 37
Mugello 34, 35, 40, 49, 80
Mugen 92, 93, 99, 110, 112, 117, 121, 132-134, 147, 151, 159, 165, 168, 171
Müller, Herbert 35
Müller, Jörg 167
Mulsanne 24, 98
Mulsanne Straight 11, 24, 35, 47, 49, 107
Murphy, Chris 90, 93, 102, 170
Murray, Gordon 11

Nagasaka, Naoki 108
Nakajima, Satoru 56
Nakako, Osamu 108
Nakano, Shinji 168
Nakaya, Akihiko 100, 115-117, 121
Naspetti, Emanuele 117
Nazareth 104, 115, 123, 138, 150, 155, 165
Needham, Hal 29
Nelkin, RJ 23, 28
Nelson 14
New Hampshire 123, 137, 150, 157, 158
Newey, Adrian 79, 86, 92
Newman, Paul 28
Newman-Freeman 8, 23
Newman-Haas 54, 73, 86, 92, 96, 114, 115, 123, 136, 137, 140, 141, 149, 150, 155, 161, 165, 168
Nicholson, John 11
Nielsen, John 98, 107
Nimrod 11
NISMO 107-110, 115, 116
Nissan 65, 66, 69, 70, 72, 73, 97-99
Nissan R90C 104-109, 115, 116
Nissen, Kris 32
NME 105-107
Nogaro 111, 117, 132
Nomex 26, 33, 47, 70, 73, 97
Nordic Racing 151, 159
Norisring 59
Nova Engineering 89, 109, 115, 116, 131, 134, 147, 165, 171
NPTI 105-107, 109, 110
Nunn, Mo 114
Nürburgring 20, 31, 35, 40, 48, 49, 56, 63, 99, 108, 132

O'Brien, Eugene 63
O'Rourke, Steve 35
O'Steen, John 62
Oatley, Neil 56, 75
Offenhauser 17
Ogawa, Hitoshi 100, 108, 112, 116, 117, 121, 133
Okada, Hideki 115, 116
Olivieri, Maximo 31
Olofsson, Anders 99, 106-108, 110, 115, 116
Omegaland 151
Ongais, Danny 15-17, 19, 36, 46
Ontario 15-18, 25

Onyx 102
Oran Park 7, 13
Osella 24, 35, 36
Österreichring 20, 79, 80
Oulton Park 14, 31-33, 44, 52, 53, 58, 59, 63, 88, 121
Oxborrow, John 51

PacWest 150, 165
Paine, Norman 31
Palm Beach 65
Palmer, Dr Jonathan 65, 83, 85
Panis, Olivier 132
Pardini, Guido 40
Pareja, Jesús 126, 129, 131
Parnelli 15-17
Parsons, Johnny 16, 18, 55
Patrese, Riccardo 24, 90
Patrick Racing 92, 96, 105, 155, 165, 168
Patrick, Pat 123
Pau 40, 56, 88, 100, 111, 159
Paul, John Jr 31, 36-39, 44-46, 55, 65, 73
Paul, John Sr 46
Paul Ricard 78, 93, 98, 102
Payton-Coyne 165
Peerless 66
Pegasus Motorsport 53
Penistone 32
Penske 8, 15-19, 25, 55, 68, 90, 92, 96, 104, 105, 114, 115, 122, 123, 136-138, 143, 145, 149-151, 155, 157, 165, 166, 168
Pérez-Sala, Luis 88
Perkins, Larry 13
Perry, Dick 53
Pescarolo, Henri 24, 37, 109
Peters, Mark 30, 31, 51, 52
Peterson, Ronnie 44
Peugeot 126, 127, 129, 131
Phillips, Simon 13
Phoenix 15-17, 19, 20, 25, 55, 56, 67, 68, 73, 74, 81, 92, 94, 104, 113, 114, 123, 136, 140, 141, 145, 149, 155, 158
Piquet, Nelson 35, 102, 123
Pirelli 35
Pironi, Didier 14, 23
Pirro, Emmanuele 80, 93
Pocono 17, 19, 25, 46, 55, 68, 74, 81, 92
Policand, Jérôme 159
Polimotor 60
Porsche 12, 35, 44, 45, 49, 59, 62, 65, 92, 99, 104, 107-109, 111
Porsche 908 24, 35
Porsche 917K/81 24, 37
Porsche 935 13, 24, 35, 36, 37, 39, 44, 45
Porsche 936 11, 36
Porsche 956 44, 48, 49
Porsche 962 59, 61, 70, 109, 126
Portland 7, 37, 46, 65, 67, 72-74, 81, 86, 92, 97, 104, 115, 123, 137, 150, 155, 165
Posey, Sam 37
Pratt, John 51-53
Preece, Titmus 8
Price, Dave 106, 107
Price, Lew 65
Prophet 8-11, 23, 28, 29

Prost, Alain 20, 22, 79
Provimi Veal 73, 97
PRS 53
Pruett, Scott 97, 110, 155, 157, 165, 166, 168

Quester, Dieter 61-63

Rahal, Bobby 10, 11, 28-30, 35, 37, 44, 55, 66, 68, 83, 86, 92, 97, 104, 105, 114, 115, 122, 123, 125, 136-138, 149, 150, 155, 157, 158, 166
Ralt 20, 28, 40, 56, 75, 89, 121
Ramsey, Rex 43
Raphanel, Pierre-Henri 90, 116
Ratcliffe, Andrew 26
Rattlesnake Raceway 28
Ratzenberger, Roland 108, 133, 134, 147
Ray 51
Raymond, Martin 13, 24
Redman, Brian 7-9, 23, 25, 34, 35, 37-39, 45-47, 49
Reed, Ian 67
Regout, Hervé 107, 108
Renault 22
Reuter, Manuel 126
Reynard 19, 31, 51, 53, 64, 93, 100, 111, 112, 117, 121, 130, 132, 133, 137, 146, 147, 149, 150, 154, 155, 157-159, 165, 166, 168-170
Reynolds, Burt 29
Ribeiro, André 145, 157, 165, 166, 168
Richmond, Tim 20
Riley, Brett 20
Riverside 8, 9, 29, 30, 34, 42, 44, 46, 55, 58, 59, 65, 72
Road & Track 66
Road Atlanta 8-10, 18, 29, 37, 42, 44, 46, 53, 58, 65, 72
Robertson, Steve 145
Robinson, Chip 72, 98, 106, 109, 110
Roc, Michael 31, 42, 43, 58, 106, 107
Roebuck, Nigel 75
Rogers, Troy 14
Röhrl, Walter 24, 35
Rondeau 36, 48, 49, 62, 63
Roos, Bertil 42
Rosberg, Keke 9-11, 23
Rose, Peter 53
Rosset, Ricardo 170
Rossi, Carlo 40, 56
Rossiter, Jeremy 14, 25, 32, 33
Rotel 20
Rothengatter, Huub 40
Rothmans 7, 13
Royale 19, 30, 31, 43, 44, 51, 52
Ruddenham, Trevor 30
Rutherford, Johnny 16-19, 25, 68

Sadler, Peter 33
Sala, Maurizio Sandro 107
Salisbury 99, 167
Salles, Gualter 145
Salo, Mika 147, 148, 154
San Antonio 66, 72

San Marino GP 83
Sanair 68, 74
Sandown Park 7, 13, 49, 59, 60
Santa Pod 170
Santin, Alessandro 80
Sardou, Max 33
Sauber 47, 49
Sauber-Mercedes 98, 99, 106, 108, 116
Schäfer, Uwe 64
SCCA 10, 14, 20, 33, 44, 53, 112
Schkee 8, 10, 28
Schlesser, Jean-Louis 99
Schnarwiler, Fredy 40
Schornstein, Dieter 35
Schubeck, Joe 66
Schulz, Doug 8
Schumacher, Michael 121, 170
Schumacher, Ralf 168
Schuppan, Vern 7, 8, 10, 11, 29
Scriven, Andy 97
Sears Point 23, 28, 42, 46, 66
Sebring 11, 44, 51, 59, 72, 73, 107, 126, 145, 168
Sekiya, Masanori 93, 116
Senna da Silva, Ayrton 43, 51, 53, 102
SERA 26, 33
Serra, Chico 20, 22
Servanin, François 49
Sharp, Scott 158
Sheldon, John 11, 14, 25
Shepherd, Dave 8
Sherman Armstrong T500 17, 18
Sherman Armstrong Team 16, 17, 25
Sherman Armstrong Wildcat Offy 17, 25
Shierson, Doug 67, 73, 104
Shrike 58
Silverstone 11-13, 14, 16, 19-22, 24, 25, 27, 31-33, 35, 39, 40, 43, 48, 49, 51, 53, 56, 58, 60, 65, 75, 80, 93, 100, 102, 106, 111, 126, 132, 146, 152, 159, 168, 170
Simon, Dick 81, 86, 92, 123, 136, 150
Skellern, Chris 19
Skoda 8, 25
Smith, Jack 10, 28, 30
Smith, Lance 8, 23
Smith, RK 53
Snetterton 19, 22, 25, 31, 33, 43, 47, 51-53, 57, 63, 66, 98
Sneva, Jerry 25
Sneva, Tom 15, 16, 18, 25, 55, 56, 67, 68
Soppe, Darrell 55
Sospiri, Vincenzo 117, 146, 159, 170
South, Stephen 23, 28, 29
Spa-Francorchamps 40, 49, 50, 56, 75, 77, 88, 99, 100, 106, 117, 146, 159
Spalding, Tom 8, 10
Spanish GP 90, 102
Spax 14
Specialised Mouldings 55, 73
Spénard, Richard 59

Spice 108
Spice, Gordon 13, 63
Spitzley, Matt 40, 56
Spyder, NF11 8-10, 23, 28, 29
St James, Lyn 150
St Jovite 8, 9
Stancombe, Colin 52, 53
Stellar Team 134, 154
Stewart, Paul 111, 117, 146
Stewart, Tony 158
Stirling, Robbie 131
Stohr, Siegfried 40
Stommelen, Rolf 37
STP 8
Stuck, Hans-Joachim 35, 47, 49
Sugo 100, 108, 112, 116, 121, 134, 147, 154
Sullivan, Danny 23, 26, 28-30, 42, 67, 68, 70, 81, 92
Suntec Team 116
Super Nova Team 167, 170
Supercup 99
Surfers Paradise 7, 13, 114, 123, 136, 143, 149, 155, 165, 168
Suzuka 40, 99, 100, 102, 106, 108, 116, 117, 121, 129, 132-134, 147, 154, 165, 168
Suzuka, Yoshi 72, 105
Suzuki, Aguri 72, 90, 93, 94, 102, 107, 108, 113, 146
Suzuki, Toshio 98, 106-110, 115-117, 134, 147, 159, 165
Swan, Dennis 14
Swift 53, 168
Symonds, Pat 56
Sytner, Frank 14, 25, 32

Taft, Raymond 58
TAG 158
Takagi, Toranosuke 165
Takahashi, Kunimitsu 100, 154
Tambay, Patrick 25, 28, 29, 42, 43, 58, 77-79
Tamiami Park 92
Tasman Motorsports 145, 165, 166, 168, 169
Tassin, Thierry 56
Taylor, Ian 14, 25, 32, 33, 58
Taylor, Mike 32, 44
Team Take One 116
Tempero, Bill 8
Tennyson, David 129
Tetu, Michel 112
Texas 43
Texas Speedway 17
Thackwell, Mike 19, 20, 40, 41, 75, 80
Thatcher, Mark 25
Theodore 13, 29, 55, 67
Thiim, Kurt 33, 44
Thruxton 14, 22, 31, 32, 39, 40, 43, 44, 52, 53, 56, 58
Thundersports 43, 44, 48, 49, 58, 59
Thyrring, Thorkild 44, 59
Tiga 14, 25, 29, 30, 33, 43, 44, 63
Toleman, Teddy 25, 40
Toleman-Hart DS1 56
Toronto 81, 96, 104, 115, 123, 137, 150, 157, 166

Touraco, Team 30, 51
Townsend Thoresen 51-53, 63
Townsend, Peter 63
Townsend, Randy 10
Toyota 20, 22, 106-109, 115, 116, 126, 129, 131
Tracy, Paul 23, 42 123, 136-138, 143, 150, 151, 155, 157, 158, 165
Travis, John 123, 147, 165, 168
Trenton 15-18
Trevelyan, John 14, 25
Trevor, Tony 58
Trimmer, Tony 58
Trisconi, François 24
Trivellato 75
Trois Rivières 8-10, 23, 29, 30, 42, 58
Trollé, Michel 88
Troost, Wolfgang 53
Trott, Richard 31
Trueman, Jim 47
TrueSports 68, 85, 86, 90, 92, 97, 105, 136, 137, 145
Tullius, Bob 46
Tully, Jim 62
TWR Jaguar 106, 107, 109, 110
Tyrrell 19, 83, 85, 112, 167

Unser, Al 9, 14-19, 23, 25, 29, 30, 42, 55, 56, 67, 124
Unser, Al Jr 42, 55, 68, 73, 74, 81, 83, 96, 97, 104, 105, 114, 115, 123, 125, 138, 149, 150, 155, 157, 158, 165, 166
Unser, Bobby 17-19, 25

Vallelunga 40, 56, 80, 93, 117
Van de Poele, Eric 100, 111
Van der Merwe, Sarel 62, 65, 66
Van der Straten, Count 114
Van Diemen 10, 19, 32, 43, 51-54, 64
Van Dievoet, Julian 43
Van Kouwen, Gerrit 63, 64
Van Silfhout, Jaap 43
Vancouver 104, 115, 137, 150, 151, 158, 166
Vandervell 20
Vasser, Jimmy 136, 155, 165, 166, 169
VDS 7, 9, 10, 28-30, 34, 42, 43, 58, 63
VDS Team 9, 10, 26-29, 114
Vega 20, 22
Vermeulen, Huub 31-33, 43, 44
Vermeulen, Jim 31, 33
Villeneuve, Gilles 48
Villeneuve, Jacques (brother of Gilles) 42, 66, 68
Villeneuve, Jacques (son of Gilles) 145, 149, 150, 155, 157, 158
Vitolo, Dennis 150
Volkswagen 44, 58, 59
Vukovich, Bill 17

Wada, Takao 93, 100, 107, 108, 115, 116

Wainwright, Wayne 14
Walger, Leon 24, 33
Walker, Derrick 123, 137, 150
Walker, Johnnie 7, 13
Wall, Andy 146
Wallace, Andy 53, 87
Walther, Salt 17
Wanneroo 14
Warner 64
Warren wind tunnel 64
Warwick, David 40
Warwick, Derek 102, 131
Warwick, Paul 121
Watkins Glen 9, 10, 17, 18, 23, 28, 29, 36, 37, 62, 63, 65, 66, 72
Watson 17, 18
Watson, John 59
Watt, Jason 168
Weaver, James 14, 32, 33
Webb, John L 33, 43
Weidler, Volker 53, 110, 112, 115-117, 121, 132-134
Weis, Franz 14, 30
Weismann 72
Wendlinger, Karl 106
Weslake 8
West Palm Beach 51
Westwood, Julian 121
Whatley, Mike 53
Whittington, Bill 37, 45
Wietzes, Eppie 37, 44
Wildcat 15, 17, 25, 55
Wilds, Mike 26, 27, 43, 44
Williams 9, 14, 23, 25, 56, 136, 140, 151
Williams, Dave 42
Williams, Mark 75, 80, 86, 88, 92, 110, 131, 146
Williams, Richard 11
Williams-Honda 83
Wilson, Desiré 14, 19, 24, 25, 33
Winkelhock, Manfred 37, 40
Winter, John 109
Winter, Spike 58
Wisconsin 68, 92
Wolber Motorsport 53
Wolf 9, 10, 13
Wollek, Bob 13, 37, 46, 99, 109
Woodcote 22, 35
Woods, Martin 43
Woods, Roy 37
Wright, John 13
Wright, Mike 89, 100

Xerox 58

Yanagida, Haruhito 72
Yokohama 112, 117

Zanardi, Alessandro 117, 165, 166
Zandvoort 19, 20, 31-33, 43, 44
Zetec 170
Zolder 20, 31, 43, 47, 53, 93
Zonta, Ricardo 167, 168
Zorzi, Renzo 22
Zwolsman, Charles 33, 44, 59, 126, 129
Zytec 166

Also from Veloce Publishing

Those Were The Days ... Series
Alpine Trials & Rallies 1910-1973 (Pfundner)
American 'Independent' Automakers – AMC to Willys 1945 to 1960 (Mort)
American Station Wagons – The Golden Era 1950-1975 (Mort)
American Trucks of the 1950s (Mort)
American Trucks of the 1960s (Mort)
American Woodies 1928-1953 (Mort)
Anglo-American Cars from the 1930s to the 1970s (Mort)
Austerity Motoring (Bobbitt)
Austins, The last real (Peck)
Brighton National Speed Trials (Gardiner)
British and European Trucks of the 1970s (Peck)
British Drag Racing – The early years (Pettitt)
British Lorries of the 1950s (Bobbitt)
British Lorries of the 1960s (Bobbitt)
British Touring Car Racing (Collins)
British Police Cars (Walker)
British Woodies (Peck)
Café Racer Phenomenon, The (Walker)
Don Hayter's MGB Story – The birth of the MGB in MG's Abingdon Design & Development Office (Hayter)
Drag Bike Racing in Britain – From the mid '60s to the mid '80s (Lee)
Dune Buggy Phenomenon, The (Hale)
Dune Buggy Phenomenon Volume 2, The (Hale)
Endurance Racing at Silverstone in the 1970s & 1980s (Parker)
Hot Rod & Stock Car Racing in Britain in the 1980s (Neil)
Last Real Austins 1946-1959, The (Peck)
Mercedes-Benz Trucks (Peck)
MG's Abingdon Factory (Moylan)
Motor Racing at Brands Hatch in the Seventies (Parker)
Motor Racing at Brands Hatch in the Eighties (Parker)
Motor Racing at Crystal Palace (Collins)
Motor Racing at Goodwood in the Sixties (Gardiner)
Motor Racing at Nassau in the 1950s & 1960s (O'Neil)
Motor Racing at Oulton Park in the 1960s (McFadyen)
Motor Racing at Oulton Park in the 1970s (McFadyen)
Motor Racing at Thruxton in the 1970s (Grant-Braham)
Motor Racing at Thruxton in the 1980s (Grant-Braham)
Superprix – The Story of Birmingham Motor Race (Page & Collins)
Three Wheelers (Bobbitt)

Great Cars
Austin-Healey – A celebration of the fabulous 'Big' Healey (Piggott)
Jaguar E-type (Thorley)
Jaguar Mark 1 & 2 (Thorley)
Triumph TR – TR2 to 6: The last of the traditional sports cars (Piggott)

Biographies
A Chequered Life – Graham Warner and the Chequered Flag (Hesletine)
A Life Awheel – The 'auto' biography of W de Forte (Skelton)
Amédée Gordini ... a true racing legend (Smith)
André Lefebvre, and the cars he created at Voisin and Citroën (Beck)
Chris Carter at Large – Stories from a lifetime in motorcycle racing (Carter & Skelton)
Cliff Allison, The Official Biography of – From the Fells to Ferrari (Gauld)
Edward Turner – The Man Behind the Motorcycles (Clew)
Driven by Desire – The Desiré Wilson Story
First Principles – The Official Biography of Keith Duckworth (Burr)
Inspired to Design – F1 cars, Indycars & racing tyres: the autobiography of Nigel Bennett (Bennett)
Jack Sears, The Official Biography of – Gentleman Jack (Gauld)
Jim Redman – 6 Times World Motorcycle Champion: The Autobiography (Redman)
John Chatham – 'Mr Big Healey' – The Official Biography (Burr)

The Lee Noble Story (Wilkins)
Mason's Motoring Mayhem – Tony Mason's hectic life in motorsport and television (Mason)
Raymond Mays' Magnificent Obsession (Apps)
Pat Moss Carlsson Story, The – The Harnessing Horsepower (Turner)
'Sox' – Gary Hocking – the forgotten World Motorcycle Champion (Hughes)
Tony Robinson – The biography of a race mechanic (Wagstaff)
Virgil Exner – Visioneer: The Official Biography of Virgil M Exner Designer Extraordinaire (Grist)

General
1½-litre GP Racing 1961-1965 (Whitelock)
AC Two-litre Saloons & Buckland Sportscars (Archibald)
Alfa Romeo 155/156/147 Competition Touring Cars (Collins)
Alfa Romeo Giulia Coupé GT & GTA (Tipler)
Alfa Romeo Montreal – The dream car that came true (Taylor)
Alfa Romeo Montreal – The Essential Companion (Classic Reprint of 500 copies) (Taylor)
Alfa Tipo 33 (McDonough & Collins)
Alpine & Renault – The Development of the Revolutionary Turbo F1 Car 1968 to 1979 (Smith)
Alpine & Renault – The Sports Prototypes 1963 to 1969 (Smith)
Alpine & Renault – The Sports Prototypes 1973 to 1978 (Smith)
Anatomy of the Classic Mini (Huthert & Ely)
Anatomy of the Works Minis (Moylan)
Armstrong-Siddeley (Smith)
Art Deco and British Car Design (Down)
Autodrome (Collins & Ireland)
Automotive A-Z, Lane's Dictionary of Automotive Terms (Lane)
Automotive Mascots (Kay & Springate)
Bahamas Speed Weeks, The (O'Neil)
Bentley Continental, Corniche and Azure (Bennett)
Bentley MkVI, Rolls-Royce Silver Wraith, Dawn & Cloud/Bentley R & S-Series (Nutland)
Bluebird CN7 (Stevens)
BMC Competitions Department Secrets (Turner, Chambers & Browning)
BMW 5-Series (Cranswick)
BMW Z-Cars (Taylor)
BMW Classic 5 Series 1972 to 2003 (Cranswick)
BMW – The Power of M (Vivian)
British at Indianapolis, The (Wagstaff)
British Cars, The Complete Catalogue of, 1895-1975 (Culshaw & Horrobin)
BRM – A Mechanic's Tale (Salmon)
BRM V16 (Ludvigsen)
Bugatti – The 8-cylinder Touring Cars 1920-34 (Price & Arbey)
Bugatti Type 40 (Price)
Bugatti Mark 1 & 2 Pictures (Price)
Bugatti 46/50 Updated Edition (Price & Arbey)
Bugatti T44 & T49 (Price & Arbey)
Bugatti 57 2nd Edition (Price)
Bugatti Type 57 Grand Prix – A Celebration (Tomlinson)
Carrera Panamericana, La (Tipler)
Car-tastrophes – 80 automotive atrocities from the past 20 years (Honest John, Fowler)
Chrysler 300 – America's Most Powerful Car 2nd Edition (Ackerson)
Chrysler PT Cruiser (Ackerson)
Citroën DS (Bobbitt)
Classic British Car Electrical Systems (Astley)
Cobra – The Real Thing! (Legate)
Competition Car Aerodynamics 3rd Edition (McBeath)
Competition Car Composites A Practical Handbook (Revised 2nd Edition) (McBeath)
Concept Cars, How to illustrate and design – New 2nd Edition (Dewey)
Cortina – Ford's Bestseller (Robson)
Cosworth – The Search for Power (6th edition) (Robson)
Coventry Climax Racing Engines (Hammill)
Daily Mirror 1970 World Cup Rally 40, The (Robson)

Daimler SP250 New Edition (Long)
Datsun Fairlady Roadster to 280ZX – The Z-Car Story (Long)
Dino – The V6 Ferrari (Long)
Dodge Challenger & Plymouth Barracuda (Grist)
Dodge Charger – Enduring Thunder (Ackerson)
Dodge Dynamite! (Grist)
Draw & Paint Cars – How to (Gardiner)
Drive on the Wild Side, A – 20 Extreme Driving Adventures From Around the World (Weaver)
Dune Buggy, Building A – The Essential Manual (Shakespeare)
Dune Buggy Files (Hale)
Dune Buggy Handbook (Hale)
East German Motor Vehicles in Pictures (Suhr/Weinreich)
Fast Ladies – Female Racing Drivers 1888 to 1970 (Bouzanquet)
Fate of the Sleeping Beauties, The (op de Weegh/Hottendorff/op de Weegh)
Ferrari 288 GTO, The Book of the (Sackey)
Ferrari 333 SP (O'Neil)
Fiat & Abarth 124 Spider & Coupé (Tipler)
Fiat & Abarth 500 & 600 – 2nd Edition (Bobbitt)
Fiats, Great Small (Ward)
Ford Cleveland 335-Series V8 engine 1970 to 1982 – The Essential Source Book (Hammill)
Ford F100/F150 Pick-up 1948-1996 (Ackerson)
Ford F150 Pick-up 1997-2005 (Ackerson)
Ford Focus WRC (Robson)
Ford GT – Then, and Now (Streather)
Ford GT40 (Legate)
Ford Midsize Muscle – Fairlane, Torino & Ranchero (Cranswick)
Ford Model Y (Roberts)
Ford Small Block V8 Racing Engines 1962-1970 – The Essential Source Book (Hammill)
Ford Thunderbird From 1954, The Book of the (Long)
Formula One – The Real Score? (Harvey)
Formula 5000 Motor Racing, Back then ... and back now (Lawson)
Forza Minardi! (Vigar)
France: the essential guide for car enthusiasts – 200 things for the car enthusiast to see and do (Parish)
Grand Prix Ferrari – The Years of Enzo Ferrari's Power, 1948-1980 (Pritchard)
Grand Prix Ford – DFV-powered Formula 1 Cars (Robson)
GT – The World's Best GT Cars 1953-73 (Dawson)
Hillclimbing & Sprinting – The Essential Manual (Short & Wilkinson)
Honda NSX (Long)
Inside the Rolls-Royce & Bentley Styling Department – 1971 to 2001 (Hull)
Intermeccanica – The Story of the Prancing Bull (McCredie & Reisner)
Jaguar, The Rise of (Price)
Jaguar XJ 220 – The Inside Story (Moreton)
Jaguar XJ-S, The Book of the (Long)
Jeep CJ (Ackerson)
Jeep Wrangler (Ackerson)
The Jowett Jupiter – The car that leaped to fame (Nankivell)
Karmann-Ghia Coupé & Convertible (Bobbitt)
Kris Meeke – Intercontinental Rally Challenge Champion (McBride)
Lamborghini Miura Bible, The (Sackey)
Lamborghini Urraco, The Book of the (Landsem)
Lambretta Bible, The (Davies)
Lancia 037 (Collins)
Lancia Delta HF Integrale (Blaettel & Wagner)
Land Rover Series III Reborn (Porter)
Land Rover, The Half-ton Military (Cook)
Lea-Francis Story, The (Price)
Le Mans Panoramic (Ireland)
Lexus Story, The (Long)
Little book of microcars, the (Quellin)
Little book of smart, the – New Edition (Jackson)
Little book of trikes, the (Quellin)
Lola – The Illustrated History (1957-1977) (Starkey)

Lola – All the Sports Racing & Single-seater Racing Cars 1978-1997 (Starkey)
Lola T70 – The Racing History & Individual Chassis Record – 4th Edition (Starkey)
Lotus 18 Colin Chapman's U-turn (Whitelock)
Lotus 49 (Oliver)
Marketingmobiles, The Wonderful Wacky World of (Hale)
Maserati 250F In Focus (Pritchard)
Mazda MX-5/Miata 1.6 Enthusiast's Workshop Manual (Grainger & Shoemark)
Mazda MX-5/Miata 1.8 Enthusiast's Workshop Manual (Grainger & Shoemark)
Mazda MX-5 Miata, The book of the – The 'Mk1' NA-series 1988 to 1997 (Long)
Mazda MX-5 Miata Roadster (Long)
Mazda Rotary-engined Cars (Cranswick)
Meet the English (Bowie)
Mercedes-Benz SL – R230 series 2001 to 2011 (Long)
Mercedes-Benz SL – W113-series 1963-1971 (Long)
Mercedes-Benz SL & SLC – 107-series 1971-1989 (Long)
Mercedes-Benz SLK – R170 series 1996-2004 (Long)
Mercedes-Benz SLK – R171 series 2004-2011 (Long)
Mercedes-Benz W123-series – All models from 1976 to 1986 (Long)
Mercedes G-Wagen (Long)
MGA (Price Williams)
MGB & MGB GT– Expert Guide (Auto-doc Series) (Williams)
MGB Electrical Systems Updated & Revised Edition (Astley)
Mini Cooper – The Real Thing! (Tipler)
Mini Minor to Asia Minor (West)
Mitsubishi Lancer Evo, The Road Car & WRC Story (Long)
Monthléry, The Story of the Paris Autodrome (Boddy)
Morgan Maverick (Lawrence)
Morgan 3 Wheeler – back to the future!, the (Dron)
Morris Minor, 60 Years on the Road (Newell)
Motor Racing – Reflections of a Lost Era (Carter)
Motor Racing, The Pursuit of Victory 1930-1962 (Carter)
Motor Racing, The Pursuit of Victory 1963-1972 (Wyatt/Sears)
Motor Racing Heroes – The Stories of 100 Greats (Newman)
Motorsport in colour, 1950s (Wainwright)
N.A.R.T. – A concise history of the North American Racing Team 1957 to 1983 (O'Neil)
Nissan 300ZX & 350Z – The Z-Car Story (Long)
Nissan GT-R Supercar: Born to race (Gorodji)
Northeast American Sports Car Races 1950-1959 (O'Neil)
Pontiac Firebird – New 3rd Edition (Cranswick)
Porsche Boxster (Long)
Porsche 356 (2nd Edition) (Long)
Porsche 908 (Födisch, Neßhöver, Roßbach, Schwarz & Roßbach)
Porsche 911 Carrera – The Last of the Evolution (Corlett)
Porsche 911R, RS & RSR, 4th Edition (Starkey)
Porsche 911, The Book of the (Long)
Porsche 911 – The Definitive History 2004-2012 (Long)
Porsche – The Racing 914s (Smith)
Porsche 911SC 'Super Carrera' – The Essential Companion (Streather)
Porsche 914 & 914-6: The Definitive History of the Road & Competition Cars (Long)
Porsche 924 (Long)
The Porsche 924 Carreras – evolution to excellence (Smith)
Porsche 928 (Long)
Porsche 944 (Long)
Porsche 964, 993 & 996 Data Plate Code Breaker (Streather)
Porsche 993 'King Of Porsche' – The Essential Companion (Streather)

Porsche 996 'Supreme Porsche' – The Essential Companion (Streather)
Porsche 997 2004-2012 – Porsche Excellence (Streather)
Porsche Racing Cars – 1953 to 1975 (Long)
Porsche Racing Cars – 1976 to 2005 (Long)
Porsche – The Rally Story (Meredith)
Porsche: Three Generations of Genius (Meredith)
Preston Tucker & Others (Linde)
RAC Rally Action! (Gardiner)
Racing Colours – Motor Racing Compositions 1908-2009 (Newman)
Rallye Sport Fords: The Inside Story (Moreton)
Roads with a View – England's greatest views and how to find them by road (Corfield)
Rolls-Royce Silver Shadow/Bentley T Series Corniche & Camargue – Revised & Enlarged Edition (Bobbitt)
Rolls-Royce Silver Spirit, Silver Spur & Bentley Mulsanne 2nd Edition (Bobbitt)
Rootes Cars of the 50s, 60s & 70s – Hillman, Humber, Singer, Sunbeam & Talbot (Rowe)
Rover P4 (Bobbitt)
Runways & Racers (O'Neil)
Russian Motor Vehicles – Soviet Limousines 1930-2003 (Kelly)
Russian Motor Vehicles – The Czarist Period 1784 to 1917 (Kelly)
RX-7 – Mazda's Rotary Engine Sportscar (Updated & Revised New Edition) (Long)
Singer Story: Cars, Commercial Vehicles, Bicycles & Motorcycle (Atkinson)
Sleeping Beauties USA – abandoned classic cars & trucks (Marek)
SM – Citroën's Maserati-engined Supercar (Long & Claverol)
Speedway – Auto racing's ghost tracks (Collins & Ireland)
Standard Motor Company, The Book of the (Robson)
Subaru Impreza: The Road Car And WRC Story (Long)
Supercar, How to Build your own (Thompson)
Tales from the Toolbox (Oliver)
Tatra – The Legacy of Hans Ledwinka (Margolius & Henry)
Taxi! The Story of the 'London' Taxicab (Bobbitt)
To Boldly Go – twenty six vehicle designs that dared to be different (Hull)
Toleman Story, The (Hilton)
Toyota Celica & Supra, The Book of Toyota's Sports Coupés (Long)
Toyota MR2 Coupés & Spyders (Long)
Triumph TR6 (Kimberley)
Two Summers – The Mercedes-Benz W196R Racing Car (Ackerson)
TWR Story, The – Group A (Hughes & Scott)
Volkswagens of the World (Glen)
VW Beetle Cabriolet – The full story of the convertible Beetle (Bobbitt)
VW Beetle – The Car of the 20th Century (Copping)
VW Bus – 40 Years of Splitties, Bays & Wedges (Copping)
VW Bus Book, The (Bobbitt)
VW Golf: Five Generations of Fun (Copping & Cservenka)
VW – The Air-cooled Era (Copping)
VW T5 Camper Conversion Manual (Porter)
VW Campers (Copping)
Volkswagen Type 3, The book of the – Concept, Design, International Production Models & Development (Glen)
Volvo Estate, The (Hollebone)
You & Your Jaguar XK8/XKR – Buying, Enjoying, Maintaining, Modifying – New Edition (Thorley)
Which Oil? – Choosing the right oils & greases for your antique, vintage, veteran, classic or collector car (Michell)
Wolseley Cars 1948 to 1975 (Rowe)
Works Minis, The Last (Purves & Brenchley)
Works Rally Mechanic (Moylan)

veloce.co.uk

First published in 2001 by Veloce Publishing Limited, Veloce House, Parkway Farm Business Park, Middle Farm Way, Poundbury, Dorchester DT1 3AR, England.
Fax 01305 250479 / e-mail info@veloce.co.uk / web www.veloce.co.uk or www.velocebooks.com
Reprinted December 2017
ISBN: 978-1-787112-58-2/UPC: 6-36847-01258-8
© 2001 & 2017 John Starkey, Esa Illoinen and Veloce Publishing Ltd

All rights reserved. With the exception of quoting brief passages for the purpose of review, no part of this publication may be recorded, reproduced or transmitted by any means, including photocopying, without the written permission of Veloce Publishing Ltd. Throughout this book logos, model names and designations, etc. have been used for the purposes of identification, illustration and decoration. Such names are the property of the trademark holder as this is not an official publication. Readers with ideas for automotive books, or books on other transport or related hobby subjects, are invited to write to the editorial director of Veloce Publishing at the above address.
British Library Cataloguing in Publication Data - A catalogue record for this book is available from the British Library. Typesetting, design and page make-up all by Veloce Publishing Ltd on Apple Mac. Printed and bound by CPI Group (UK) Ltd, Croydon, CR0 4YY.